J.W. (John West) MacMeeken

History of the Scottish Metrical Psalms

J.W. (John West) MacMeeken
History of the Scottish Metrical Psalms
ISBN/EAN: 9783744784962
Printed in Europe, USA, Canada, Australia, Japan
Cover: Foto ©Lupo / pixelio.de

More available books at **www.hansebooks.com**

The Scottish Metrical Psalms.

HISTORY

OF THE

Scottish Metrical Psalms;

WITH AN ACCOUNT OF

THE PARAPHRASES AND HYMNS,

AND OF THE

MUSIC OF THE OLD PSALTER.

ILLUSTRATED WITH

TWELVE PLATES OF MS. MUSIC OF 1566.

BY

REV. J. W. MACMEEKEN,

LESMAHAGOW.

PRINTED FOR SUBSCRIBERS ONLY.

GLASGOW:
M'CULLOCH & CO., PRINTERS, 7 ALSTON STREET.
1872.

In
Psalmorum Laudem.

Chorus.   1. *Angelorum*, &, 2. *Hominum*.

Chorus. The Psalms *are Paradises Spring;*
  Streaming Refreshments every way.
    They,   1. Wine,   2. Oyl,   1. Milk,   2. And Honey bring,
      1. To Cheer,   2. To Cure,   1. To Feed,   2. T' Allay.
    1. When we are merry, Psalms we sing,
    2. When we're afflicted, Psalms we say.
    1. They Heav'n's,   2. And Earth's Devotions wing,
    1. While Angels Praise,   2. Or Men do Pray.

Chorus. The Psalms *are Paradises Spring,*
  Streaming Refreshments every way, &c.

From the Italian of Gio. Francesco Loredano, 1656,
by Lord Coleraine. 1665.

In Token of

SINCERE REGARD,

AND

IN GRATEFUL ACKNOWLEDGMENT OF

LENGTHENED, GENIAL, AND MUCH-PRIZED

COURTESY AND KINDNESS,

This Work is Inscribed to

J. B. GREENSHIELDS, of Kerse, Advocate,
F. S. A. SCOT., ASSOCIATE OF THE BRIT. ARCH. ASSOCIATION,
ETC., ETC.

BY

THE AUTHOR.

CONTENTS.

		PAGE
Preface,		ix
Introduction,		xi
Chapter I.	The Earliest Versions, 1548-64,	1
,, II.	Complete Authorised Version, 1564-1635,	11
,, III.	King James' Version, 1631-37,	15
,, IV.	Sir William Mure's Version, 1639,	23
,, V.	Francis Rous' first issues, 1641-43,	27
,, VI.	William Barton's Version, 1644,	32
,, VII.	Zachary Boyd's Version, 1646-48,	37
,, VIII.	Rous' last Labours on the Psalter, 1646-49,	43
,, IX.	Authorised Version, 1650, with Notice of Versions by Brady and Tait, and by Dr. Watts,	48
,, X.	Gaelic Translations of Psalms and Paraphrases, 1648-1826,	61
,, XI.	Paraphrases, 1648-1781,	71
,, XII.	Hymns,	88
,, XIII.	The Music of the Old Psalters,	95

APPENDIX.

No. I.	Prefatory Remarks by Whittingham to Version 1556,	121
,, II.	Royal Licences to Printers. "Cum Privilegio," &c.,	123
,, III.	Duty of possessing Bible and Psalm Book rigidly enforced,	130
,, IV.	The Authorship of the Old Psalms,	131
,, V.	The "Conclusions," with Specimens of Prayers, Ed. 1595,	137
,, VI.	Baillie defending the use of the "Gloria Patri,"	150
,, VII.	Knox's Liturgy described, with the Spiritual Songs in full,	155
,, VIII.	Reasons against the Reception of King James' Metaphrase,	175
,, IX.	Letter to Sir William Mure,	183
,, X.	Extracts from Will of Francis Rous,	184
,, XI.	Boyd Caricatured,	185
,, XII.	Logan and Bruce,	189
,, XIII.	Versions of Psalms by the Free Church,	190
,, XIV.	Music Schools,	192
,, XV.	Rochester's estimate of the singing of Sternhold and Hopkins' Psalms,	196
,, XVI.	The decadence and revival of the Psalter Music,	197
,, XVII.	The various measures used in the Old Psalter,	200
,, XVIII.	The XXIII Psalm in Forty-two Versions,	207

The Plates, and List of Subscribers' Names.

PREFACE.

THE recent introduction of the "Scottish Hymnal," on the authority of the General Assembly, as a supplementary manual of praise in the Church of Scotland, gave rise to considerable discussion and comment throughout the district in which the Author resides. By one party the step was condemned as an unwarrantable innovation, interfering with the conservatism of good old ecclesiastical forms, whilst by another it was vindicated as a *re*-novation instead of an *in*-novation— a returning to the practice of the Church as inaugurated by the First Reformation. The Author embraced the opportunity thus afforded of calling attention, by means of a short article in a local newspaper, to the Liturgy introduced by Knox, and used in the Reformed Church;—quoting the titles of the fourteen spiritual songs which appear immediately after the Psalms, with instructions as to the tune to which each was to be sung. The Article concluded with this paragraph:— "Some of our readers will, doubtless, be astonished to think that John Knox used a Liturgy; but such is the fact. On a future occasion we may give a short historical detail of the steps by which our metrical version of the Psalms has been developed into its present authorised condition."

In accordance with the purpose thus indicated, a series of Chapters on the "History of the Scottish Metrical Psalms" forthwith appeared in the columns of the Paper referred to. These excited considerable attention, and were favourably received by many under whose notice they were brought; so much so that, during their progress, the Author was frequently urged to issue them in a separate form. With these solicitations he resolved to comply—more especially as much additional matter, consisting of important, interesting, and curious facts and incidents relating to the subject, had accumulated in his hands;—matter which, he felt, could not fail to enhance the value of the work, if judiciously wrought into the original articles, and used as an Appendix. This the Author has now attempted to do, but with what success must be left to the decision of those into whose hands the work may fall. Whilst the labour connected with research, compilation, &c., has not been little, the personal gratification has been very great.

The Author begs to tender his most grateful acknowledgments to the many friends who have encouraged him in his undertaking, amongst whom he would specially mention J. B. GREENSHIELDS, Esq. of Kerse, and WILLIAM EUING, Esq., Glasgow—who, with remarkable kindness, gave him free access to their rare and valuable stores of Biblical lore—and JOHN KIRSOP, Esq., Glasgow, Rev. ALLAN MACNAUGHTAN, D.D., Lesmahagow, and JOHN GIBB, Esq., Banker, Lesmahagow, from whom he had the use of several works bearing on the subject. The warm and courteous hospitality accorded to him by these gentlemen is much appreciated.

J. W. M.

LESMAHAGOW,
May, 1872.

INTRODUCTION

VARIOUS Instrumentalities were in operation during the first half of the sixteenth century, to promote the reformation of the Church in Scotland; and undoubtedly the first place is to be assigned to the fact that the Scriptures, and scripture knowledge embodied in religious publications, were widely distributed throughout the country in the vernacular language. The grand secret of the prosperity which had been attained and so long enjoyed by the system of Priestcraft, was the ignorance in which it shrouded the minds of the people. Every avenue by which truth might enter was carefully guarded. Heresy was denounced as the legitimate offspring of learning; and heretics—separatists from the Church of Rome—were depicted in the most frightful colours, and exhibited to the populace as an emphatic warning against the terrible consequences of following their example. But the slightest ray of light indicates the existence of the sun, and suggests the certainty that—how deep soever the present darkness—it will increase in power and beauty until it reaches meridian splendour. The thirst for knowledge once excited must be gratified, notwithstanding the most active vigilance and opposition of those who would prevent it. A beam of the "bright light in the cloud" had shone into the darkened minds of men raised and endowed by the Head of the Church for the emergencies of the occasion— men who would not be satisfied until their whole understanding was enlightened, and the precious rays of truth shed forth on the intellects and hearts of all within their reach. Through means which the enemy could neither avert nor counteract—because the hand of God was there—the Scriptures were introduced into our country. Merchants trading from the Continent and England to Scottish ports brought with them Tindal's translation of the Bible, with many Protestant books ; which were industriously circulated throughout the land, and perused with the utmost earnestness aud avidity.

One of the most attractive and influential forms in which the truths of Scripture were brought to bear on the popular mind was that of Poetry. He who said "Let me make a nation's *songs* and who will may make its *laws*," was not ignorant of the mysteries by which the emotions and actings of mankind are prompted and regulated. The gift of song, consecrated to the truth, either in the way of plain exposition of its doctrines and precepts, or in that of satirizing and holding up to ridicule the impurities and distortions of falsehood and error, is a most powerful and effective instrument for good—as was signally verified at the time of the Reformation. The earnest study of God's holy word had endowed the heart with a new and spiritual life which was intensified and irresistibly poured out and carried along in a continuous stream of popular sacred song—spreading its blissful influence widely and penetrating deeply. This agency was in active operation long before the Romish Church dreamt of the danger that was threatening her. Intoxicated with the fancied security of their high position, or lulled asleep by sluggish indolence, the Clergy either could not see the peril to which they were exposed, or treated it with haughty indifference and contempt. Personages of honoured name and exalted rank, did not scruple to encourage a Poet to exert his genius in the way of lampooning the priesthood, and showing off the immoralities of their conduct, and the absurdities of their creed. The same individuals who, with all the earnestness of bigoted fidelity to mother church would assist at an *auto-da-fe*, in which heretics were committed to the flames, would perhaps next day countenance by their presence the acting of a pantomime or play, the leading object of which was to caricature the Romish system, and hold it up to ridicule in all its peculiarites. This practise became so common that it could no longer be resisted, and contributed greatly to the progress of the Reformation.

The use of this formidable instrumentality for the advancement of the good cause was not confined to one district or one country. It was of universal adaptability, and was universally applied. " In Italy from the Gulf of Genoa to the Adriatic Sea—in the deep valleys among the purple Appenines—in the air-hung villages which gleam among the pine and chesnut trees on the southern slopes—and even in queenly Florence, which a few years later sent the bold Friar of San Marco to Heaven in a chariot of fire, simple Italian ballads containing some of the elementary truths of the Gospel were rapidly winning their way among the common people." (Sunday Magazine for July, 1866.) Dante, Petrarch, Boccaccio, and other Italian writers, had done much to disturb and weaken the veneration in which the Clergy had been held, by descanting on their ambition, their luxury, and their scandalous habits; thus awakening in the popular mind a deep consciousness of the necessity of a change. Luther's genuis as a Poet as well as his skill and fortitude as a theological dialectitian and intrepid Christian hero, had an effect decidedly beneficial. His Psalms and Hymns, with those of Eber, Sachs, Weisse, Wackernagel, and other poets, wedded to popular music, aroused the German Churches to the warmest enthusiasm, and were "treasured in the households of the faithful from the mountains of Switzerland to the swamps of Holland and the shores of the Baltic, and from the banks of the Rhine to those of the Vistula and the Danube." Their influence is yet felt not only in "Fatherland," but in our own and other countries where translations into the native languages are possessed and prized, not only as memorials of past triumphs over sore trials, but as aids to present piety, and incentives to present duty. "By the middle of the sixteenth century the Reformed Hymnology of Denmark had assumed such a position as to call for a history from the pen of Thomässon." In France, the effect was no less striking. The Psalms and other spiritual songs were translated by Clement Marot and Theodore Beza into French verse, and set to simple and appropriate music, at the suggestion of Calvin. They were greatly appreciated by the French Protestants, and sung with relish even in the dissolute and ungodly court of France. These French Psalms and songs were closely connected—were in fact invariably bound up with the Liturgy of Calvin, at whose instignation the translation was made.

But it is with the Reformation Poetry of our own country that our subject leads us chiefly to deal. And its influence here, was not less observable nor less beneficial than elsewhere. The influence of sacred song in spreading the new faith, and quickening to new and deeper life was not less decided and conspicious in our native land, than in continental countries; and after the prayerful study of the Word of God there was not, during the twenty years of struggling and suffering which preceded the establishment of the Reformed Church, any instrumentality which contributed so much to keep alive the faith of the sufferers, to spread their doctrines, and to bring their opponents and their teaching into the contempt they merited, as the godly and spiritual songs, the tragedies, and ballads of those whom God had endowed with the gift of poesy, and whose hearts He had touched with the love of His truth. It is acknowledged by the apostate Hamilton, that one of the earliest and most effectual means of promoting these ends was the circulation of certain books in the vernacular dialect, exposing the vices of the Clergy, which were printed in England and surreptitiously introduced into the country. Early in the century the Reformed sentiments had been diffused by metrical and dramatic writings. The Latin Satires against the Friars, by the celebrated Buchanan, were elegant and pungent, but of course almost a dead letter to the common people. The instinctive passion for Scottish Poetry, however, was not allowed to wear itself out, neglected and unnourished. It was abundantly fed and cherished by friends of the Reformation. It is told of one Kyllor, that he composed a Scripture Tragedy on the crucifixion of Christ, which was enacted in the presence of James V. at Stirling, about the year 1535, in which it was very easily perceived that the Romish Clergy, in opposing the truth and persecuting its friends were boldly delineated as the modern representatives of the Jewish Priests in their treatment of the Saviour and his followers. Shortly after this period, Alexander, Lord Kilmaurs, "painted forth the hypocricy of the Friars in rhmyme" in "An Epistle directed from the Holy Hermite of Larite (Loretto) to his brethren the Grey-Friars." James Stewart, son of Lord Methven, composed Poems and Ballads in a similar strain after the death of the Vicar of Dollar. And with the same purpose, Robert Alexander, advocate, published the Earl of Errol's "Testament" in Scottish metre. All these must have aided, in a greater or less degree, to secure the special object aimed at—the advancement of the

Reformation by exposing and ridiculing the Romish System, and the character and conduct of its abettors.

But another name appears on the roll of these worthies—a name of which honoured mention is made in the record of the sayings and doings that helped forward the great cause to the desired issue—SIR DAVID LINDSAY of the Mount. He has been represented as *par excellence* the Poet of the Reformation. He was a patriot, a statesman, and a theologian, as well as a poet. *Reform* appears to have been the one object of his existence—*Reform* everywhere, in Church and State, in the municipality and in the family—Reform among all classes of individuals, from the Monarch and his lordly Prelates down to the meanest and most insignificant of the commons of the realm.

Sir David Lindsay, or Lyndsaye, was born at the paternal seat near Cupar, in Fifeshire, in 1490. After being educated at the University of St. Andrews, and making the tour of Europe, he was introduced to the Court, appointed Gentleman of the Bedchamber to the King, and Tutor and Companion to the young Prince—afterwards James V., by whom he was knighted and made Lyon King-at-Arms, in 1530. Having devoted a goodly portion of his public life to the service of his king and country, he retired to the seclusion of his ancestral halls where he spent his latter days in rural tranquility, and died in the year 1553. His principal poetical productions, abound in racy pictures of the times, in humorous and burlesque description, and in keen and cutting satire. The facetious and undaunted satirist lashes the vices of the clergy with an unsparing hand, and a whip of scorpions. And from his exalted and public position, and the plainness and boldness of his ridicule and invective, he must very materially have advanced the reformed opinions.

His *Play*, "The Satire of the Three Estaitis," is a most remarkable production; a Satire on the whole of the three Orders—Monarch, Barons, and Clergy—brimming with pungent exposure and rebuke. It was acted at Cupar in 1535; at Linlithgow, before the King and Queen, the Court and Country in 1540; and at Edinburgh, before the Queen-regent, a great part of the nobility, and a vast number of people, in 1554. When acted at Linlithgow, the Parliament Hall of the Palace was the Theatre; and among the royal, noble, and distinguished personages who constituted the audience, Gavin Dunbar, the Archbishop of Glasgow, was present. "It was at a time when Beaton and the Bishops had rid themselves, either by banishment or the stake, of every preacher in the kingdom. And what did Lindsay do on that occasion? By a happy stroke of his genius he converted the stage itself into a pulpit, and brought in a Lutheran Doctor as one of the *dramatis personae*, and made him pour in a volley of sound doctrine upon the mitred churchmen, which must have made every man among them flinch, and all their orthodox ears to tingle. The effect upon the King himself has been recorded. The play was no sooner over than he commanded the Bishops to follow him into the royal closet, and there told them roundly that they must henceforth 'reform their fashions and manner of living, and that unless they did so, he would send ten of the proudest of them to his uncle Henry of England, and as those were ordered (or handled), so he would order all the rest that would not amend.'"

The following quotations are from this Play—"*The Satyre of the Three Estaitis.*" They tell their own tale with a vengeance, and are as plain as they are pithy and pointed. Throughout the Play, Lindsay assumes to himself the designation of "*King Correctioun.*" Here is a telling exposure of the nefarious exaction of Corpse-dues. It is the explanation by PAUPER, in answer to a question by DILIGENCE *how that he had happinit on their unhappie chances:*—

> Gude man, will ye gif me your charitie;
> And I sall declair yow the black veritie.
> My father was ane auld man and ane hoir,
> And was of age fourscore of yeiris, and moir.
> And Mald, my mother, was fourscore and fyftene,
> And with my labour I did thame baith sustene.
> We had ane meir, that caryt salt, and coill
> And everilk yeir, scho brocht us hame ane foill.
> We had thre ky, that was baith fat, and fair
> Nane tydier into the toun of Air.
> My father was sa waik of blude, an bane
> That he deit, quharefor my mother maid gret mane;
> Then scho deit, within ane day or two;
> And thare began my povertie and wo.

Introduction.

Our gude gray meir was baitand on the field,
And our lands laird tuke hir, for his heryeild,
The vickar tuke the best cow be the heid
Incontinent, when my father was deid.
And quhen the vickar hard tel how that my mother
Was deid, fra hand, he tuke to him ane uther:
Then Meg, my wife, did murne baith evin, and morrow,
Till at the last scho deit, for verie sorrow;
And quhen the vickar hard tell my wyfe was deid
The third cow he cleikit be the heid.
Thair upmest clayis, that was of raploch gray,
The vickar gart his clark bere thame away.
Quhen all was gane, I micht, mak na debeat,
Bot, with my bairns, past, for till beg my meat.
Now, haif I tald yow the black veritie,
How I am brocht into this miserie.

Here again is a cutting Satire, ridiculing the assumed virtue of *relics*, and the prerogative of trafficking in *indulgences*. It is part of the speech of PARDONER, a doughty champion, who designates himself Schir Robert Romeraker.

Bona dies! Bona dies!
Devoit pepill, gude day, I say yow
Now tane ane lytill quhyll, I pray yow,
    Till I be with yow knawin;
Wat ye weill how I am namit?
Ane nobill man, and undefamit,
    Gif all the suith war schawin
I am schir Robert Rome-raker,
Ane perfyte publik pardoner,
    Admittit be the Pape:
*   *   *   *   *   *
[*Heir sall he lay doun his geir upon ane buird; and say:*]
My patent pardouns, ye may see
Cum fra the Can of Tartarie,
    Weill seald, with oster-schellis.
Thocht ye haif na contritioun
Ye sall haif full remissioun
    With help of bukes, and bellis.

Heir, is ane relict lang and braid
Of Fyn Macoull the richt chaft blaid
    With teith and al togidder:
Of Collins cow, heir is ane horne,
For eating of Makconnals corne
    Was slane into Balquhidder.
Heir is ane cord, baith gret and lang,
Quhilk hangit Johne the Armistrang,
    Of gude hemp soft and sound:
Gude, halie pepill, I stand for'd
Quhaever beis hangit, with this cord,
    Neidis never to be dround.
The culum of Sanct Bryds kow
The gruntill of Sanct Antonis sow,
    Quhilk bure his haly bell:
Quha ever he be heiris this bell clink;
Gif me ane ducat for till drink
    He sall never gang to hell.

Introduction.

Without he be of Beliall borne,	Of that cummer, I sall mak yow quyte
Maisters, trow ye, that this be scorne?	Howbeit your selfis be in the wyte,
Cum win this pardoun, cum.	And mak ane fals narratioun.
Quha luffis thair wyfis nocht with thair hart	Cum win the pardoun, now let se
I haif power thame for till part,	For meill, for malt, or for monie
Me think yow deif and dum.	For cok, hen, guse or gryse.
Hes nane of yow curst wickit wyfis	Of relics, heir I haif ane hunder;
That halds yow intil sturt and stryfis	Quhy cum ye nocht? this is ane wonder:
Cum tak my dispensatioun:	I trow ye be nocht wyse.

After this manner does this fearless "*King Correctioun*," hold up to public ridicule and scorn the various corruptions of the days in which he lived. His efforts were ably seconded by the *Wedderburns* in Scotland, and *Myles Coverdale* in England—the former by their "Compendious Book of Psalms and Spiritual Songs" commonly known as "The Gude and Godlie Ballates;" and the latter by his "Goostly Psalms and Spirituall Songes."

The WEDDERBURNS—brothers, James, John and Robert—were natives of Dundee and flourished about the middle of the 16th century. They appear to have been specially fortunate in their teachers. The College of St. Leonard's in St. Andrews, where they prosecuted their studies, had been recently founded, under the principal regency of Mr. Gavin Logie, who all but openly laboured to instruct his pupils in the principles and doctrines of the Reformers; whilst at the same time St. Mary's College—where at least John studied for a session or two—was privileged with the services of Patrick Hamilton, which doubtless had a precious influence throughout the whole University. And in Dundee they received the instructions of Friar Hewat, a Dominican Monk in the monastry of that order, by which they were trained to deeper and clearer views of the truth. Thus they were led to acknowledge and profess the principles of the Reformation; and brought to its defence and propagation the invaluable gift of poesy with which they were endowed.

JAMES WEDDERBURN, the eldest of these brothers, we are told by Calderwood, —"had a good gift of poesie and made diverse comedies and tragedies in the Scotish tongue, wherein he nipped the abusses and superstitioun of the time. He composed in the forme of tragedie the beheading of Johne the Baptist, which was acted at the West Port of Dundie, wherin he carped roughlie the abusses and corruptions of the Papists. He compiled the Historie of Dyonisius the Tyranne, in form of a comedie, which was acted in the playfield of the said burgh, wherein he otherwise nipped the Papists." He composed another play, which cost him a life-long exile from his native land. It appears that some time previously, the King's confessor, Friar Laing had attempted the "conjuring of a ghaist" at Kinghorn. James Wedderburn burlesqued this ridiculous attempt;—in consequence of which he was delated to the King, and letters of caption directed against him. He however escaped to France, became a merchant in Dieppe, where he lived in prosperity and died in peace—saying to his son on his deathbed, "We have beene acting our part in the theater; you are to succeed; see that you act your part faithfullie."

Regarding JOHN, the second brother—we are informed that "being persuaded by his friends, albeit against his will, he took on the order of preesthood, and was a preest in Dundie. But soon after he began to profess the reformed religioun. Being summouned, he departed to Almaine (Germany), where he heard Luther and Melancton, and became verie fervent and zealous. He translated manie of Luther's dytements into Scotish meeter, and the Psalmes of David. He turned manie bawdie songs and rymes in Godlie rymes. He returned after the death of the King, in December 1542, but was againe persued by the Cardinall, and fled to England."

ROBERT, the youngest of the three, was also admitted to priest's orders, and ultimately succeeded Robert Barrie, his maternal uncle, as Vicar of Dundee. He also, at all events during the life of Cardinal Beaton, had to seek safety in flight to a foreign land. He is said to have superintended the editing of the "Gude and Godlie Ballates" after his brother's death, and to have taken great pains to provide for the various metres pleasant and appropiate tunes.

The authorship of this remarkable compendium is chiefly ascribed to John Wedderburn, the second of these brothers—though there is little doubt that the poetic genius of the other two, has also to some extent, found vent in it. Indeed it is surmised on the ground of strong probability, that some stray effusions of other authors form part of the compilation. It consists to a great

extent of translations and adaptations of German Songs and Psalms—such as
"Luther's Dytements" as Calderwood tells us. The refugees being brought
into close contact with the evangelical and stirring hymnology of Germany,
and observing its effects on the people and the prosperity of the Church,
could scarcely fail to appropriate to the use of home and country an agency
so powerfully beneficial.

The date of the first issue of these songs in a collected form cannot be
accurately ascertained—but it must have been earlier than 1578—for an edition
of that date makes reference to a former one. It must have existed in some
shape or other, many years previously; and in all probability it was originally
scattered throughout the country in leaflets and detached portions. Knox, in
his history of the Reformation, records the fact that Wishart, on the night
before he was apprehended at Ormiston—"after supper, held comfortable purpose
of the death of Goddis chosen childrin and merrily said? 'Methink that I desyre
earnestlye to sleep;' and thairwith he said 'will ye sing a Psalme?' and so
he appointed the 51st Psalme, which was put in Scotishe meter and begane
thus:—'Have mercy on me now good Lord, After they great mercy,'"[a]&c.,
lines which occur in the second verse of that Psalm in the Wedderburn
collection. Some of these Psalms, therefore, must have been published before
16th January, 1545-6.

This "Compendious Book" consists of three classes of compositions. The
first is Doctrinal, including a Catechism, the Creed, &c., in metre, with various
Spiritual Songs. The second contains versions of twenty-two Psalms, and a
number of Hymns. And the third, which gives its peculiar character to the
collection, consists of secular songs, but converted from profane into religious
poetry. McCrie, in referring to the title "Gude and Godlie Ballates," gives
the following information "This title sufficiently indicates their nature and
design. The air, the measure, the initial line or chorus of the ballads most
commonly sung by the people at that time, were transferred to hymns of
devotion. Unnatural, indelicate, and gross as this association appears to us,
these spiritual songs edified multitudes in that age. We must not think that
this originated in any peculiar depravation of taste in our reforming countrymen.

Spiritual songs constructed upon the same principle, were common in Italy. At the beginning of the Reformation, the very same practise was adopted in Holland as in Scotland."

This is a specimen of the "Ballates":—

The False Fire of Purgatorie.

Of the false fire of purgatorie,
Is nocht left in ane sponke;
Therefore, says Gedoe, woes mee,
Gone is priest, frier, and monke.

The reik, sa wonder deir, they salde
For money, gold, and landes;
Whill halfe the riches on the molde
Is seaset in their handes.

They knew nothing but couetice,
And loue of paramours,
And let the saules burn and bis
Of all their foundatours.

At corps presence they would sing
For riches to slocken the fire;
But all pure folk that had nae thing,
Was scaldit bane and lyre.

Yet sat they high in parlement,
Like Lordes of hie renowne;
While now that the New Testament
Hes it and them brought downe.

And thocht they snuffe at it, and blaw
Ay while their bellies ryue;
The mair they blaw, full wel they knaw
The mair it does misthryue.

The following, from the "Gude and Godlie Ballates," tell their own tale very plainly. We can conceive them sung with considerable animation by parties who had long groaned under Popish tyranny.

"God send euery Priest ane wife."

God send euery priest ane wife,
And euery nunne a man,
That they may liue that haly life,
As first the kirk began.

Sanct Peter quhom nane can repruve
His life in mariage led:
All gude preists quhom God did lufe
Their maryit wyfes had.

Greit causis then I grant had they
Fra wyfes to refraine;
Bot greiter causis haue they may
Now wyfis to wed againe.

For then suld noght sa mony hure
Be vp and downe this land;
Nor zit sa many beggers pure
In kirk and mercat stand.

And not sa meikill bastard seid,
Throw out this cuntrie sawin;
Nor gude men vncouth fry suld feid
And all the suith were knawin.

Sen Christs law and common law,
And doctours will admit
That priests in that zock suld draw;
Quha dar say contrair it?

From "*The Paip, that pagane full of pryd.*"

* * * * *

The sisters gray, before this day
Did crune within their closter:
Thay feeit ane frier their keyis to beir,
The feind ressaue the foster:
Syne in the mirk, he weill culd wirk
And kittile them wantonly
Hay trix, trim goe trix
    under the greene-wod-tree.

The parson wald nocht hae an hure,
But twa, and they were bony;
The viccar, thocht he was pure,
Behuift to hae as many.
The parish priest, that brutall beist
He polit them wantonly.
Hay trix, trim, &c.

The bishop wald not wed ane wife,
The abbot not perseuane
Thinkand it was ane lustie life,
Ilk day to hae ane new ane,
In euery place, an vncouth face
His lust to satisfie.
Hay trix, trim, &c.

Of Scotland well the friers of Faill
The limmery lang has lastit,
The monks of Melros made gude kaill,
On Fryday quhen they fastit:
The silly nunnis cast vp their bunnis,
And heisit their hippes on hie.
Hay trix, trim, &c.

These, one might think, are sufficiently pointed and cutting—but not more so than the following by a different author—viz., Wm. Warner, 1589—(from "ALBION'S ENGLAND.")

> It was at midnight when a Nonne in travell of a childe,
> Was checked of her fellow Nonnes for being so defilde;
> The Lady Prioresse heard a stirre, and starting out of bed
> Did taunt the Novasse bitterly, who, lifting up her head,
> Sayd, 'Madame, mind your hood;' for why, so hastily she rose,
> That on her head, mistooke for hoode, she donde a Canon's hose.
>   *See Collier's Bibliographical Catalogue, ii.* 483-86.

"The Goostly Psalmes and Spiritual Songs," by Coverdale—about 1546, partake very much of the character of this Compendious Book. There is such a remarkable similarity between a great many of the pieces in the respective volumes as to lead one to the conclusion that the authors have been culling flowers in the same garden, and drinking at the same fountain :—whilst the general style of versification and objects aimed at, are almost identical. This perhaps was to be expected when it is remembered that they were sufferers for the same cause, exiles in the same foreign land, brought much into each others company, endowed with the same spirit, and aiming at the same end.

In a lengthened address to the Christian reader, Coverdale thus apologises for the character of his book. "Wolde God that oure mynstrels had none other thynge to play upon, neether our carters and plowmen other thynge to whistle upon save Psalmes, Hymnes, and such godly songs as David is occupied withal. And yf women syttynge at theyr rockes or spynnynge at the wheles had none other songes to passe theyr tyme withall then soch as Moses sister, Elchanahs wife, Debora, and Mary the Mother of Christ have songe before them, they shulde be better occupied than with hey nony nony, hey troly loly, and soch lyke fantasies."

The following two verses must suffice as a specimen of Coverdale's songs. They are the opening lines of a long poem which is more of a satirical cast than the others, and is the last in the volume :—

LET GO THE WHORE OF BABYLON.

Let go the whore of Babilon,
  Her kyngdome falleth sore;
Her merchauntes begyne to make theyr mone
  The Lorde be praysed therefore.
Theyr ware is naught, it wyll not be bought
  Great falshood is found therein
Let go the Whore of Babilon
  The mother of al synne.

No man wyll drynke her wyne any more
  The poyson is come to lyghte;   [sore
That maketh her merchauntes to wepe so
  The blynde have gotten theyr syghte.
For now we se Gods grace frelye
  In Christ offred us so fayre
Let go the Whore of Babilon
  And bye no more her ware.

That Wedderburn and Coverdale either "drank from the same fountain," or that the one imitated the other, will appear from the following specimens of their versions of the Psalms. The first are their respective renderings of

Ps: CXXX—obviously modified translations of Luther's version of this Psalm. Coverdale's version is declared by Professor Mitchell to be the most favourable specimen of his powers as a translator and versifier:—

DE PROFUNDIS PSALM CXXX.

WEDDERBURN.	COVERDALE.
Fra deip, O Lord, I call on thee,	Out of the depe cry I to thee
Lord, heir my inuocatioun	O Lorde, Lorde, hear my callynge;
Thy eiris thow inclyne to me	O let thyne eares enclyned be
And heir my lamentatioun:	To the voyce of my complaynynge.
For gif thow will our sin impute	If thou, Lorde, wilt deal with stratenesse,
Till vs, O Lord, that we commit	To marke all that is done amysse,
Quha may byde thy accusatioun?	Lord, who may abyde thy reckonynge?
Bot thow art mercyfull and kynde,	But there is mercy ever with thee,
And hes promittet in thy write,	That thou therefore mayst be feared;
Them that repent with hart and mynde	I will abyde the Lord patiently;
Of all thair sin to mak them quyte.	My soul looketh for him unfaynted,
Thocht I be full of sinfulnes,	And in his word is all my trust;
Zit thow art full of faithfulnes,	So is my hope and comforte most
And thy promeis trew and perfyte.	His promise shall be fulfylled.
My hope is steidfast in the Lord,	As the watchemen in the mornynge
My saul euer on him traist,	Stonde lokynge longe desyrously;
And my beleue is in thy word,	That they myght see the faire daysprynge;
And all thy promittis maist and leist.	So waytteth my soul for the Lord dayly.
My saull on God waitis and is bent	Therefore let Israel wayte styll,
As watcheman wald the nicht wer went,	Until it be the Lorde's wyll,
Bydand the day to tak him rest.	To lowse them from adversitie.
Israell, in God put thy beleue,	For with the Lord, there is mercy,
For he is full of gentilnes,	And great plenteous redempcyon;
Fredome, gudnes, and sal releue	Although we synne oft wickedly,
All Israel of thair distres:	Yet hath he for us a sure pardon.
He sall delyuer Israel,	He shall redeme poore Israel
And all thair sinnes sall expell,	And him shall he delyver full well
And cleith them with his richteousnes.	From all the synnes that he hath done.

The following are the versions, given by each, of Psalm LXVII. It will at once be observed that with very trifling exceptions, all the difference between the two lies in the fact that the one uses the Scotch and the other the English form of certain words :—

DEUS MISEREATUR. PSALM LXVII.

WEDDERBURN.

O God be mercyfull to vs,
   And send to vs thy blissing;
Thy face schaw vs sa glorious,
   And be euer to us luiffing;
That men on eird may knaw thy way,
   Thy sauing heill and richteousnes,
That they be nocht led nicht nor day
   Fra thy preceptis, and trew justice,
To seik saluatioun quhair nane is.

Thairfoir the pepill micht magnifie;
   O God, all folke, and honour thy Name;
Let all the pepill rejoice glaidlie,
   Becaus thow dois richt without blame:
The pepill dois thow judge trewlie,
   And ordouris euerie Natioun:
Thow hes declarit the Eird justlie
   Euer sen the first Creatioun,
Throw thy godlie prouision.

The pepill most spred thy name sa hie,
   All pepill (O God) mon giue thee honour:
The eird alswa richt plenteouslie,
   Mot incres euer moir and moir;
And God, quhilk is our God ouer all,
   Mot do vs gude and plesour.
God mot bless us greit and small,
   And all the warld him honour
Alway, for his micht and power.

COVERDALE.

God be mercifull unto us,
   And send over us his blessynge;
Shew us his presence glorious,
   And be ever to us lovynge;
That men on earth may know thy way,
   Thy saving health and righteousnesse;
That they be not led by nyght nor day,
   Throw the pretexte of trew justice
To seek salvacyon wher none is.

Therefore the people mought magnifie thee:
   O God, let all folke honour thy name:
Let all the people rejoyce gladly,
   Because thou dost ryght without blame.
The people dost thou judge truly
   And ord'rest every nacyon;
Thou hast directe the earth justly,
   Ever sense the first creacyon,
With thy godly provision.

O God, let the people praise thee;
   All people, God, mought give thee
The earth also ryght plenteously [honoure;
   Mought increase ever more and more;
And God which is our God over all,
   Mought do us good and pleasure,
God bless us now both great and small,
   And all the world him honoure,
Fearynge alwaye his myght and power.

There is evidence that Wedderburn's "Gude and Godly Ballates"—especially those in which the errors and superstitions of Popery were exposed—were much relished by an indignant populace, struggling to throw off the shackles of an unscrupulous and intolerant priesthood. His Psalms and spiritual songs, along with those of Coverdale, set to simple music, were eagerly appropriated and used in religious services to give expression to the devotional workings of the heart. True, they do not appear to have been employed as *church songs*, properly so called, nor to have received ecclesiastical sanction. Nevertheless they were sung by individuals, and in all probability by families, in the worship of Jehovah; and doubtless did good service in preparing the way for the public authoritative adoption of the version of the Psalms by Sternhold and Hopkins, with the first instalment of which the History of the Scottish Metrical Psalms commences. The worshippers in the Romish Church had nothing to do with the musical service. They were not allowed to take any share in it. They could only listen—it might be to the drawling intonations of the priest, to the artistic chanting of a surpliced choir, or to the music of the organ in all its grandeur. But now that they had been led to feel, by the means we have been endeavouring to sketch, the enrapturing effects of taking part in sacred psalmody with the living voice, they would not be content until permitted to join with one voice and one heart in the public service of song. This was one of the ruling principles of the Reformation. The hearts of an enlightened people, freed from the darkness of Romanism, must find vent for joy and gratitude in song. Possessed of Psalms and Hymns in their own language, and set to suitable music, they found in them the appropriate expression of their new-born spiritual light and life.

Wherever these Psalms and Sacred Songs were introduced, their influence on the character and conduct of the people was the same. Calvin's original version, translated by Marot and Beza, speedily attained a most extraordinary popularity—a popularity which it continues still to command. Until the great reformer secured more appropriate music for them, these psalms were rapturously sung by all ranks and classes to their own profane ballad tunes, fairly taking possession of the people and superseding every other kind of song. The Emperor Francis, to suit his proclivities for the chase, adopted as his hunting song—"As pants the hart for water brooks." And one of his cast-off favourites sang as specially suiting her case—"Out of the depths to thee I cried." The Camisards chose as their war-song, which they raised with loud and enraptured voices whenever they marched forth to battle, one of the most stirring Psalms in the collection—the sixty-eighth. The first verse, the part generally used on such occasions, is thus translated:—

Let God but rise and shew his face,
And in a moment from the place
    Our foes are disappearing.
Their camp dispersed, bereft their pride,
Astonished, pressed on every side,
    They flee at his appearing.

We shall behold their scattered tents
Fade like a vapour dark and dense
    Their nothingness resuming:
As melts the wax in fervent heat
So melt the wicked when they meet
    Our God, their strength consuming.

An incident in the religious wars of the Huguenots is characteristic and to the point. When the town of Montauban, which had been for many years their stronghold, was besieged in 1623, all attempts to capture it proved ineffectual. At length it was determined to raise the siege. On the evening before this purpose was put in execution, the people of the town were apprised of the approaching decampment of the army, by a Protestant soldier, who played upon his flute the air of this war-song—the sixty-eighth Psalm. The besieged took this for the signal of their deliverance, and were not mistaken. (See "Baird on Liturgies.")

"Ah, how they penetrate the very soul at such moments," exclaims a brilliant delineator of the Huguenot character, "these rude songs of our fore-fathers! These psalms are our epic; and the most profoundly truthful epic that has ever been written or sung by any nation; an endless work, of which each of us becomes afresh the author; a sacred treasure, where are gathered beside our patriotic remembrances, the remembrances, hopes, joys, and griefs of each. Not a verse, not a line, which is not a whole history, or a whole poem. This was sung by a mother, at the cradle of her first-born; that was chanted by one of our martyrs as he marched to his death. There is the song of the Vaudois returning armed to their country; here that of the Camisards advancing to battle. This was the line interrupted by a ball; this was half murmured by an expiring father, who went to finish it among the angels. O our psalms! our psalms! Who in human language could ever tell what you say to us in our solitudes, upon the soil crimsoned with our blood, and under the vault of heaven, from whose height look down upon us those who with us have wept, and sung, and prayed!"

THE SCOTTISH METRICAL PSALMS.

I.

The Earliest Versions, 1548 till 1564.

By STERNHOLD AND HOPKINS.

IT is believed that a short historical account of the origin of our Metrical Version of the Scottish Psalter, and its gradual development into the authorised condition in which it now exists for use in divine worship, will prove interesting and acceptable to the general reader. The records bearing on the subject are not easily accessible; and when collected into a concise and chronological narrative, as is proposed to be done in the following notices, they cannot fail to be appreciated. The authorised version, at present in use, has maintained its honoured position for nearly two centuries and a quarter, and is the result of immense labour on the part of translators and versifiers, thoroughly qualified by talent, piety, and learning for the work entrusted to them; and every step of their progress was taken under the careful superintendence of the highest authorities of the country, both civil and ecclesiastical.

The work of preparing the first metrical version of the Psalter as a whole extended over a period of about fourteen years—viz., from 1548 till 1562—and although the book was popularly known as "Sternhold and Hopkins'" version, it was the joint production of at least eight translators and versifiers. The date of the first edition of Sternhold's version is not certainly known, but it is believed to be 1548. The following is its title—"Certayne PSALMES chosē out of the PSALTER of DAVID, and drawē into English metre, by Thomas Sternhold grome of yᵉ Kynges Maiesties roobes. Excudebat Londini Edvardus Whitchurche." The work is remarkably rare, and contains only 19 Psalms, viz.:—Ps. 1, 2, 3, 4, 5, 20, 25, 27, 29, 32, 33, 41, 49, 73, 78, 103, 120,

The Scottish Metrical Psalms.

122, 138. The volume contains a Dedication to King Edward VI., of which the following is a portion:—

"To the most noble and verteous King, oure Soueraygne Lord, King Edward vj Kinge of Englande, France, and Ireland, &c., Thomas Sternholde, Grome of Hys Maiestie's robes, wysheth increase of healthe, honour, and felycytie. Althoughe moste noble Soueraigne, the grosnes of my wit doth not suffyce to searche out the secrete mysteryes hidden in the boke of Psalmes whyche by the opinion of many learned men comprehēdeth the effect of the whole Bible; yet trusting to the goodnesse of God whyche hathe in hys hands the key thereof, which shutteth and no man openeth, and openeth and no man shutteth, albeit I cannot geue to youre Maiestye great loaues thereof, or bring into the Lord's barne ful handefulles; yet to thintent, I woulde not appear in the haruest vtterly ydle and barraine, being warned with the exaumple of the drie figtre, I am bold to present unto youre Maiestie, a fewe crummes which I have pycked vp from vnder the Lorde's borde.—Seeing further, that youre tender and godly zeale dooeth more delight in the holye songes of veritie then in any fayned rymes of vanytie, I am encouraged to trauayle further in the said booke of psalmes; trustynge that as your Grace taketh pleasure to heare them song sometymes of me, so ye will also delight not only to see and reade them youre selfe, but also to commaunde them to bee songe to you of others; that as ye haue the psalme it selfe in youre mynde, so ye maye iudge myne endeuoure by youre eare."

In the following year an edition was issued containing 37 Psalms by Sternhold, and seven by Hopkins, with this title—"*Al suche Psalmes of* DAVID *as* Thomas Sternholde late grome of y*e* Kinges Maiesties Robes didde in hys lyfe tyme draw into English metre. *Newly emprinted by Edwarde Whitchurche, cum privilegio ad imprimendum solum.* London 1549." Sternhold's Psalms—thirty-seven in number—terminate with the words, "Finis. *Here end the psalmes drawen into Englisshe metre, by M. Sternholde.*" On the reverse is a preface by John Hopkins, announcing his addition of seven others, as translated by himself; and these are followed by the words—"Finis. *Imprinted at London by Edwarde Whitchurche the XXIIII day of December.* ANNO DOM. 1549." At the end of the book is a spare leaf containing a woodcut of the church in a state of glory, with this line in the inner margin, "All fayre and white art thou my churche, and no spotte is in thee." This edition is also of excessive rarity. It contains

44 Psalms, and was re-issued two years afterwards, viz., in 1551, the full title being similar to that of the previous edition. Hopkins, the editor, speaks with great modesty regarding the merits of the seven which he has contributed. He says, in a short preface—" *Thou haste here (gentle Reader) vnto y*ᵉ *psalmes that were drawen into English metre, by M. Sternhold, vii moe adioined. Not to the intēt that they shoulde bee fathered on the dead man, and so through his estimacion to be the more hyghly esteemed: neyther for that they are, in myne opinion (as touching the metre) in any part to be compared with his most exquisite doings. But especially for that they are fruiteful, although they bee not fine; and comfortable vnto a Christyan mind, although not so pleasaunt in the mouthe or eare. Wherefore, yf thou (good reader) shal accept and take thys my doyng in good part, I have my heartes desire herein. Farewell. J. H.*"

The following is a specimen of Sternhold's versification, as it appears in this Work:—

PSALM XIX. (*Sternhold*, 1549).

1.

The heavens and the fyrmamente
  do wondersly declare:
The glory of God omnipotent,
  Hys woorks and what they are,

2.

Eche day declareth by hys course,
  an other day to come:
And by the nyght we knowe lykewise,
  a nyghtly course to runne.

3.

Ther is no lãguage, tong, or speche,
  wher theyr sound is not hearde:
In al the earth and coastes therof
  Theyr knowledge is conferd.

4.

In them the Lord made royally,
  a settle for the sunne:
Wher lyke a Gyant joyfully
  he myght hys iourney runne.

5.

And all the skye from ende to ende
  he compast round about:
No man can hyde hym from his heate
  but he wil fynd hym out.

Various editions of this work, all nearly similar, were published until the year 1556, when a slightly enlarged version appeared with this title—" ONE AND FIFTIE PSALMES OF DAVID in Englishe metre, wherof 37. were made by

The Scottish Metrical Psalms.

Thomas Sternholde; ād the rest by others. Cōferred with the hebrewe, and in certeyn places corrected as the Text and the sens of the Prophete required with musical notes." Below it is Crespin's device, viz., a large Y, with an old man holding up a rod in one hand, and with the other pointing to a scroll which appears to encircle the Y, and contains the words, "Intrate per arctam viam.— Jam. 5. Yf any be afflicted let him pray, and it any be merye let him sing Psalmes." The Psalms here printed are Sternhold's 37, and 7 by Hopkins, as in the edition of 1549, to which are now added—appearing here for the first time—Ps. 23, 51, 114, 115, 130, 133, 137—all which appear to have been the production of W.W.—initials of William Whittingham. This Psalter forms part of the Geneva Collection, comprising the Form of Prayers, Confession of Faith, Order of Discipline, Calvin's Catechism, &c. At the end of the *Catechism*, which is the last in the volume, the Printer's device is repeated, with the words, "Imprinted at Geneva by John Crespin, Anno D., M.D.LVI. the tenthe of february." *(Appendix I.).*

Four years afterwards—viz., in 1560—a version was issued, containing 65 Psalms. Title:—"Psalmes of David in Englishe metre, by Thomas Sterneholde and others; conferred with the Ebrue, and in certein places corrected, as the sense of the Prophete required; and the Note ioyned withall. Very mete to be used of all sorts &c. Newly set fourth and allowed, according to the order appointed in the Quenes Maiesties Iniunctions. James v. 13. Col. III. 16. 1560." The Psalms published in this version are followed by the Hymns—Benedictus, Magnificat, and Nunc Dimittis, in metre; the commandments, "with an addition; the Lords Prayer, and the XII Articles of the Christen fayth."

In 1561, the work was still further enlarged and appeared as "FOURSCORE AND SEVEN PSALMES, by Thomas Sternhold and others; together with the SONG of SIMEON, the TEN COMMANDMENTS, &c.—Geneva, printed by Zacharie Durand—1561." And the entire Psalter appears to have been issued in the following year—1562—with this title, "THE WHOLE BOOKE OF PSALMES, collected into English metre, by T. Sternhold, J. Hopkins, and others; conferred with the Ebreu; with apt notes to sing them withall. London, by JOHN DAYE, 1562." Mr. Lea Wilson was under the impression that Day's Edition of 1563 was the *first collected Edition of the whole* 150 *Psalms;* but Herbert distinctly specifies this of 1562 ; mentioning, at the same time, that towards the close of the year 1561, Day had license to print "the resydewe of the Psalmes not heretofore printed.

So that this maketh up the hole." So that during the following year he might well put forth an entire edition.

In 1563, another entire version was issued by Day, viz.:—"THE VVHOLE BOKE OF PSALMES, collected into English metre by Thomas Starnhold, J. Hopkins, and others; conferred with the Ebrue, with apt notes to synge them with all. Faithfully perused and alowed according to the order appoynted in the Queenes Maiesties Iniunctions. Very mete to be used of all sorts of people privatly for their solace and comforte; laing a part all ungodly songs and Ballades, which tende only to the norishing of vice and corrupting of youth (2 scrip: texts). Imprinted at London by John Day, dwellynge over Aldersgate, beneath Saynt Martyns *Com gratia et privilegio Regiae Maiestatis perseptennium.* An. 1563." This version contains—besides "A treatise by Athanasius," "Veni Creator," &c., " A shorte introduction into the Science of Musicke, made for such as are desirous to have the knowledge thereof, for the singing of the Psalmes." During the same year, and again in 1565, Day published the "WHOLE PSALMES, in foure parts," of which the following is a brief description:—Title of the *First Part*, within a flowered border, "MEDIUS OF THE WHOLE PSALMES IN FOURE PARTES, whiche may be song to al musicall instrumentes, set forth for the encrease of vertue and abolishyng of other vayne and triflying ballades. Imprinted at London by John Day dwelling over Aldersgate, beneath Saynt Martyns. Cum gratia &c. 1563." The reverse shows a woodcut of the Royal Arms between two pillars, on the pedestals of which are the initials I. D. On the next leaf begins *Veni Creator,* followed by *Venite, Te Deum, Benedicite, Benedictus, Quicunque Vult,* and other hymns, followed by the Psalms. The *Second* volume is "CONTRA TENOR OF THE WHOLE PSALMES," the remainder of the title as in the first, The *Third* "TENOR," and the *Fourth* "BASSUS, OF THE WHOLE PSALMES," &c., as before. The musical notes appear in every page. The work is in oblong 8vo. This version, the same substantially as that of the previous year (1562) was adopted on public authority by the Church of England, by whom it continued to be used until it was superseded by Brady and Tait's Version in 1696.

In 1564 an important Version was printed at Edinburgh, under sanction of the General Assembly of the Church of Scotland. The book is now remarkably rare and valuable. The Psalms have no separate title page, but form part of a volume designated and described as follows:—"THE FORME OF PRAYERS AND

The Scottish Metrical Psalms.

MINISTRATION OF THE SACRAMENTS, &c., vsed in the English Church at Geneua, approued and receiued by the Churche of Scotland. Whereunto besydes that was in the former bokes, are also added sondrie other prayers with the whole Psalmes of Dauid in English meter. The contents of this boke are conteined in the page following. 1. Corinth. iii. 'No man can lay any other foundation, then that which is laid, even Christ Jesus.' Printed at Edinburgh by Robert Lekpreuik. M.D.LXIIII." On the reverse of the title page are:—"The contents of the boke. 1. A Kalender with an Almanack for 12 years. 2. The Confession of the Christian Faith. 3. The Order of Electing Ministers Elders and Deacons. 4. The Assemblie of the Ministerie everie Thursday. 5. An Order for interpretation of the Scriptures and answering of doutes, observed one day in the weke. 6. A confession of our sinnes used before the Sermon. 7. Another Confession used in the Churche of Edinburgh. 8. A confession used in tyme of extreame ttouble (*trouble*). 9. A general prayer after the Sermō for the whole state of Christs Churche. 10. Other sortes of prayers to be used after the Sermon, the Sonday, and day of publick prayer. 11. Prayers used in the tyme of persecution by the Frenchemen, and when the Lordes Table is ministered. 12. A Thanksgiving for our deliverance, with prayers for continuance of peace. 13. A prayer used at general and perticuler assemblies. 14. The Ministration of Baptisme and the Lordes Supper. 15. The forme of Mariage. the visitation of the Sicke, with a prayer for the Sicke, and the maner of Buryall. 16. An order of Ecclessiastical Discipline. 17. The 150 Psalmes of David in meter. 18. The Catechisme of M. Calvin. 19. A brief examination of Children before they be admitted to the Lordes Table. 20. Sundrie sorts of prayers. 21. A prayer for Scollers. 22. A prayer for labourers." The Catechisme has a separate title—" The Catechisme or maner to teache children the Christian religion. Wherein the minister demandeth the question, and the chylde maketh answere; made by the excellent Doctor and Pastor in Christs Church, John Calvin. Ephes. 2. The doctrine of the Apostles and Prophetes is the foundation of Christs Church. Imprinted at Edinbrough by me, Robert Lekprivik. 1564. Cum privilegio." (*App. II.*). The work is in 12mo. Very considerately, to aid in the production of this version—" The Kirk lent Robert Lekprevick, printer, twa hundredth pounds (Scottish money) to help to buy Irons, ink, and paper, and to fee craftsmen for printing of the Psalmes." On the 25th of December, 1564, the Assembly ordained "That every Minister,

Exhorter, and Reader, sal have ane of the Psalme Books latelie printed in Edinburgh, and use the order contained therein in Prayers, Marriage, and Ministration of the Sacraments." (*App. III.*). This is the earliest edition of the Psalms printed *for the use of the Kirk of Scotland* which is known to exist. The book is of extreme rarity. It will thus be observed that at an early period the Scottish Reformers made Congregational Psalmody a stated portion of public worship— following the example of some of the churches abroad—and that for this purpose they adopted the metrical version commenced by Sternhold in the reign of Edward the Sixth, and enlarged and completed during the following reign by the English exiles at Geneva. It is to be remarked, however, that in course of its development from Sternhold's first 19—onward to the entire 150—a great number of variations were introduced, and that the Scottish version is in many respects different from that adopted by the English church, the variation consisting chiefly in the substitution of different versions of 41 Psalms. (*App. IV.*).

THOMAS STERNHOLD, the originator, and one of the principal contributors to this version, was born in Hampshire and educated at Oxford, after which he became Groom of the Robes to King Henry VIII. and to his successor, Edward the VI. He died in 1549.

JOHN HOPKINS is described as having been a clergyman and schoolmaster in Suffolk. After the death of Sternhold he appears to have acted as Editor of the infant Psalter. His name is mentioned as among the exiles during Queen Mary's reign, but his place of refuge is not correctly known. He obviously had no connection with those who left Frankfort for Geneva.

WILLIAM KETHE is spoken of as a native of Scotland. He joined the exiles at Geneva in November, 1556, and was employed by them after the death of Queen Mary in carrying on negotiations with some other English congregations. He afterwards went to England and was Chaplain to the forces under the Earl of Warwick, in 1563 and 1569. He became Minister of Child-Ockford, in Dorsetshire, about 1571. His rendering of the 94th Psalm was published 1558, attached to a Tract by John Knox. Warton styles him "no unready rymer." He wrote some popular religious ballads, the most noted of which was "A Ballad on the whore of Babylon, called Tye thy Mare Tom boy." We are told that, about the end of January, 1559, "When, as Kethe was returned to Geneua with answer from the Congregations and Companies that were dispersed in sundry places off Germany and Heluetia, the congregation prepared themselves to depart, sauing certeine whiche remained behinde the rest, to witt, to finish the bible and the psalmes, both in meeter and prose, which were already begon, at the charge of such as were off most habilitie in that congregation. And with what successe these workes were finished I must leave it to the Judgements of the godly learned." It appears that Kethe was one of those who remained, and that he was specially engaged on the metrical translation of the psalmes—as the whole of the 25 additions published in 1561 were produced by him.

WILLIAM WHITTYNGHAM was born in the county of Chester in 1524, and educated at Oxford. He joined the company of exiles at Frankfort, and adhered to those who left that city in 1556 for Geneva, where he married the sister of Calvin, and in 1559 succeeded Knox as pastor. He returned to England in 1560; and in 1563, though still adhering to Puritan views, was, by the friendship of the Earl of Warwick, made Dean of Durham, which office he held till his death in 1579.

THOMAS NORTON was born in Bedfordshire, and became a barrister-at-law, and whilst he wrote several tracts on the religious controversies of his age (a "forward and busy Calvinist," as Wood calls him) he enjoyed considerable poetical reputation, and is best known as the joint author with Sackville, Lord Bathurst, of the Tragedy of Gordabuc.

JOHN PULLEYN, or PULLAIN, was a native of Yorkshire. In 1547, at the age of 30, he became senior student of Christ's Church. He became an exile, after preaching the Reformation privately at St. Michael, Cornhill, 1556. On his return to his native country he was made Archdeacon of Colchester, and died 1565.

ROBERT PONT was a native of Culross, Perthshire; entered College at St. Andrews in 1543. He was a member of the first General Arsembly in 1560, and continued to take an active interest in the business of the Church. He was successively Commissioner of the Diocese of Moray, Provost of Trinity College, and Minister of St. Cuthberts, Edinburgh. He was also for some time a Senator of the College of Justice, but was deprived of his seat on the bench in consequence of an Act prohibiting " all persons exercising functions of ministrie within the Kirk of God, to bear or exercise any office of civil jurisdiction."

JOHN CRAIG (I. C.) became Minister of Holyrood House, and of the King's Household, after an absence from his native country of 24 years. He had been a Monk of the Order of St. Dominic at Bologna, in Italy; but having embraced

Earliest Versions, 1548-64.

the Protestant faith narrowly escaped martyrdom. He died on 4th December, 1600, aged 88.

The following brief specimens of the poetical talent of three of these contributors to our old version will be read with interest. It will be seen that considerable use has been made of that version in preparing our present one; and indeed our 100th Psalm, in long metre—*All people that on earth do dwell*; and 124th, in peculiar metre—*Now Israel may say*, stand as they were originally produced, with the exception of a few slight changes on account of style:—

From the Edition printed at Edinburgh, by Lekprevik, 1564.

PSALM LVII. 1-3. BY ROBERT PONT.

1. Be mercifull to me O God
   be merciful to me
   For why? my soule in all assaults
   shall euer trust in thee.
   And till these wicked stormes be past
   which rise on euerie syde:
   Vnder the shaddowe of thy wings
   my hope shall alwayes byde

2. I will therefore call to the Lord,
   who is most high alone:
   To God who will his worke in me
   bring to perfection.

3. He will sende down from heauen above,
   to saue me, and restore
   From the rebukes of wicked men,
   that fayne wolde me deuoure.

PSALM XC. 1-6 BY WILLIAM KETHE.

1. O Lord thou hast bene our refuge,
   and kept us safe and sounde:
   From age to age, as witness can
   all we which true it founde.

2. Before the mountaines were foorth brought
   yer thou the earth didst frame:
   Thou wast our great eternal God
   and stil shalt be the same.

3. Thou dost vaine man strike downe to dust
   though he be in his floure
   Again thou saist, Ye Adams sonnes,
   returne, to shewe your power.

4. For what is it a thousand yeares
   to count them in thy sight:
   But as a day which last is past,
   or as a watche by night?

5. They are, so sone as thou dost storme,
   euen lyke a slepe or shade,
   Or lyke the grasse, which as we knowe,
   betymes away doth fade.

6. With pleasant dewes, in breake of day
   it groweth vp full grene:
   By night cut downe, it withreth, as
   no beautie can be sene.

The Scottish Metrical Psalms.

Psalm CXLV. 1-6. By I. C. (John Craig).

1. O Lord thou art my God and King,
   Vndoubtedly, I will the praise:
   I will extoll and blessings sing,
   Vnto thyne holy name alwayes.
2. From day to day I wil thee blesse,
   And laude thy name worlde without end.
3. For great is God, most worthy praise,
   Whose greatnes none may comprehend.
4. Race shal thy workes praise vnto race:
   And so declare thy power, ô Lord.
5. The glorious beautie of thy grace,
   And wondrous workes, will I record.
6. And all men shall the power (ô God,)
   Of all thy fearful Actes declare:
   And I to publishe all abrode,
   Thy greatnes at no tyme will spair.

II.

Complete Authorised Version, 1564 till 1635.

By STERNHOLD AND HOPKINS.

WE have remarked that Sternhold's version of 1563 was adopted by the Church of England. The fact that almost incessant editions of it continued to be poured forth from the press during the first 150 years of its reign, gives an impressive idea of the great hold it had obtained upon the English mind. In the list given by Dr. Cotton, in his most elaborate and interesting work, "*Editions of the Bible and parts thereof*," we find mention made of about 309 distinct issues (and the Doctor does not imagine he has given them all) previous to the year 1700, when the more recent version of Brady and Tait began to divide the public favour with it, and by degrees nearly drove it from the field.

In Scotland, the reign of the version adopted by the Scottish Church—1564— was not so protracted; neither was it, perhaps, so quiet and undisturbed. It was very frequently republished, amid repeated proposals to have it revised or replaced, until it was finally and entirely superseded by the authorised version in 1650—the version still in use—although it appears to have been used by the Scottish congregations in Holland till a later period. We would here simply indicate some of the more important editions that continued to be issued for the Kirk of Scotland onward till 1634, when the experiment of a new version was attempted. The press of Day, or Daye (John, Richard, and assignees), London, seems to have been specially busy—scarce a year having passed without witnessing one new edition, and very often two. Lekprevick, of Edinburgh, reissued his version of 1564 in the following year. In 1569, THE PSALMES, BY STERNHOLD, &c., conferred with the Ebrue, with notes, was printed at Geneva, by John Crespin. In 1575 we have the following:—"The whole Boke of Psalmes collected into Englishe metre by T Sternholde, W. Whitingham. I. Hopkins and others; conferred with Hebrue, with apt notes to syng them withall. Newly set forth and allowed to be Song of all the people together, in all churches before and after mornyng and Euening prayer, as also before and after the Sermons, and moreover in private houses, for their godly solace and comfort, laying apart all ungodly songes and balades which tend onely to the nourishyng of vyce and corrupting of youth—James V. Collossi. III. Imprinted ..t London by John Daye, dwelling over Aldergate. Cum priuilegio Regiae Maiestatis per Decennium. 1575. Forbyddying all others to print these Psalms or any part of them." The volume contains "A treatise made by Athanasius the great, wherein is set foorth howe and in what maner ye may use the Psalmes." Also the following songs set to music—" Veni Creator." " Venite Exultemus." " The Song of S. Ambrose called Te Deum." " The Song of the Three Children." " The Song of Zacharias called Benedictus." " The Song of the blessed Mary, called Magnificat." " The Song of Simeon called Nunc Demittis." " The Creed of Athanasius, called Quicunque Vult." " The Lamentation of a Sinner." " The humble suit of a Sinner." " The Lords Prayer or Pater Noster." " The X Commandments Audi Israel—Exod XX" In the same year was printed at Edinburgh, " THE CL PSALMES OF DAVID IN ENGLISH METER. WITH THE FORME OF PRAYERS and ministration of Sacraments &c used in the Churche of Scotland—Whereunto, besydes that was in the former bookes, are added also sundrie other Prayers, with a new and exact Kalender for XVI yeres next to come (compiled by Robert Pont) Printed at Edinburgh by Thomas Bassandine, dwelling at the Nether Bow—1575.—Cum privilegio." Bassandine issued another edition in 1578, containing the book of Common Order and Calvin's Catechism. In the same year an edition of the Geneva version was printed by Denham, viz.:—" The Booke of Psalmes, wherein are contained prayers, meditations, prayses, and thanksgiving to God for hys benefits towards his Church." A version was printed in 1587, for the Kirk of Scotland, by T. Vautrollier, London. The book contained " divers notes and tones augmented to them." The following appeared in 1594, in 8vo, the same printer issuing an edition in 12mo, in 1602:—" THE CL PSALMES OF DAVID IN METRE (for the use of the Kirk of Scotland) with divers notes and tunes augmented to them. James V. 13. If any be afflicted &c. Middleburgh. Imprinted by Richard Schilders, printer to the States of Zealand—1594."

An editition ranking among the first in importance, and forming one of the chief stages in the history of the Psalter, was issued in the following year.

Authorised Version, 1564-1635.   13

The work contains two titles—a *general* and a *special*. The general title is as follows:—" THE CL PSALMES OF DAVID IN METER, with Prayers and Catechism, according to the forme vsed in the Kirk of Scotland. With sundrie other things quhilk sall be declared in the Table next following the Kalender. Edinburgh. printed by Henri Charteris 1596. Cum priuelegio regali." The special title to the Psalmes is :—" THE PSALMES OF DAVID IN METRE. According as they are sung in the Kirk of Scotland. Together with the Conclusion, or Gloria Patri, eftir the Psalme: and alsua ane Prayer eftir eurie Psalme agreeing with the mening thairof. JAMES V. &c. Prented at Edinburgh be Henrie Charteris 1595. Cum Privilegio Regali." The chief distinguishing characteristic of this version is the fact, that it contains a remarkable series of Prayers, and metrical Doxologies adapted to each Psalm. The prayers are in the Scottish dialect, one annexed to each Psalm, and agreeing with "the mening thairof;" and the Doxologies—or conclusions as they are sometimes called—being as various as the different styles of metre, the purpose being that each Psalm should be terminated by one of them. *(App. V., VI.).*

In 1597 an edition of the Psalms for the Kirk of Scotland was printed at Middelburgh, for John Gibson; and two years thereafter, Smyth of Edinburgh printed the following:—" THE CL PSALMES OF DAVID in Meiter, with the form of Prayeris and administratioun of the Sacraments &c. usit in the Kirk of Scotland. Quhair unto ar addit sundry other prayeris with the Catechisme of M. Johne Calvin. and ane Kalender. Edinburgh, printed be Robert Smyth dwelling at the nether Bow. 1599. Cum privilegio regali." *(App. II.).* In 1601 we have " THE CL PSALMES OF DAVID in prose and metre. For the use of the Kirk of Scotland. At Dort, printed by Abraham Canin, at the expenses of the aires of Henry Charteris and Andrew Hart, 1601. Cum Privilegio." This version contains the usual Almanac; The Calendar; Use of Epact; Fairs in Scotland; Confession of Faith, &c. The prose is the Genevan version; the verse, Sternhold's. *Raban,* of Aberdeen, published the Scottish version in 1629, 1632, and 1633. The following is the title of the last of these:—" THE PSALMES OF DAVID, in Prose and Meter; *according to the Church of* SCOTLAND. The Psalms in Prose, on the margine, according to the New Translation, 1610.—(Psal. 96. 1. 2.) IN ABERDENE, Imprinted by EDWARD RABAN, *for David Melvill,* 1633. WITH PRIVILEDGE." Woodcut of King David with a Harp.

The Edinburgh editions of the Psalter, printed by Hart or his heirs, appear

14 The Scottish Metrical Psalms.

to have enjoyed special reputation. Early in this century Hart appears as the leading printer of the Psalter. His first edition seems to have been printed in 1609. In 1611 he printed a version with this title:—"THE CL PSALMES OF Dauid in Prose and Meeter. WHEREVNTO IS ADDED, Prayers commonly vsed in the Kirkes and privat houses. With a perpetuall Kalendar, and all the changes of the moone that shall happen for the space of 19 yeeres to come. Duelie calculated to the meridian of Edinburgh. David with Harp. EDINBVRGH, printed by Andro Hart. 1611." In 1614 another edition appeared; and again, in 1615, we have—"The CL PSALMES OF DAVID in prose and meeter, with their whole usual tunes newly corrected and amended. HEREUNTO IS ADDED the whole Church Discipline, with many godly prayers, and an exact Kalendar for xxv yeeres; and also the Song of Moses in meeter never before this time in print. David with Harp. EDINBVRGH, printed by Andro Hart, Anno 1615." Other editions appeared in 1617 and 1621. In this latter year Andro Hart of Edinburgh died, and several editions of the Psalter were subsequently printed by his heirs, onwards till 1635, when an edition was issued in which "the Psalter reached its climax by the increase of the common tunes, and the addition of harmouy to the entire musical materials." The following is the title of this impression:—"THE PSALMES OF DAVID *in Prose and Meeter* with their whole tunes in foure or mo parts, and *some Psalmes in Reports*. Whereunto is added many godly Prayers and *an exact Kalendar for* xxv yeeres to come. King David, with Harp. Printed at EDINBURGH by the heires of ANDREVV HART, ANNO DOM. 1635." In a woodcut, at the top of the page where the music commences, there is an ingenious monogram of the printer's name—a shield, with the letter A interlacing the figure of a heart. *(App. VII.).*

III.

King James' Version, 1631 till 1637.

E have now to direct attention to a remarkable version which, in the meantime, had been completed under Royal patronage, in the vain endeavour to supplant the old one in the estimation of the Scottish Church. We refer to the version of King James VI. of Scotland and I. of England. When this monarch ascended the English throne he was actuated by the desire of promoting uniformity of worship between the churches in his dominions—subsidiary to his purpose of arbitrary rule over one Prelatic establishment. With this object in view he entrusted the revising of the English translation of the Bible to forty-seven ministers—" the most learned divines of the Church" —who were engaged in the work for three years. The translation now in general use throughout the country is the fruit of their labours. His Majesty deemed that, to serve his purpose, the metrical psalms also required re-modelling, and " vain of his theological learning" and poetical genius, he undertook the task himself of perfecting a new version for general use.

In "HIS MAJESTIES POETICALL EXERCISES at Vacant Hours"—a work printed in 1591—the Royal author thus addresses the Reader:—" Rough and unpolished as they are I offer them unto thee: which *being well accepted*, will move me to haste the presenting unto thee of my Apocalyps, and also *such nomber of the Psalmes as I have perfited, and encourage me to the ending out of the rest.*"

We are, besides, informed by Archbishop Spottiswoode, in his Church History, that when it was proposed at the General Assembly, held at Burntisland in 1601, to have a new translation of the Bible, and a revisal of the Psalms in metre, " King James did urge very earnestly, and with many reasons did persuade the undertaking of the work, shewing the necessity and the profit of it and what a glory the performing thereof should bring to this church: . . . and when he came to speak of the Psalms he did recite whole verses of the same, shewing both the faults of the metre and the discrepance from the text. It was the joy of all that were present to hear it, and bred not little admiration in the whole assembly. . . . But nothing was done in the one or the other; yet did not the King let this his intention fall to the ground. . . . The revising of the Psalms he made his own labour, and at such hours as he might spare from the public cares, went through a number of them, commending the rest to a faithful and learned servant, who hath therein answered his Majesty's expectation."

The faithful and learned servant here referred to was Sir William Alexander of Menstrie, afterwards Earl of Stirling, who held a respectable place among the poets of his time, and doubtless has a better claim than his royal patron to the authorship of this work. He was the author of the stately "Monarchicke Tragedies." In a letter to his friend, William Drummond of Hawthorden, 18th April, 1620, he says:—" Brother, I received your last letter, with the Psalm you sent, which I think very well done: I had done the same long before it came; but He (King James) prefers his own to all else; tho' perchance, when you see it, you will think it the worst of the Three. No Man must meddle with that Subject, and therefore I advise you to take no more Pains therein."

His Majesty died in 1625, some years before the version was completed. The Bishop of Lincoln, in his Funeral Sermon for him, entitled "*Great Britain's Salomon*," tells us how far he had proceeded in this undertaking. After remarking that in James was "observed all that was admirable in the eloquence of Salomon," he thus quaintly proceeds:—" For, beside his prose, *Iter ad carmen nouerat*, hee made a verse also when he pleas'd, and that (as became Buchanan's best scholler) *Sanissimi coloris*, of a most dainty and elaborate composition. An everlasting honour to the Muses! . . . So the greatest potentate of all the Earth may now stoope to a Verse, being the usuall Recreation of King David, together with this first and second Salomon. The King our Master, was in hand (when God called him to sing Psalmes with the Angels) with the translation of our Church Psalmes, which he intended to have finished, and dedicated withall to the onely saint of his devotion, the Church of Great Britaine, and that of Ireland. This worke was staied in the one and thirty Psalme."

James was succeeded by his son, Charles I. The son proved perhaps more anxious than the father that Prelacy—under himself as arbitrary head—should be the uniform religion in his domains; and to aid him in carrying out his measures, he warmly cherished the desire of perfecting his father's version of the Psalms. With this object, he wrote to the Archbishop of St. Andrews in the following terms:—" Whereas it pleased our late dear Father, of famous and eternall memorie, considering how imperfect the Psalmes in meeter presentlie vsed ar, out of his zeal to the glorie of God, and for the good of all the churches within his dominions, to translate them of new, Therefor, as we have given commandement to our trustie and weilbeloved Sr. William Alexander Knycht, to consider and revew the meeter and poesie thereof, So our pleasour is, that zow, and some of the most learned Divynes in that our kingdom, confer them with the originall text, and with the most exact translations, and thairefter certifie back zour opinions vnto ws concerning the same, whether it be fitting that they be published and sung in churches, instead of the old translation or not.—Windsore, 25 August, 1626." This version was published five years after this date, with the engraved title:—" THE PSALMES OF KING DAVID, TRANSLATED BY KING IAMES. *Cum Privilegio Regiae Maiestatis*," and a device representing King David on one side with a harp, and King James on the other with his sceptre, and both holding a book. There is another engraved leaf with the Royal arms and the King's authority for these Psalmes "to be sung in all the Churches of our Dominions," and the volume is closed with this imprint—" Oxford, Printed by William Turner, Printer to the famous University—M.DC.XXXI." The *Authorization* engraved under the Royal Arms is in the following terms:—" CHARLES R.— *Haueing caused this Translation of the Psalmes (whereof our late deare Father was Author) to be perused, and it being found to be exactly and truely done, wee doe hereby authorise the same to be Imprinted according to the Patent graunted thereupon, and doe allow them to be sung in all the Churches of oure Dominiones, recommending them to all our goode Subjects for that effect.*" Three years previously, viz., on 28th December, 1627, Sir William Alexander, the King's " faithful and learned servant," had received the "*Privilegium Regiae Maiestatis*"—the patent of exclusive right—for the space of thirty-one years to print this version, in consideration " of the great paynes already taken and to be taken in collating and revising the same, and in seeing the first impression thairof to be carefullie and well done." *(App. II.).*

Copies of this Royal Translation were sent to so many of the Presbyteries as had sent members to the previous convention, and these were appointed to report their opinion to the next Diocesan Assembly. The indignation of many of the Presbyterians was excited. One of their number—believed to be Calderwood— drew up and widely circulated " Reasons against the Reception of King James' Metaphrase of the Psalms." In these he objected to the "harsh and thrawen phrases, new coined and court terms, poetical conceits, and heathenish liberty which occurred in the new meeter, and served to mak people glaik." *(App. VIII.)*. Probably incensed by the opposition thus aroused, or it may be hoping thereby to quell it, Charles, in December, 1634, enjoined the Privy Council of Scotland "that no other Psalmes of any edition whatsoever be either printed heirefter within that our kingdom, or imported thither, either bound by themselff or otherways, from any forrayne parts." Accordingly, two years afterwards, this version was published under the same title, and containing music notes:—" The Psalmes of King David, translated by King Iames. London, Printed by Thomas Harper— 1636." It seems, however, worthy of observation that, though this latter edition is given simply as a republication of the former—both professing to be translated by King James—there is a marked distinction between the two—a distinction so striking as to lead one to consider them two *separate versions*, rather than two *editions* of the same version.

The following examples will not only serve as a specimen of these translations, but will illustrate the difference beween the two printed versions, and the fact, at the same time, that the versions differ from that of the King's original MS.*

PSALME I.

FROM KING JAMES' MS.

1. That mortal man most happy is and blest
Who in the wickeds counsals doth not walk,
Nor zit in sinners wayis doth stay and rest,
Nor sittis in seatis of skornfull men in talk,
2. Bot contrair fixis his delicht
Into Jehouas law
And on his law, both day and nicht
To think is neuer slaw.

---

* A Volume of Psalms, in the Scottish dialect, written in his Majesty's own hand, is preserved in the British Museum. MSS. Reg. 18 B. XVI. They consist of versions of Psalm I. to XXI. inclusive (except the VIII.), XXIX., XLVII., C., CII., CXXV., CXXVIII., CXXXI., CXXXIII., CXLVIII., and CL., along with a metrical paraphrase of Ecclesiastes, Chap. XII., of the Lord's Prayer, and of the Song of Moses.

King James' Version, 1631-37.

3. He salbe lyk a plesant plantit tree,
   Vpon a reuer syde incressing tal,
   That yieldis his frute in saison dew, we see;
   Whose plesant leif doth neuer fade nor fal.
   Now this is surely for to say
   That quhat he takis in hand,
   It sal withoutin doute alway
   Most prosperously stand.

4. Bot wickit men ar nowayis of that band;
   But as the caffe quhich be the wind is tost:
5. Thairfor they sall not in that iugement stand
   Nor yett among the iust be sinneris lost.
   6. For gret Jehoua cleirly knowis
   The iust mens way vpricht
   But sure the wickeds way that throwis
   Sall perish be his micht.

PSALME 1.

(*Edit.* 1631. *Oxford*).

1. The man is blest that doth not walke
   where wicked councells guide;
   Nor in the way of sinners stands,
   nor scorners sits beside:
2. But of the Lord he on the law
   doth ground his whole delight;
   And on his law doth meditate
   devoutly day and night.
3. He shall be like a planted tree,
   the streames of waters neare;
   Whose pleasant boughs bring timely fruit
   in season of the yeare.
4. His leafe it never wither shall
   as Winters blasted prey;
   And whatsoever he designes,
   shall prosper every way.

PSALME I.

(*Edit.* 1636. *London*).

1. The man is blest who to walke in
   th' ungodlies counsell hates,
   And stands not in the sinners way,
   nor sits in scorners seats.
2. But in the Lord's most holy law
   he hath his whole delight,
   And in his law doth meditate
   devoutly, day and night.
3. He shall be like a tree that grow'th
   the streames of waters neare,
   Whose pleasant boughs bring timely fruit
   in season of the yeare;
4. His leafe shall never withered be,
   as Winters blasted prey,
   And whatsoever thing he doth,
   shall prosper every way.

5. But wicked men are nothing so,
    for they as chaffe shall prove;
    Which whirling windes doe drive away
    and from the earth remove.

Psalm VIII.

(Edit. 1631. Oxford).

1. O Lord, our Lord, how gloriously
    thy name o're all doth sound!
    Whose glory plac'd aboue the heavens,
    no time, nor bounds can bound!
2. From infants mouthes and sucking babes
    thy praise with power doth goe;
    Because of foes, to silence thus
    the proud avenging foe.
3. When I look vp vnto the heavens,
    workes which thy finger wrought;
    The lightning moone, the sparkeling starres,
    which thou from darknesse brought.
4. Ah, what is man (poore wretche) that he
    should come within thy mind?
    Or yet the sonne of dying man,
    that thou to him art kinde?
5. Thou him then Angells in degree,
    more low a little plac'd;
    With glory and with majestie
    thou hast him crown'd and grac'd.

5. They who are wickedly dispos'd,
    no such assurance finde;
    But like unto contemned chaffe,
    are tossed with the winde.

Psalm VIII.

(Edit. 1636. London).

1. O Lord, my God, how doth thy name
    in all the earth excell?
    Who hast thy glory set above
    the heavens where light doth dwell!
2. From infants mouths and sucking babes
    thou dost great strength ordain,
    Because of foes, that soe thou might'st
    th' avenging foe restraine.
3. When I looke up unto thy heavens,
    thy fingers workes which be
    The lightning moon, the sparkling stars
    which were ordain'd by thee.
4. A what is man (poor wretch) that he
    should come within thy mind?
    Or yet the sonne of dying man,
    that thou to him art kind?
5. For thou a little lower him
    than Angels mad'st to be
    With glory and with honour too
    he crowned is by thee.

Psalm CXLVIII. From King James's MS.

1. Sing laude unto the Lord
    Heavens Indwelliris, I say
    To do the same accord
    In places hie and stay
2. And so alwayse
    Ye Angellis all
    Great hostes and tall
    Jehoua prayse.

3. Praise him both sunne and moone
    And starres of shyning light
    The same of you be done
    Ye heavens of heavens most bryght
4. Set forth his fame
    Ye wateris eaven
    Aboue this heaven
    And praise his name.

5. All ye who by his will
   And word created bene
   Praise great Jehoua still,
   Who dois you ay contein
   In stablisht rest.
   Whose just decree
   Can nowyse be
   By oght transgrest

(*Edit.* 1631. *Oxford*).

1. From heavens harmonious rounds
   give praise vnto the Lord;
   And in the parts most high,
   to him due praise afford.
   2. And praise him most
      You Angells pure;
      His praise procure,
      All you his hoast.

3. His praise at length dilate
   you flaming Lord of light:
   And with the starres in state,
   pale Lady of the night.
   4. Heavens, heavens, him praise,
      And all you floods,
      Enclosed in cloudes,
      His glory raise.

6. Praise him eche levyng beast
   That on the earth dois go;
   Thou deape, with most and least
   Of fishe, and whailes also;
   Thou glancing lowe,
   Hail roundlie rolde,
   Snow, whyte and colde,
   His praise furthe showe.

(*Edit.* 1636. *London*).

1. Praise ye the Lord, praise ye,
   even from the heavens the Lord
   In parts that highest be
   to him due praise afford.
   2. And praise him most
      You Angells pure;
      His praise procure
      All you his hoast.

3. His praise at length dilate
   thou sun that shin'st so bright,
   Praise him with stars in state,
   thou moon that clear'st the night.
   4. Heavens, heavens, him praise.
      Ye clouds that move
      The heavens above
      His glory raise.

Every effort to force this version on the Scottish Church proved in vain. For many years that church had submitted to the impost of the Episcopal form of *government;* and Charles, backed by his adviser, Laud, thought the time now come to enforce submission to the Episcopal forms of *worship* also. Accordingly, a more than semi-popish Service Book, known as Laud's Liturgy, with this version of the Psalms attached, was prepared for use in Scottish congregations. By royal mandate, all ministers were to commence the use of it on Sabbath, 23rd July, 1637. But when the Dean of Edinburgh attempted to obey the injunction, the stool of the famous Jenny Geddes hurled at his head, with her exclamation—" Villain, dost thou say mass at my lug !"—raised a storm throughout the land that subsided only on the entire abolition of Prelacy in Scotland, and the establishment of the church more firmly than before, on the basis of Presbyterianism.

In the library of the University of Glasgow there are no fewer than four copies of this remarkable version (K. Iames, 1636). In one of these the following note occurs, inscribed by a former zealous possessor:—" This is the book called the 'Service Book,' that was pressed upon the Kirk of Scotland by the Prelates of that tyme, in one thousand six hundred and thirty-seaven: a book full of errors, and may be called 'the masse in English.' The reason I kept it undestroyed is, that all generations following may take heed of novacions in the Kirk, and praise God for our preservation.—Alexander Blockhead (sic)."

IV.

Sir William Mure's Version, 1639.

IN tracing the development of our metrical psalms, we have now arrived at a memorable era in the history of our country. At the close of our last chapter, we indicated the result of the injudicious attempt to obtrude Laud's Liturgy, with King James'. Psalter attached, on the Church of Scotland. It has been quaintly remarked—" There may be no harm in a prayer book. There is no harm in a pair of crutches. Crutches enable one to walk a little who cannot walk at all; and a prayer book may help those to pray who cannot pray without it; but no tyrant in his freak ever thought of compelling all men (lame or not lame) to walk on crutches. It was Charles' pleasure, however, that all his subjects should pray by his book—and so he ordered it to be." The spirit of the Scots was roused. They could not brook the indignity of tamely submitting to this unscrupulous measure. In a few days nineteen twentieths of the nation had appended their names to a parchment (the National Covenant), binding themselves by solemn oath to oppose the revival of Popish errors in Scotland, and to unite for the defence of their laws, their freedom, and their king. The commotion speedily spread throughout England as well as Scotland; and was not laid until the King's head rolled on the scaffold—a fifty years' struggle resulting in the establishment of the glorious privilege of British freedom. Free Parliaments and Free Assemblies were demanded and enforced by a long outraged people. The famous Assembly of Divines, which was held so long and did such important service at Westminster, was convened by "Ordinance" of both Houses of Parliament—acting on their own responsibility, and setting the King's arbitrary denunciations at defiance. Its first meeting took place on July 1st, 1643. The object was now, from a Presbyterian stand-point, but by constitutional means, the same as that aimed at by Charles with his Prelatic Liturgy—viz., to bring about a uniformity in the doctrine, discipline, and form of Church Government and Worship throughout the Three Kingdoms. A few weeks later, to aid in furthering the same object, "The Solemn League and

Covenant" was cordially attested by the General Assembly and Convention of Estates in Scotland, and by both Houses of Parliament, and the Westminster Assembly in England. A new version of the psalms was specially recommended to the notice of all concerned, as necessary to secure the end in view. The Independents were opposed to the use of any psalter in particular, but the Presbyterians were in favour of such a measure, and the Commissioners from the Assembly of the Scottish Church entered very heartily into the question. Dr. Robert Baillie (one of the Commissioners), made the remark—"The Psalter is a great part of our uniformity, which we cannot let pass till our Church be well advised with it;" and on another occasion he adverted to a "Psalter which," said he, "to my knowledge cost the Assembly much pains, and is like to be one necessary part of the Three Kingdoms' uniformity." The result was a protracted investigation of the claims of a variety of translations, and the adoption of one after it had been subjected to a severely testing ordeal, and altered and amended in repeated meetings of Committee. The versions to which we have now to direct attention, therefore, are the following—given in chronological order:—Sir William Mure's of Rowallan; Francis Rous' earliest edition; William Barton's; Zachary Boyd's; and Francis Rous' revised edition.

Sir William Mure, whose version thus stands first in order, was the lineal representative of a very old and notable Ayrshire family of that name—proprietors of "The Barronies of Rowallan and Pokelly, the lands of Limflare and Lowdown hill, with oyr considerable possessions"—"the proper inheritance of the house of Rowallane at the surname of Mure." It is stated at the close of "The Historie and Descent of the House of Rowallane," that "This Sir William was pious and learned, and had ane excellent vein in poyesie; . . . He lived Religiouslie and died Christianlie in the yeare of his age 63, and the yeare of our Lord 1657." (*App. IX.*). He was a member of the Parliament held at Edinburgh in 1643; and of the "Committee of Warre," for the Sheriffdom of Ayr in 1644, in which year he was present, in command, with the Scottish army in England, and actively engaged in some encounters between the Royal and Parliamentary forces. Literary pursuits seem, however, to have chiefly engaged his attention—especially poetical compositions. His manuscript poetry is considerable. Amongst his largest and most ambitious productions are:—a "Translation of some Books of Virgil;" a religious poem which he calls "The joy of tears;" another, "The Challenge and Reply;" and an entire version of the Psalms, to

which he seems to have devoted himself with much assiduity, on the entreaty—
it is believed—of Principal Baillie, and other influential friends, by whom a
revised version was deemed a desideratum. So far as has been ascertained, this
version exists only in manuscript. It is not known ever to have been printed.
Nevertheless it was favourably noticed by the General Assembly of the Church
of Scotland when making arrangements for a version to which they might give
their sanction. In the *Act* of Assembly—Edinburgh, 28th August, 1647—" for
revising the Paraphrase of the Psalmes brought from England"—the Committees
for revising were "recommended for this purpose, to make use of the travels
of Rowallane." And Baillie, on more than one occasion, spoke in highly
approving terms of it;—as when writing from London on January 1st, 1644,
to his constituents in Scotland, he said—" I wish I had Rowallane's Psalter here,
for I like it better than any I have yet seen." This translation seems to have
been completed in 1639—having been commenced about 10 years previously.
In a short preface the author says:—" It is not to be presumed that this version
in the first draught, attained the intendit perfection. Let the reader observe and
comport with this essaye, till (the Lord furnisching greater measure of light, and
better convenience of tyme) they be amendit."—July 12, 1639.

"To all the sinceare seekers of the Lord, and in him spirituall furniture from the
riche fountaines of his holy word.

"Let not seeme strange that here no studied phrase
Charme thy conceat, and itching eare amaize.
Simplicitie of words, still grave, bold, plaine,
The spirit (doubtless) did not chuise in vain.
Pure streams, from puirest fountaines to present,
in davids language, davids mind to vent
My purpose is. Though for this task but able,
as we, a liveing face see on a Table
in charcoale draughts; or as a body true,
the eye takes up, when but its shade we view,
Yett, for this chairge (in strength how ere uneavin,)
as God hath furnischt, I againe have given,
Where, so thou lyff, and power, from him perceave
both for thy good and mine, my end I have.

for, if I can, whiles I with david sing,
to david's harp, my hart in consort bring,
and profite thee, so god the glorie gett,
to my weak ayme, no end beside is sett."

The following are specimens of the manner in which the psalms are rendered in this version:—

Psalm XV.

Who in thy Tabernacle stay,
Lord who sall dwell with thee
2. upon thy holie mount? the man,
that walketh uprightlie;
Who just is in his works and wayes
whose mouth and mynd aggree
3. in uttring of the treuth; whose tonge
is from backbyting free.

Hee who no evill to his freend
intends; hee, who taks head
his neighboure, nor defam'd to heare,
nor his reproache to spread.

4. Vyle personnes in whose pureer eyes
contemptible appeare,
but faithful men, that fear the Lord,
are honord and held deare.

Hee, to his hurt, thogh having sworne,
whose faith no change doth staine.
5. by biteing usury, who makes
not by his money gain.
hee, 'gainst the innocent, for brybs
who hath not partiall prov'd,
The man who these things shall attayne
Shall in no time be mov'd.

Psalm CXXII.

I joy'd, when to the hous of God
we'l go, to me they said.
Jerusalem within thy gates
our feet thy courts shal tread.
Thou built art o Jerusalem,
as comlie citties be,
Whose pairts compactlie all contriv'd
togither do aggree.

Thither the Tribs, Jehouah's tribs
to prayse his name repair,
to Israel's glory they go up,
the testimonie there.

for throns of Judgement there, the throns
of david's hous are sett.
pray for her peace: Jerusalem,
much good thy lovers gett.

Tranquilitie and weelfare have
they, Peace be in thy fort
Prosperitie thy palices
may fill above report.
O peace be in thee, for my mates
and brethrens sake I'le say,
and for the hous of God our Lord
thy good I'le wish alway.

V.

Francis Rous' first issues, 1641-1643.

FRANCIS ROUS, whose earlier version we have now to notice, as coming next in order, was born at Walton, in Cornwall, in 1579—a younger son of Sir Anthony Rous, Knight. He was several times returned a member of Parliament, and was chosen one of the lay commissioners to the Assembly of Divines at Westminster. On the 29th January, 1643-44, it was "Ordered, that Mr. Prideaux do bring in an ordinance for the settling of Mr. Rous in the place of the provost of Eaton College, and to receive and enjoy all profits, privileges, and emoluments thereunto belonging." This lucrative appointment was held by him for about fourteen years, viz., till his death on the 7th January, 1658. (*App. X.*). He adhered to Cromwell, his original intention being to form the English Commonwealth after the model of the Jewish; but as a Theocracy was rejected, he made the proposal that Parliament should resign the Government into Cromwell's hands, under the title of Protector, whom he looked upon as a compound of the characters of Moses and Joshua. In return, he was declared one of the Protector's Privy Council. His works which are numerous, and all of a religious character, were printed at London in 1653— dedicated to the Saints and to the Excellent throughout the earth. He was a man of great learning and distinction, and eminently qualified by piety and poetic genius to produce a metrical translation of the psalms—a work to which he appears to have been invited both by the English Parliament and the Assembly of Divines. Various versions, or revised editions, were produced by him; and after careful scrutiny, side by side with those of William Barton and Zachary Boyd (which shall be noticed in course) his revised version received authoritative sanction and was adopted by the Church.

Rous' first version bears date 1641. The following is its title:—" The Booke of Psalmes in English meeter. By Francis Rous (a Hebrew quotation, signifying, 'sing ye praises with understanding.') London, printed by R. Y. for Philip Nevil, at the signe of the Gun, in Ivie-Lane, 1641." Preface on sign A. 2.—To the

Reader on A. 5.—The Text, p. 1-312: a Table, 4 leaves. Regarding this translation, Dr. Cotton, in his "Editions of the Bible," says:—"This first edition of Rous' Version of the Psalms is a little book of uncommon rarity; indeed, it seems to have disappeared from view, almost immediately after its birth. Few, if any, writers on the subject speak as if they had personally examined it. I never saw a copy in any library, public or private, except that of Dr. Bliss. It is probable that the General Assembly's *limited* approval of this first attempt of Rous, coupled with some suggestions for its improvement, caused it to be withdrawn." The following is a short specimen of this very rare production, being part of

Psalm XIX.

1. The glory of Almighty God
 the heavens do speak and shew
 The firmament his handy worke
 presenteth to our view.

2. Day unto day doth speak and tell
 his wisdom and his might;
 And a true knowledge of the same
 night sheweth unto night.

3. Both tongue and language bears the voice
 which they abroad do send
 Their speech through all the earth, their words
 go to the wide world's end.

4. A tabernacle for the Sun
 in them prepared hath he;
 Whom, as a bridegroom coming forth
 we from his chamber see.

5. In glorious brightness forth he comes
 from his appointed place.
 As a strong man he doth rejoice
 Swiftly to run his race.

6. And all the skie from end to end
 he compasseth about,
 Nothing can hide it from his heat
 but he will find it out.

After the space of about two years, another version of Rous' Psalter was issued by order of the Commons House of Parliament. It is also, as well as the first, of great rarity. The following is its title:—" The Psalmes of David in English meeter, set forth by Francis Rous. Psal. 47, ver. 7, (a Hebrew phrase, meaning, 'sing ye praises with understanding.') April 17, 1643. It is this day ordered by the Committee of the House of Commons in Parliament for printing, that this Book, entitled, *The Psalms of David*, &c. (according to the desires of many reverend Ministers) be published for the generall use; And for the true correcting of it be printed by these the author shall appoint.—John

Francis Rous' first issues, 1641-43.

WHITE. I do appoint *Philip Nevill and Peter Whaley* to print these Psalmes.—FRANCIS ROUS. London, Printed by James Young for Philip Nevill, at the signe of the Gun in Ivie-lane, 1643." This edition contains, besides the title—Preface, six pages—To the Reader, four pages—The Text, p. 1-312—Psalmes of harder and less usuall tunes corrected, and the tunes not altered, sixteen pages unnumbered—a Table to find each Psalm, eight pages. The author states in the preface that many passages in the old version "seemed to call aloud for amendment," of which he selected "some patterns;" but "apprehending many years past (which experience had shewed to be a true conjecture) that a forme wholly new would not please many, who are fastened to things usual and accustomed, I assaied only to change some pieces of the usual version, even such as seemed to call aloud, and, as it were undeniably for a change. These being seen, it was desired that they should be increased; which being done, they are here subjoined."

This version, thus corrected and amended by the author, was forthwith submitted to the consideration of the Assembly of Divines, and of the House of Commons. In Lightfoot's Journal of the Westminster Assembly, this notice occurs, under date 22nd November, 1643:—"The first thing done this morning was, that Sir Benjamin Rudyard brought an order from the House of Commons wherein they require our advice, whether Mr. Rous's Psalms may not be sung in churches; and this being debated, it was at last referred to the three Committees to take every one fifty psalms." The following notices also occur in the Journals of the House of Commons:—" 20th Novembris, 1643.—Ordered that the Assembly of Divines be desired to give their advice, whether it may not be useful and profitable to the church, that the Psalms set forth by Mr. Rous be permitted to be publickly sung, the same being read before singing until the books be more generally dispersed." Again, December 16, 1644—"The House being informed that divers Divines of the Assembly were at the door, they were called in, and Dr. Burgesse presented the advice of the Assembly of Divines, now by Ordnance of Parliament sitting at Westminster, concerning Visitation of the Sick. He further informed the House, that touching the Directory of all parts of public worship, in ordinary, they have brought up all the parts to the House, save only some Propositions touching the singing of Psalms;" and under date, the 27th of the same month (Dec., 1644), we have this entry—"The House being informed that some of the Divines of the Assembly were at the door, they were called in. Dr. Burgesse presented the remaining parts of the Directory for Public Worship,

The Scottish Metrical Psalms.

concerning the Keeping Days of Public Fasts, of Publick Thanksgiving, and some Propositions touching the Singing of Psalms." The following are specimens of this version:—

PSALM I. *(London, 1643.)*

1. The man is blessed, that to walk
in wicked waies doth feare ;
And stands not in the sinners path
nor sits in scorners chaire.
2. But in the perfect Law of God
he greatly doth delight ;
And on that Law doth meditate
with pleasure, day and night.

3. He shall be like a tree by streames
of waters planted neare,
Which in his season doth not faile
his pleasant fruit to beare.
Whose leaf shall never fade nor fall,
but flourish still and stand :

Even so all things shall prosper well
that this man takes in hand.
4. So shall not the ungodly men,
they shall be nothing so ;
But as the dust, which from the earth
the wind drives to and fro.
5. Therefore shall not the wicked men
in judgment stand approv'd
But sinners from the just shall be
divided, and remov'd.
6. Because the way of righteous men
God doth with favour know
Whereas the way of wicked men
ends in their overthrow.

PSALM LVII, 1-4. *(London, 1643.)*

1. Be merciful to me, O Lord,
be merciful to me ;
Because, according to thy word,
my soule doth trust in the
2. Yea she unto the shadow flies
of thy wings her to cover ;
Until these sad calamities
be wholly passed over.

3. To God most High my earnest cry
in praier sent shall be
Even to that God, who graciously
performeth all for me.
4. From heaven shall his power descend
to save me from their spight
That would devoure me, God shall send
his mercy, truth, and might.

PSALM XCIII. *(London, 1643.)*

1. The Lord doth raign and cloth'd is he
with majesty and light ;
His works do shew him cloth'd to be
and girt about with might.

4. The flouds, O Lord, have lifted up,
they lifted up their voice :
The flouds have lifted up their waves,
and made a mighty noise.

2. For this round world by his great strength
established hath he:
Yea, he so surely hath it set
that mov'd it cannot be.

3. Of old most firmly stablisht is
thy throne of majestic;
And thou without beginning art
from all eternitie.

5. The Lord this noise of many flouds
in might exceedeth farre;
The Highest overcomes the sea,
when his waves mighty are.

6. Thy testimonies are most sure,
and surely lead to blisse
And holinesse for ever, Lord,
in thine house comely is.

VI.

William Barton's Version, 1644.

HERE seems to have been a considerable degree of rivalry between Francis Rous and William Barton as to the honour of producing a version of the psalms which would be most highly appreciated by the public; and, although the influence of the General Assembly prevailed to secure the preference to the translation by "the old Presbyterian Provost of Eton," that by Barton was much commended. William Barton was a celebrated scholar of Oxford, where he took his degree of B.A. on the 23rd of October, 1633. In 1656 he was appointed minister of St. Martin's, Leicester, and had the rectory of Cadeby bestowed on him by Cromwell, whence, however, he was ejected in 1662. He died sometime between 1672, when he published "Two Centuries of Select Hymns and Spiritual Songs"—and 1682, when an edition was printed of his "Book of Psalms," bearing on the title to be "as he left it finished in his lifetime."

Barton's first edition was published in 1644, under the title—"The Book of Psalms in metre; close and proper to the Hebrew; smooth and pleasant for the metre; plain and easie for the tunes; with musical notes, &c., by W. Barton. London: Printed by Matthew Simmons, for the Companie of Stationers." This edition was afterwards much altered, and was republished in 1645-46-54, &c., down to 1768. The edition of 1645 is designated "The Book of Psalms in metre, lately translated, with many whole ones, and choice collections of the old Psalms added to the first impression. Printed by order of Parliament, and now much augmented and amended with the cream and flower of the best authors, &c., with the approbation of more than fourty eminent divines of the city, and the most of them of the Assembly.—By William Barton, Mr. of Arts, and minister of John Zecharies, London. London: by G. M." This version is considerably altered, and contains numerous additions. The title is followed by metrical addresses to sundries, and twelve complimentary sonnets to the author; the text, p. 1-123; variations in the metre; and a table, 13 pages.

The following notices will be read with interest, as shewing that the struggle between this version and that of Rous, which was finally adopted, was keen and protracted. In the Journals of the House of Lords, this entry occurs:—"Oct. 7, 1645.—Upon the humble petition of Wm. Barton, Master of Arts, read this day in the House, it is ordered that two books of David's Psalms, composed in English metre by the petitioner, and presented to their lordships, are hereby referred to the Assembly of Divines, to be read over and judged by them; and the result of their judgments thereupon returned to this House, that such further direction may be given respecting the same, as shall be meet." Regarding these instructions, the Assembly sent a message to the House, on the 14th November, embodying the following memorial:— .

"To the Right Honourable the House of Lords, assembled in Parliament.—The Assembly of Divines having received from this Honourable House an order, bearing date October 7, 1645, to read over and judge of two books of David's Psalms, composed in English metre by Mr. William Barton, and thereupon to return their judgment to this Honourable House, do humbly certify that they had long before received an order from the Honourable House of Commons, bearing date November 20, 1643, to give their judgment touching the Psalms composed in metre by Mr. Rouse, a member of that House; and that thereupon, there was a Committee appointed by this Assembly to consider of these Psalms; and that the same Committee had with much care perused, and with great diligence concurred with the same learned gentleman, to amend and perfect his copy, and had fully finished that Work before they received the said order from the Honourable House of Lords; and withall, that the greatest part of this version was sent to the General Assembly of the Church of Scotland, and there put into the hands of a Committee, and by that Committee, so far as they have examined it, very well approved; yet, in obedience to the order of this Honourable House, they appointed a Committee to consider thereof; and, upon the whole matter, do find reason to certify this Honourable House, That albeit the said Mr. Barton had taken very good and commendable pains in his Metaphrase, yet the other version, so exactly perused and amended by the said Mr. Rouse and the Committee of the Assembly with long and great labour, is so closely framed according to the original text as that we humbly conceive it will be useful for the edification of the

Church.—CORNELIUS BURGES, *Prolocutor pro tempore.* HENRY ROBROUGH, *scriba.* ADONIRAM BYFIELD, *scriba.*"

The members of the House of Lords appear to have been not altogether satisfied with this decision of the Assembly. Barton seems to have petitioned them anew in favour of his version; and this entry appears in their Journals.— "March 26, 1646.—Upon reading the petition of Mr. Wm. Barton, concerning his Translation of his Book of the Psalms, it is ordered to recommend the same to the Assembly of Divines, to certify to this House why these Psalms may not be sung in churches, as well as other Translations, by such as are willing to use them." In reference to this recommendation, the Assembly of Divines forwarded a message to the House, on April 25, 1646, containing the following memorial:—

"TO THE RIGHT HONOURABLE THE HOUSE OF LORDS ASSEMBLED IN PARLIAMENT.—The Assembly of Divines received, April 9th, from this Honourable House, an order bearing date March 26th, 1646, to certify this Honourable House why the Translation of the Psalms made by Mr. Barton may not be used and sung in Churches by such as shall desire it, as well as any other Translation, do hereby return this answer:—That whereas on the 14th of Nov., 1645, in obedience to an order of this Honourable House, concerning the said Mr. Barton's Psalms, we have already commended to this Honourable House one Translation of the Psalms in Verse, made by Mr. Rous, and perused and amended by the same learned Gentleman, and the Committee of the Assembly, as conceiving it would be very useful for the Edification of the Church, in regard it is so exactly framed according to the Original Text, and whereas there are several other Translations of the Psalms already extant, we humbly conceive that, if liberty should be given to people to sing in Churches, every one that Translation which they desire, by that means several Translations might come to be used in the same congregation at the same time, which would be a great distraction and hinderance to edification,—CORNELIUS BURGES, *Prolocutor pro Tempore.*"

Although Barton failed in his endeavours to have his Psalms adopted by the Scottish Church, some attempts still continued to be made in its favour in England, as appears from the following entry in the Journals of the House of Commons:—"Sept. 27, 1650.—The humble Petition of Wm. Barton, Preacher of God's Word, was this day read; ordered that it be referred to Mr. Carill, Mr. Nye, Mr. Bond, Mr. Stronge, Mr. Sedgewick, and Mr. Byfield, or any three

of them, to peruse and consider of the Translation of the Psalms set out by
Mr. Rous, and since reviewed by the said Wm. Barton; and if they shall approve
of the same, then to license the printing thereof." About four years thereafter,
a version appeared, printed by authority, with this title—" The Book of Psalms
in Metre; close and proper to the Hebrew: smooth and pleasant for the metre.
To be sung in usuall and known tunes. By WILLIAM BARTON, Master of Arts,
London. Printed by Roger Daniel, 1654." Prefixed is this authority for
printing it:—" Wednesday January 11th, 1653-4.—At the Councill at White-
hall. Ordered by his Highness the Lord Protector and the Councill, that Mr.
Wm. Barton have the sole printing of the Translation of the Psalms." This
version is materially different from Barton's first edition—licensed by the Committee of the House of Commons concerning printing, April 2nd, 1644—and, in
fact, from all his previous issues. Later editions contain " Amendments and
addition of many fresh Meters." In the copies subsequent to 1654, the author—
who takes credit to himself for having "compiled the whole Book as near as
may be, in the same order of words with the original, *and for the most part in as
perfect prose as verse*"—has introduced this sentence into the middle of his preface
to the reader:—" The Scots of late have put forth a Psalm-Book, most-what
composed out of mine and Mr Rouse his, but it did not give full satisfaction, for
somebody hath been at charge to put forth a new edition of mine, and printed
some thousands of mine in Holland, as it is reported; But whether they were
printed there or no I am in doubt; for I am sure that 1500 of my Books were
heretofore printed by stealth in England, and carried over to Ireland."

The following is a specimen from Barton's first edition (1644), with various
readings of some of the lines as they appear in the edition of 1706:—

PSALM XIX. WM. BARTON.

Edition 1644. *Various Readings. Edit.* 1706.

1. The heavens give to understand
   the glory of the Lord
   The operations of his hand
   the firmaments record.

2. Night unto night hath knowledge show'n
   and day with day confer'd :
   And speech or language there is none
   Where their voice is not heard.

    Day unto day hath made it known
    and night to night declar'd

3. Their line doth close and comprehend
   the vast earth round about :
   Unto the world's remotest end
   their words are passed out.

4. Their line is gone throughout the earth
   their words as far extend
   And there's his royal tent set forth
   the Sun to comprehend.

4. The Lord a TABERNACLE there
   did for the Sun compose ;
   Which as a Bridegroom doth appear
   that from his chamber goes,

5. Which as a bridegroom bravely clad
   doth leave his lodging place :
   And giant-like with gesture glad
   Sets out to run his race.

5. Rejoycing for to run a race
   like to a champion stout :
   At heavens furthest distant place
   begins his going out.

6. And he to heavens utmost end
   his circuit makes compleat :
   And there is nothing can defend
   or hide it from his heat.

6. He reacheth heaven's vast extreams
   making his course compleat.
   And nothing can by any means
   be hidden from his heat.

VII.

Zachary Boyd's Version, 1646 till 1648.

ZACHARY BOYD, whose services in versifying the psalms we have now to notice, was descended from the Boyds of Pinkill, a family of some standing in Carrick, Ayrshire, and a cadet of the noble family of Kilmarnock. He was cousin to Andrew Boyd, Bishop of Argyle, and to Principal Boyd of Trochrig. It is believed that he was born in the town of Kilmarnock in the year 1585, and received his earliest education at the public school there. He afterwards passed through part of his academical course in the College of Glasgow, where he matriculated in 1601, after which he studied at the University of St. Andrews from 1603 to 1607, when he took his degree of Master of Arts. It was a common practice at that time for students to finish their studies at some of the seats of learning on the Continent; accordingly Mr. Boyd, when 22 years of age, entered the College of Saumur in France, which was the chief Protestant seminary of that country. Having spent sixteen years in France, during four of which he was a preacher of the Gospel, he was obliged, in consequence of the persecution of the Protestants, to return to his native country. In 1623 he was appointed minister of the Barony Parish, Glasgow, where he continued till his death, which happened in 1657. After having been eight years a minister, he was found almost uninterruptedly occupying some of the highest offices in the University. In 1631 he was chosen Dean of Faculty. In 1633 he was re-elected Dean. In 1634, and again in 1635, he was chosen Rector. In 1636 he was for a third time Dean of Faculty. He was a member of the several commissions of visitation named by the General Assembly in 1640-42 and 43. By the beginning of 1644, if not earlier, he had been appointed Vice-Chancellor. In 1645 he was for a third time named Rector, and in the following years, down to the time of his death, he continued to officiate as Vice-Chancellor, in which capacity he sat and voted in the Faculty, though not otherwise a member.

The honourable distinction which Boyd thus obtained in the University would

The Scottish Metrical Psalms.

doubtless in some measure help to influence him in his repeated benefactions in its favour, which were most munificent. He bequeathed to it his large and valuable library, besides his immense stock of manuscripts, and £20,000 Scots—equal to about £1666 13s. 4d. sterling—no small sum in those days. In commemoration of his liberality, by the Act of 24th February, 1655, nearly two years after his death, the " Moderator ordain yt the statue of Mr Zacharias Boyd, done in marble be set up in some convenient place of the said new building, with an inscription in gold letters, bearing the munificence of the said Zacharias towards this University." The statue or bust was erected ever the gateway within the College court, with the following inscription:—

"MR ZACHARIAS BODIVS, FIDELIS ECCLESIÆ,
SVBVRBANÆ PASTOR, 20,000 LIB. QVA AD ALENDOS
QVOTANNIS TRES ADOLESCENTES THEOLOGIÆ
STVDIOSOS: QVA AD EXTRVENDAS NOVAS,
HAS ÆDES VNA CVM VNIVERSA SVPELLECTILI,
LIBRARIÆ ALMÆ MATRI ACADEMIÆ LEGAVIT."
NAT. 1590.   OB. 1654.

Judging from the immense mass of his manuscripts, carefully written, besides his published works, which are in considerable variety, Boyd must have been a devoted student. In all his writings, both in prose and poetry, he was animated by a spirit of sincere piety. Many of his subjects are discussed with much ingenuity and originality of thought, and abound in racy metaphor and colouring. One of his most popular attempts to render himself serviceable to his country was in preparing a metrical version of the Psalms for the use of the Church. He must have been engaged in this work for some years previous to 1646, for in that year was published—"'The Psalms of David in meter. By Mr. Zachary Boyd, Preacher of God's Word. The third edition. Printed at Glasgow by George Anderson, anno, 1646."

In the minutes of Assembly of date 11th February, this entry occurs—"The Commission appoynts a letter of encouragement to be written to Mr. Zachariah Boyd for his pains in his paraphrase of the Psalmes, shewing that they have sent them to their Commissioners at London, to be considered and made use of there by those that are upon the same work." Another minute dated Edinburgh, 8th July following, "recommends to Mr. John Adamsone to revise Rous's paraphrase of the Psalmes, and Mr. John Rowe's observations thereupon, and to have his opinion thereof ready for the next Assembly;" and again, on 28th August same year, "for this purpose recommends them to make use of the travels of Rowallen, Master Zachary, or of any other on the subject . . . . The Assembly doth further recommend that Mr. Zachary Boyd be at the pains to translate the other Scripturall songs in meetre, and to report his travels also to the Commissioners of the Assembly." Baillie, about this time, wrote—"Our good friend Mr. Zachary Boyd hes putt himself to a great deal of paines and charges to make a psalter, but I ever warned him his hopes were groundless to get it receaved in our churches, yet the flatteries of his unadvysed neighbours makes him insist in his fruitless design. The Psalms were often revised and sent to presbyteries. Had it not been for some who had more regard than needed to Mr. Zachary Boyd's psalter, I think they had passed through in the end of last Assembly."

In 1648 another Edition of this work was issued, viz., "THE PSALMES OF DAVID IN MEETER: With the Prose interlined. By MR. ZACHARY BOYD, Preacher of GOD'S WORD. PSAL. 119, vers. 54, *Thy statutes have been my songs in the house of my pilgrimage.* PSAL. 34, vers. 2 (a Hebrew quotation, signifying, 'my soul shall make her boast in the Lord'). Printed at GLASGOW by the Heirs of GEORGE ANDERSON. *Anno* 1648." We quote the following from Boyd's address, prefixed to this edition:—

"To the right Reverend, the faithfull ministers of God's Word in Britain and Ireland. RIGHT REVEREND, Grace be to you, and peace from God our Father, and from the Lord Jesus Christ. At the direction of the Generall Assembly at Edinburgh, anno 1644, I put my hand to the work of the Psalmes; whereof I give to you now this last Edition. The work is for the publike service of God in his Church, and it concerns you especially to endeavour by all meanes that this work may be done for the glory of God, and edification of his people, whose soules are committed to your charge."

"Now right Reverend, this is my last labour which I have set down, with the text interlined, that the judicious reader may have under his eye both the text and the verse, and may the more easily confer them together, and discerne.

"I desire that no man esteem that in a mercenery way I am seeking gain by those my labours, though the work hath been both painfull and chargeable, I with a most willing mind offer all in a freewill offering to the Lord, seek gains who will, I will have none, nor do I stand in need, praised bee the Lord: I hope the judicious Reader shall find this last edition mended in many things: If any thing hath been observed by any in the former editions let them consider if it bee mended in this last, which, as I have hitherto done, I submit in all humility to the judgment of my Brethren in the ministry. *The spirits of the prophets are subject to the prophets.* 1 Cor. 14, 32. From GLASGOW, the day 1648. Your humble servant in the LORD. M. ZACHARY BOYD."

On the 1st of May, 1648, Boyd was one of a committee of ministers and elders "revising Rous's paraphrase." And on 10th August following, "the Assembly recommends to Mr. John Adamson and Mr. Thomas Craufurd to revise the labours of Mr. Zachary Boyd upon the other Scripturall songs." A minute dated Edinburgh, 1st January, 1650—the year in which the present version was authorised, sets forth that—" The Commissioners of the Assembly, understanding the paines of Mr. Jo. Adamson, Mr. Zachary Boyd, and Mr. Rot. Lowrie have been at in the translation of the Psalmes and other Scriptural songs in meeter, and how useful their travels have been in the correcting of the old paraphrase of the Psalmes, and in compiling the new, do therefore return their heartie thanks for these their labours, and that the Moderator show this to Mr. J. Adamson, Mr. Robert Lowrie, and wrytte to Mr. Zacharie Boyd to this purpose." Thus it appears that our author was at considerable labour and expense on this subject, and doubtless anticipated the introduction of his version into the service of the Church. This testimonial in "wrytte," conveying the thanks of the Church, so highly complimentary to his talents, could not fail to be gratifying to his feelings. Nevertheless he and his friends by whom he was encouraged in this service, must have been somewhat disappointed that he failed to obtain the laurels to which he aspired. *(App. XI.).*

The following are specimens of Boyd's rendering of the Psalms:—The version of Psalm I., from the Edition 1646, with the same Psalm as it appears in Edition 1648, and the version of Psalm C., from Edition 1648—

Zachary Boyd's Version, 1646-48.

PSALM I. (*Edition* 1646).

1. Blest is the man that walks not in
   th' ungodlies counsel ill,
   Nor stands in ways of sinners, nor
   in scorners seat sits still.
2. But in the law of God the Lord
   is chiefly his delight;
   And also he doth meditate
   in his law day and night.

3. He shall be like a planted tree,
   rivers of waters by ;
   That in his season bringeth foorth
   his fruit most plenteously.
   His leaf also at any time
   not wither shall at all
   And whatsoever thing he doth
   it prosper surely shall.

4. The men ungodly are not so
   but in their wicked way
   Are like the chaffe which stormy wind
   doth quickly drive away.
5. Therefore the ungodly shall not stand
   in judgment steadfastly
   Nor sinners in th' assembly of
   all such as righteous be.

6. For the Lord knoweth well the way
   even of the righteous all
   But the way of ungodly men
   most surely perish shall.

PSALM I. (*Edition* 1648).

1. Blest is the man that walks not in
   th' ungodlies counsell ill
   Nor stands in sinners way, nor doth
   in scorners seat sit still.
2. But in the law of him that is
   the Lord, is his delight,
   And in his law he meditates
   both in the day and night.

3. And he shall be like to a tree
   that by the water springs
   Is planted, and that forth his fruit
   in his own season brings.
   His leafe not wither shall, and what
   he doth shall prosper ay :
4. The ungodly are not so, but driven
   like chaffe by winde away.

5. Therefore not in the judgment stand
   th' ungodly shall at all :
   Nor in the congregation
   of righteous, sinners shall.
6. For well the Lord the way doth know
   of those that righteous be,
   But of ungodly men the way
   shall perish utterlie.

PSALM C. (*Edition* 1648).

1. O all ye lands, unto the Lord
   make ye a joyfull noise ;
2. Serve God with gladnes, him before
   Come ye with singing voice.
3. Know ye the Lord that he is God
   he made us and not wee;
   His people and the sheep likewise
   we of his pasture be.

4. Enter his gates with thanks, and in
   his courts his praise proclame :
   Unto him also thankfull be,
   and do ye blesse his Name.
5. For he that is the Lord is good;
   his mercy's eternall ;
   And als his truth it doth endure
   to generations all.

VIII.

Rous' Last Labours on the Psalter, 1646-49.

THE few notices of our metrical psalter to which we have now to invite attention, extend over a period of about four years, during which time the version of Francis Rous, which was already considerably altered, was carefully collated with those of Rowallen, Barton, and Boyd, and, after repeated revisals and corrections, finally sanctioned and adopted by the Church. The following extracts from official documents will serve to shew the nature of the process to which the Psalter was subjected ere this consummation was reached :—

Rous' version, to which we now allude, was re-issued under this title :—" THE PSALMS OF DAVID IN ENGLISH METER. (Psal. 47, v. 7—in Hebrew, signifying '*sing ye praises with understanding.*') London : printed by Miles Flesher, for the Company of Stationers, 1646." Though the author's name does not appear on the title-page, the work is sufficiently identified by an extract on the opposite page in the following terms :—" Die Veneris, 4th Novemb., 1645.—It is this day ordered by the Commons assembled in Parliament, That this Book of Psalms, set forth by Mr. Rous, and perused by the Assembly of Divines, be forthwith printed; and that it be referred to Mr. Rous to take care for the printing thereof; and that none do presume to print it but such as shall be authorised by him.—*H. Elsinge, Cler. Parl. Dom. Com.*" This resolution of the Commons is thus prefaced in their minutes :—" The House being informed that some of the Assembly of Divines were at the door, they were called in ; and Mr. Wilson acquainted the House, That, according to a former Order of this House, they had perused the Psalms set out by Mr. Rouse, and as they are now altered and amended, do conceive that they may be useful to the Church."

In the meantime, as we have already seen, strong efforts were made, especially in the House of Lords, to have Barton's version adopted. The Commons, however, by a resolution on April 15, 1646, renewed their order "That the Book of Psalms set forth by Mr. Rous and perused by the Assembly of Divines, be forthwith printed in sundry volumes; And that the said Psalms and none others, shall, after the first day of January next, be sung in all Churches and Chapels within the Kingdom of England, Dominion of Wales, and Town of Berwick-upon-Tweed; and that it be referred to Mr. Rous to take care for the true printing thereof." The concurrence of the Lords having been sought in this proceeding, their Lordships on April 18th committed the book, after it had been twice read, to the "consideration of these Lords following, who are to report their opinions to the House.—Comes Essex, Comes Sarum, L. Viscount Say and Seale, Comes Lyncolne, Comes Suffolke, Comes Midd., Ds. North, Ds. Willoughby, Ds. Bruce, Ds. Wharton—any three to meet."

On the 21st January, 1647, Principal Baillie submitted to the Commission of the General Assembly at Edinburgh a paper prepared by the Commissioners at London, of which the following is an extract:—" And becaus the singing of Psalms in churches is a part of the public worship of God, We desire that the Paraphrase of the Psalms in metre, as it is now examined, corrected, and approved by the Assembly of Divines here, and by the Commissioners of the General Assembly in Scotland, may be lykwise authorised and established by Ordinance of Parliament." After a short delay in getting the work through the press, the following communication from the Commissioners in London was laid before the Commission in Edinburgh, on 23rd February, 1647:—

"Wee now send yow the new edition of the Paraphrase of the Psalmes, as it was approved by the Assembly heir, and by yourselves: the animadversions which yow sent us being taken in their propper places, as the worthy Gentleman who hath taken most paines in the work assureth us. If yow be now satisfied with the work as it is, wee shall desire to know so much. One Psalme-book in the three Kingdoms will be a considerable part of uniformity, if it can be agreed upon both there and here ; and we believe it is generally acknowledged there is a necessitie of some change, there being so many just exceptions against the old and usuall Paraphrase. And we humblie conceive there will be as little controversy that this which we now send yow, as it hath come through the hands of more examiners, so it will be found as neir the originall as any Paraphrase in meeter can readily be, and much nearer than other works of that kynd, which is a good compensation to make up the want of that Poeticall liberty and sweet pleasant running which some desire.—Your most affectionat brethren to serve yow, G. WYNRAME, SAMUEL RUTHERFORD, GEO. GILLESPIE."

This communication was at once acknowledged by the Commissioners in Scotland, who at the same time preferred the request to their representatives in London :—" You will be pleased to send down a number of copies of this late Edition to our Clerk, whom we have appointed to cause dispatch them to Presbyteries with diligence, to be considered by them, which we think the best and surest way to obtain a full approbation of the work heir; whereof we make little question if you send a competent number of copies in tyme." In answer to this application, information was forwarded from London to Edinburgh, of date March 9, 1647 :—" We have now fourscore copies in readiness to be sent by the first ship to your clerk, that by him they may be directed to the severall Presbyteries." About four months afterwards:—"At Edinb., 8th July, 1647." —The Assembly " recommended to Mr. Johne Adamsone to revise Rowe's Paraphrase of the Psalmes, and Mr. John Rowe's observations thereupon, and to have his opinion thereof ready for the next Assembly." And at Edinburgh, 28th August of same year, the Assembly ordained the following :—

" ACT FOR REVISING THE PARAPHRASE OF THE PSALMES, BROUGHT FROM ENGLAND," &c.—The General Assembly having considered the report of the Committee concerning the Paraphrase of the Psalmes sent from England, and finding that it is very necessary that the said Paraphrase be yet revised : Therefore doth appoint Master John Adamson to examine the first fourty Psalmes; Master Thomas Craufurd, the second fourty; Master John Row, the third fourty; and Master John Nevey, the last thirty Psalmes of that Paraphrase ; and in their examination they shall not only observe what they think needs to bee amended, but also to set down their own essay for correcting thereof, and for this purpose recommends to them to make use of the Travels of Rowallen, Master Zachary Boyd, or any other on that subject; but especially of our own Paraphrase, that what they find better in any of these works may be chosen, and likewise they shall make use of the animadversions sent from Presbyteries, who for this cause are hereby desired to hasten their observations unto them ; and they are to make report of their labours herein to the Commission of the Assembly for Public Affaires against their first meeting in February next ; and the Commission, after revising thereof, shall send the same to provincial assemblies to be transmitted to Presbyteries, that by their further consideration the matter may be fully prepared to the next Assemblie. And because some Psalms in that Paraphrase, sent from England, are composed in verses which do not agree with the common tunes, therefore it is also recommended that these Psalms be likewise turned in other verses which may agree to the common tunes ; that is, having the first line of eight syllabs, and the second line of six, that so both versions being together, use may be made of either of them in congregations as shall bee found convenient."

Following up the resolution thus enacted, the Commission, on 14th Aprile, 1648, appointed the ministers of Edinburgh, or any three of them, a committee to examine the work of these revisers, and to confer thereupon ; and to report. Again, on the 20th of the same month the following were appointed to the same duty, viz., Mrs. John Adamson, Doctor Colvill, James Hamilton, John Smith, John Neve, Patrick Gillaspie, and James Gutterie. And once more, on 1st May, 1648—" The Commission appoynts Mr. Robert Douglas, George Gillaspie, William Colvill, James Hamilton, John Smith, with Mr. John Adamson, to revise Rouse's Paraphrase of the Psalmes in meeter, the animadversions thereupon, and to Report their opinions."

At the meeting of the Assembly, Edinburgh, 10th August, 1648, sess. xxxviii., it was enacted that—" The Generall Assemblie appoints Rouse's Paraphrase of the Psalmes, with the corrections thereof now given in by the persons appointed by the last Assemblie for that purpose, to be sent to Presbyteries, that they may carefully revise and examine the same, and thereafter send them with their corrections to the Commission of this Assemblie to be appointed for publick affairs, who are to have a care to cause re-examine the Animadversions of Presbyteries and prepare a report to the next Generall Assemblie." On the 5th of January, 1649, the Commission ordered a " competent number " of copies of the work " corrected according to these Animadversions," and now printed, to be sent down to Presbyteries, that they might revise and examine the same, and report.

These returns must have been sent in by Presbyteries before the 7th of June, for on that date—" The Commission appoints the Reports of the corrections on Rouse's Paraphrase of the Psalmes to be delyvered into the Clerk, that he may lend them out to Mr. Johne Adamsone, to be considered against the next Assembly." The next assembly took place in July of that year (1649), when steps were taken to have the work vigorously prosecuted and closed ; and the Commission was " authorised with full power to conclude and establish the

Paraphrase, and to publish and emit the same for public use." The Commission met on 20th November, and after four days' deliberation, enacted the Establishment and Authorisation of the new Psalms on the 23d of November, the Act to take effect on the first day of May, 1650. The detail of these steps, with extracts from the corresponding Records, cannot fail to be interesting to the curious reader.

IX.

Authorised Version, 1650, with Notice of Versions by Brady and Tait, and by Dr. Watts.

AT the meeting of the General Assembly, which commenced its sittings in Edinburgh on the 7th July, 1649, measures were adopted for having the metrical Psalms completed and issued with all promptitude and despatch. · The labours of Translators and of revising Committees had been protracted and arduous; and it was deemed desirable by all parties that they should now be brought to a termination, and the Church put in possession of a Psalter bearing the sanction of her highest authority. Various difficulties had to be encountered in forwarding the work. Baillie refers to some of these in a letter written on 26th January, 1647. "The Translation of the Psalms is past long agoe in the Assemblie; yet it sticks in the Houses. The Commons past their order long agoe; but the Lords joyned not, being solicited by divers of the Assemblie, and of the Ministers of London, who love better the more poetical Paraphrase of their colleague, Mr. Barton. The too great accuracie of some in the Assemblie, sticking too hard to the originall text, made the last edition more concise and obscure than the former. With this the Commission of our Church was not so well pleased; but we have gotten all these obscurities helped, so I think it shall pass." At the last session of the Assembly of 1649, August 6th, the following Act was passed:—

"REFERENCE TO THE COMMISSION FOR PUBLICKE AFFAIRES, FOR RE-EXAMINING THE PARAPHRASE OF THE PSALMES, AND EMITTING THE SAME FOR PUBLICKE USE:—The General Assembly having taken some view of the new Paraphrase of the Psalmes in Meeter, with the corrections and animadversions thereupon, sent from several persons and Presbyteries, and finding that they cannot overtake the review and examination of the whole in this Assembly; therefore now, after so much time and so great paines about the correcting and examining thereof, from time to time, some yeares bygone, that the work may come now to some conclusion, they do ordain the Brethren appointed for perusing the same during the meeting of the Assembly, viz. :—Masters James Hamilton, John Smith, Hew Mackail, Robert Trail, George Hutcheson, and Robert Lowrie, after the dissolving of this Assembly, to goe on in that worke carefully, and to report their travels to the Commission of the Generall Assembly for Publick Affaires, at their meeting at Edinburgh in November. And the said Commission, after perusall and re-examination thereof, is hereby authorised with full power, to conclude and establish the Paraphrase, and to publish and emit the same for publick use.— A. KERR."

The dissolution of the Assembly for the season took place on the same day. The Commission met on the day following—August 7th—and set themselves at once to carry out these instructions, as will appear from this enactment, under that date—" The Commission recommends to the Brethren appointed by the Generall Assembly for correcting the Psalmes to hasten their corrections; and so soon as they have done, that the Moderator conveen the Commission, or a quorum of these that are nearest, to consider their travells and prepare the matter against the Quarterly Meeting." On the same occasion, another duty was imposed upon these Brethren :—" The Commission of Assembly, considering the power they have from the late Assembly to give a competent and honest acknowledgment and reward to the young man that hes been employed in wrytting of the several copies of the Paraphrase of the Psalmes, corrected from time to time, doe therefore appoint the Brethren appointed to revise that Paraphrase, who can best know his paines, to consider what shall be given unto him, and to report their opinions therein to the next quarterly meeting."

In regard to the stage which this matter had now reached, and the aspect in which he viewed it, Baillie thus writes to his friend the Rev. William Spang, under date September 14, 1649 :—" I think at last we shall gett a new Psalter. I have furthered that work ever with my best wishes; but the scruple now arises of it in my mind, the first author of the translation, Mr Rous, my good friend, hes complyed with the Sectaries, and is a member of their republick : how a Psalter of his framing, albeit with much variation, shall be received by our Church, I do not weel know; yet it is needful we have one, and a better in haste we cannot have. The Assemblie hes referred it to the Commission to cause print it after the last revision, and put it in practise."

The quarterly meeting of the Commission commenced its sittings in Edinburgh on the 20th of Nov., 1649, when they appear to have entered heartily and without delay on the work thus referred to them by the Assembly. The revising committee were prepared with their report. The first session, 20th Nov.—*Post meridiem*—" was spent only in the reading and examining the Paraphrase of the Psalmes." Edin., 21st Nov., 1649.—*Post meridiem:*—" A number of the Psalmes of the new Paraphrase this day surveyed." Edin., 22d Nov., 1649 :— " A number of the Psalmes this session surveyed." *Eodem die post meridiem:*— " A number of the Psalmes this day surveyed and examined." Edin., 23d Nov., 1649 :—" The rest of the session spent in reading of the Psalmes." And *Eodem die, post meridiem*—The Commission brought their labours on this business to a close ; and, as empowered by the General Assembly, authorised the new Psalmes to be used in Divine Worship, and ordered precautionary measures anent their being printed and published ; and on the 18th January, 1650, they were approved by the Committee of Estates, and appointed to be used by the Kirk. The following are the Acts detailing these Resolutions. They, along with the Act of Assembly, 6th August, already quoted, are prefixed to the Version of the Psalms to which they refer :—

"ACT FOR ESTABLISHING AND AUTHORISING THE NEW PSALMS.—The Commission of the Generall Assembly having with great diligence considered the Paraphrase of the Psalmes in Meter, sent from the Assembly of Divines in England by our Commissioners whilst they were there, as it is corrected by former Generall Assemblies, Committees from them, and now at last by the Brethren deputed by the late Assembly for that purpose ; and, having exactly examined the same, doe approve the said Paraphrase as it is now compiled ; and, therefore, according to the power given them by the said Assembly, doe appoint it to be printed and published for publick use ; hereby authorising the same to be the only Paraphrase of the Psalmes of David to be sung in the Kirk of Scotland ; and discharging the old Paraphrase and any other than this new Paraphrase, to be made use of in any congregation or family after the first day of Maij in the year 1650 ; and for Vniformity in this part of the worship of God, doe seriously recommend to Presbyteries to cause make public intimation of this Act, and take special care that the same be tymeously put in execution and duely observed."

"COMMISSION TO THE MINISTERS OF EDINBURGH FOR ORDERING THE PRINTING OF THE NEW PSALMES, AND FOR SATISFYING THE TRANSCRIDERS.— The Commission of the Generall Assembly, for the better ordering of the printing

Authorised Version, 1650.

of the new Paraphrase of the Psalmes, that they may be correctly printed, and that the people be not extortioned by Printers or Stationers in the prices, doe hereby give power to the Moderator and Ministers of Edinburgh, or any three of them, with the Clerk, to order the printing of said new Paraphrase, and to sett doune prices thereof, and to take such course with Printers and Stationers as they may neither wrong the people, nor any of them another. Recommending especially to them to have a care that copies be correctly transcribed for the presse, and that the printed copies be well corrected. Giving them also power to determine and modifie what they think reasonable to give to the transcriber for all his pains he has or shall be at."

"ACT BY THE COMMITTEE OF ESTATES.—Edinburgh, 8th January, 1650.— The Committee of Estates having considered the English Paraphrase of the Psalmes of David in Meeter, presented this day unto them by the Commiss. of the General Assembly, together with their Act, and the Act of the late Assembly, approving the said Paraphrase, and appointing the same to be sung through this Kirk. Therefore the Committee doth also approve the said Paraphrase, and interpone their authority for the publishing and practising thereof; hereby ordaining the same, and no other, to be made use of throughout this Kingdom, according to the tenour of the said Acts of the Generall Assembly and Commissioners.—T. HENDERSON."

The new version of the Psalms, thus at length completed, thus sanctioned and appointed to be used in this country in the public and private worship of God, was forthwith issued under this title :—

"THE PSALMS OF DAVID *in Meeter*, newly translated and diligently compared with the Original Text and former Translations, more plain, smooth, and agreeable to the Text than any heretofore. Allowed by the authority of the General Assembly of the Kirk of Scotland, and appointed to be sung in Congregations and Families. Edinburgh : Printed by Evan Tyler, Printer to the King's Most Excellent Majesty, 1650." Small 8vo, pp. 15 and 308. Prefixed are the Acts quoted above, authorising it to be used from and after the 1st of May, 1650.

The following specimens from Rous' version of 1646, when collated with the corresponding passages in the authorised version—which we need not quote— will serve to indicate the nature and the result of the work in which the revising and correcting committee had been engaged during the four intervening years :—

Psalm I. (*Edit.* 1646).

1. The man is blest that in th' advice
 of those that wicked are
 Walks not, nor stands in sinners path
 nor sits in scorners chaire
2. But in God's law delights, on's law
 both day and night doth think;
3. He shall be like unto a tree,
 set by the river's brink,

 Whose fruit's in season, leaf fades not
 all that he doth shall thrive:

4. Not so the wicked; but like chaffe
 which wind away doth drive.
5. In judgment therefore wicked men
 shall not stand justify'd;
 Nor in the assembly of the just,
 the sinners shall abide.

6. Because the way of righteous men
 the Lord with favour knowes
 Whereas the way of wicked men
 unto destruction goes.

Psalm LVII. 1-3. (*Edit.* 1646).

1. Be merciful to me, O God
 thy mercy unto me
 Do thou extend, because my soul
 doth put her trust in thee;
 Yea in the shadow of thy wings
 my refuge I will place
 Untill that these calamities
 do wholly overpasse.

2. My cry I will cause to ascend
 unto the Lord most hy;
 Even unto God who all things doth
 for me work perfectly.
3. He shall from heaven send, and me
 from his reproach defend
 That would devour me; God his truth
 and mercy forth shall send.

Psalm XCIII. (*Edit.* 1646).

1. God reigns; God's cloth'd with majesty;
 God is with strength array'd;
 He girds himself therewith; the world
 moves not, it is not stay'd.
2. Thy throne is fixt of old, and thou
 art from eternity.
3. The flouds, Lord, raise, flouds raise their
 voice;
 flouds raise their waves on hy.

4. But yet the Lord that is on hy
 is more of might by farre,
 Than noise of many waters is,
 or great sea-billows are.
5. Thy testimonies every one
 in faithfulnesse excell;
 And holinesse for ever, Lord,
 thine house becometh well.

The edition of the Psalter, authorised for public use, and issued in 1650, having been revised, corrected, and made "more plain and agreeable to the text than any heretofore," was the first edition of that still used by the Kirk of Scotland and all her Presbyterian offshoots. Other editions were printed by Tyler in the same year; and during the 220 years that have elapsed, the busy, teeming press has poured it forth in countless numbers unvaried, unless in some slight points of orthography.

The reader who has had the patience to follow us thus far in these notices, cannot fail to be struck with the vast amount of care and labour that have been bestowed upon it. The courts of our country, civil and ecclesiastical, obviously felt that a duty of no ordinary magnitude and entailing no small degree of responsibility, devolved on them when they undertook the preparation of a new version of the Psalms—a feeling with which the parties appointed to give effect to their purpose in translating and revising, warmly sympathised. They gave their whole heart to the work, and the grateful approval and appreciation of their labours by all classes throughout the country for successive generations, is sufficient testimony to their success.

The Psalms had always possessed a firm hold of the religious heart of the people of Scotland, and, as thus rendered, that hold was certainly not relaxed but manifestly intensified. One of the reasons—if not the chief reason—why the earlier versions were not altogether satisfactory to Scotchmen, was that the translation was not sufficiently literal—sufficiently "plain and agreeable to the text." And the fact that this version of 1650 is a translation almost as close to the original, as literal and expressive, as the prose, constitutes its strength and excellence, and invests it with a special charm to the Scottish mind. Stern veneration for the pure Word of God has always been a marked characteristic of Scottish Christians, who contemplate with something akin to horror the idea of addition thereto, or detraction therefrom. They have long cherished the conviction that no words can be a vehicle of divine praise equal to the words of Scripture itself; and though the stiffness of Scottish prejudice is proverbially unbending, in this aspect of it we cannot condemn them. The caricaturist may find much in these old Psalms with which to humour his unworthy genius. The fastidious hypercritic may be dissatisfied with some expressions, plain, blunt, and uncouth, and rhymes rough and rugged. But these defects, if defects they be, are surely not of such magnitude as to crush out the admiration which its severe and manly simplicity is so well fitted to excite. A poet might easily produce a version of certain passages of greater poetic beauty, smoother in numbers, more perfect in refinement, and more elegant in expression, but he would overlay and bury out of sight the plain simplicity and truthfulness to the original, in which their beauty and value lie ; and he would find a very great many which, for exquisite sublimity and thrilling pathos, it would test the capabilities of his muse to equal, not to say surpass.

Besides those arising from its intrinsic merits, the present version of the Psalms possesses claims on the veneration and regard of Scottish Christians which no other can possibly have, how high soever its poetic excellence and beauty. It has given expression to the patriotism and piety of our ancestors in the dismal days of persecution, when to worship God according to His Word and the dictates of a sanctified and enlightened conscience, was punishable with death. Its "grave sweet melody" has awakened the echoes of our glens and mountains, and been swept in plaintive wail on moorland breezes, the worshippers compelled to seek such solitudes for safety to pay their devotions to the God of heaven. It has been instrumental in quickening the faith and stimulating the fortitude of our fathers under trials peculiarly affecting, trials of which we in these days happily know nothing. Its strains have been poured into the ear of the martyrs' God from the dungeon, the scaffold, and the stake, expressive of the martyrs' heavenward hope, and reinvigorating them in every heavenly grace. Thousands and thousands have passed away to that better land with its cheering language on their lips. For generations our fathers have given expression to their souls' deepest feelings in the praises of God in its inspiriting language. It has been impressed upon our hearts in the morning and evening service of song around the family altar. We have learned it at a parent's knee. It has formed an element in our education at public schools. It is inextricably interwoven with our religious literature, and has acted an important part in the formation of our religious character. Its expressions spring most readily to our lips when we seek to give utterance to our religious feelings and experiences. Doubtless it will become antiquated and obsolete. But whatever changes may take place in the English language, whatever alteration or improvement may be made in the service of the sanctuary, centuries will come and go before this old version is lost sight of and forgotten by the Christian folk of Scotland.

The following testimonies to the value of these Psalms are by men in whose thorough judgment and good taste all must have confidence:—Dr. Beattie, writing to Dr. Blair on the "Improvement of the Psalmody," in 1778, uses this language:—" This version, notwithstanding its many imperfections, I cannot help thinking the best. The numbers, it is true, are often harsh and incorrect; there are frequent obscurities and some ambiguities in the style; the Scotch idiom occurs in several places; and the old Scotch pronunciation is sometimes necessary to make out the rhyme. Yet in this version there is a manly, though severe, simplicity, without any affected refinement; and there are many passages so beautiful as to stand in no need of emendation." In 1828, Sir Walter Scott wrote in the following terms to Principal Baird, convener of the General Assembly's Committee on Psalmody. The erroneous impression appears to have gone abroad that the Assembly contemplated the alteration of the Psalter. "The expression of the old metrical translation"—says Sir Walter—"though homely, is plain, forcible, and intelligible, and very often possesses a rude sort of majesty which perhaps would be ill exchanged for mere eloquence. Their antiquity is also a circumstance striking to the imagination, and possessing a corresponding influence upon the feelings. They are the very words and accents of our early reformers—sung by them in woe and gratitude in the fields, in the churches, and on the scaffold. The parting with this very association of ideas is a serious loss to the cause of devotion, and scarce to be incurred without the certainty of corresponding advantages. But, if these recollections are valuable to persons of education, they are almost indispensible to the children of the lower ranks, whose prejudices do not permit them to consider, as the words of the inspired poetry, the versions of living or modern poets, but persist however absurdly, in identifying the original with the ancient translation. I would not have you suppose, my dear sir, that I by any means disapprove of the late very well chosen Paraphrases. But I have an old-fashioned taste in sacred as well as profane poetry; I cannot help preferring even Sternhold and Hopkins to Tate and Brady, and our own metrical version of the Psalms to both. I hope, therefore, they will be touched with a lenient hand." This communication from the celebrated Baronet was read in the Assembly, when Dr. Chalmers said:—" I entirely coincide in the opinion so well expressed in the letter of Sir Walter Scott, which at once combined high poetical feeling with humble piety. I consider our metrical version to have a charm peculiar to itself; besides, these Psalms were deeply identified and incorporated with the feelings of the people, who would consider it sacrilege to make any alteration on them. The majority of the people—the peasantry in particular—made a *vade mecum* of the Psalms; they expressed their thoughts in their language by the wayside as they journeyed—they uttered their last words on their death-beds in their hallowed accents. The present version of the Psalms was thus interwoven with the sentiments and devotional ideas of the people in humble life to an extent that, even though better poetry were introduced, an alteration would inflict a wound on the feelings of many of the best men in our land, that no new version, however superior, could atone for."

On looking into such a work as " Dr. Cotton's Editions of the Bible," one feels amazed at the vast number of different entire versions and detached portions of the Psalms that have been published during the last two centuries, chiefly in England. And although it is with the Scottish Psalter we are professing to deal, we may be pardoned if we refer briefly to two of the most important of these.

The version at present in use in the Church of England—which superseded that of Sternhold and Hopkins in 1696—is popularly known as Brady and Tate's version, being the joint production of these parties. Nicholas Brady—an eminent Divine, and a poet of considerable distinction—was born at Brandon, Ireland. He studied at Westminster School, and afterwards at the Colleges of Oxford and Dublin. He was a zealous promoter of the revolution, taking an active part on the side of the Prince of Orange. By his interest with King James' general, he thrice prevented the burning of his native town. After enjoying several preferments in Ireland, he settled in London, and became chaplain to the king. He died May 20, 1726. Nathan Tate was born in Dublin in 1652, and educated in the college of his native city. On coming to London, he assisted Dryden in some of his works, and succeeded Shadwell as poet-laureate to King William. He wrote a variety of poetical works, but is best known by the version of the Psalms, which he executed in conjunction with Brady.

A specimen of this work, containing only the first eight Psalms, was issued previous to 1695; and in that year an enlarged specimen was published, entitled "The first XX Psalms in Verse—being an Essay of a New Version—by N. Brady, D.D., and N. Tate, London. Printed for the company of stationers." This version was licensed to be sung in churches, and differed in many places from that which was afterwards adopted—viz., the version of 1696, which was

Brady and Tait's Version, 1696.

published under this title:—"A New Version of the Psalms of David. Fitted to the Tunes used in CHURCHES. By N. Tate, and N. Brady. London: Printed by M. Clark; for the Company of Stationers. 1696." This Edition, whilst differing in many respects from the specimens previously issued, was itself considerably altered at various times afterwards. It bears the following dedication to the King:—" To His Most Excellent Majesty WILLIAM III. of *Great Britain, France,* and *Ireland,* KING, Defender of the Faith, &c. THIS NEW VERSION of the PSALMS of DAVID is most Humbly Dedicated by His Majesty's Most Obedient Subjects and Servants, N. Brady. N. Tate." In an Advertisement at the close of the Volume, the Authors indicate the methods by which they "have endeavoured to make such a version of the Psalms as may be fit for common use."

King William gave his royal authority for the use of this version in the following terms:—"AT THE COURT AT KENSINGTON, Dec. 3, 1696.—Present: the KING'S Most Excellent Majesty in COUNCIL. Upon the humble petition of N. Brady and N. Tate, this day read at the board, setting forth,—That the petitioners have, with their utmost care and industry, compiled *A new version of the Psalms of David in English metre, fitted for public use;* and humbly praying his Majesty's Royal Allowance that the said version may be used in such congregations as think fit to receive it.

His Majesty, taking the same into his Royal consideration, is pleased to order, in Council, that the said *New version of the Psalms in English metre* be, and the same is hereby, allowed and permitted to be used in all churches, chapels, and congregations as shall think fit to receive the same.—W. Bridgeman."

On the 23rd of May, 1698, the following recommendation of these Psalms was given by the Bishop of London:—"His Majesty having allowed and permitted the use of a New Version of the Psalms of David by Dr. Brady and Mr. Tate, in all churches, chapels and congregations; I cannot do less than wish a good success to his Royal indulgence; for I find it a work done with so much judgment and ingenuity that I am persuaded it may take off that unhappy objection which hath hitherto lain against the Singing Psalms, and dispose that part of divine service to much more devotion. And I do heartily recommend the use of this version to all my brethren within my diocese. H. LONDON." The following is a specimen of this version, along with various readings of the verses as they appear in subsequent editions:—

PSALM XIX. (*Edition* 1696).

1. The Heavens declare thy Glory Lord
   Which that alone can fill;
   The Firmament and Stars express
   Their great Creator's Skill
2. Revolving Days, with every Dawn,
   Fresh Beams of knowledge bring
   From darkest nights succeeding Rounds
   Divine Instructions spring.
3. Their powerful Language to no Realm
   Or Region is confined
   'Tis Nature's Voice and understood
   Alike by all mankind.

4. Their Doctrine's sacred Sense itself
   Through earth's extent displays;
   Whose bright Contents the circling Sun
   Around the World conveys.

5. No Bridegroom for his Nuptials drest
   Has such a cheerful Face;
   No Giant does like him rejoice
   To run his glorious Race.
6. From East to West, from West to East,
   His restless Circuit goes
   And through his Progress cheerful Light
   And vital Warmth bestows.

Various readings in subsequent Editions:—

2. The dawn of each returning day
   fresh beams of knowledge brings;
   And from the dark returns of night
   divine instruction springs.

4. Their doctrine does its sacred sense
   through earth's extent display
   Whose bright contents the circling sun
   does round the world convey.

The only other version of the Psalms to which we shall here allude is that by the learned and celebrated Nonconformist divine, poet, and miscellaneous writer, Dr. Isaac Watts, who was born at Southampton, July 17, 1674. Educated for the ministry, he was ordained in 1702 to the pastorate of the dissenting congregation of Mark Lane, London, the church of which the famous Dr. John Owen had formerly been pastor. In consequence of repeated attacks of illness, his health broke down in 1712, when, for rest and change, he was received into the household of his friend, Sir Thomas Abney—where he remained for 36 years—until his death in 1748, November 25—preaching occasionally to his congregation as his strength allowed. In his retirement he gave himself assiduously to study, and produced the very numerous theological and literary works which have so well served the cause of religion and education. Dr. Watts has, however, probably exerted his widest influence, and earned his most enduring celebrity by his hymns and his metrical version of the Psalms.

The first public appearance of Dr. Watts, as a versifier of the Psalms, seems to have been made in 1712, when he published Psalm cxiv. in the *Spectator*. At this time, his biographer assures us, he had the whole version about half composed, and in 1719 it was published under this title:—" The Psalms of David, imitated in the language of the New Testament, and applied to the Christian state and worship: By Isaac Watts, D.D. London : Printed for J. Clarke and others." This version has been continually reprinted, and has all along been greatly admired, especially by the author's Nonconformist friends. Within the year, when the first edition was issued, four thousand copies were sold. In one of his prefaces the Dr. says:—" If an author's own opinion may be taken, he esteems it to be the greatest work that ever he has published, or ever hopes to do, for the use of the churches;" and Dr. Rippon, in a sermon preached November 17, 1802, bears this testimony in their favour:—" They (these psalms) had not long appeared at the bar of the public before the general voice (with one or two illustrious exceptions) pronounced a flattering verdict on them—a verdict, the wisdom and justice of which have now been sanctioned by the imprimatur, I had almost said, of half a world."

A version of these Psalms was issued in New Brunswick, in 1789—sanctioned by Ecclesiastical Authority, as a manual of praise in Divine worship—according to this enactment:—" Philadelphia, May 24, 1787. The Synod of New York and Philadelphia did allow Dr. Watts Imitation of David's Psalms, as revised by Mr. Barlow, to be sung in the Churches and Families under their care.— Extracted from the records of Synod by George Duffield, D.D., Stated Clerk of Synod."

The following is a specimen of this work. It is to be observed that almost throughout the entire production, the Psalms are composed in two, and very frequently in three versions—" the three most useful metres to which our Psalm tunes are fitted." Thus the xix. Psalm is rendered in three versions. We subjoin three stanzas of each:—

PSALM XIX. (S.M.)

1. Behold the lofty sky
   Declares its maker God.
   And all his starry works on high
   Proclaim his power abroad.

PSALM XIX. (L.M.)

1. The heavens declare thy glory Lord
   In every star thy wisdom shines;
   But when our eyes behold thy word
   We read thy name in fairer lines.

2. The darkness and the light
   Still keep their course the same;
   While night to day and day to night
   Divinely teach his name.

3. In every different land
   Their general voice is known;
   They shew the wonders of his hand
   And orders of his throne.

2. The rolling sun, the changing light,
   And nights and days thy power confess;
   But the blest volume thou hast writ
   Reveals thy justice and thy grace.

3. Sun, moon, and stars convey thy praise
   Round the whole earth, and never stand;
   So when thy truth begun its race,
   It touch'd and glanc'd on every land.

PSALM XIX. (PROPER METRE.)

1. Great God the heavens well-order'd frame
   Declares the glories of thy name;
   There thy rich works of order shine;
   A thousand starry beauties there
   A thousand radiant marks appear
   Of boundless power and skill divine

2. From night to day, from day to night,
   The dawning and the dying light
   Lectures of heavenly wisdom read;
   With silent eloquence they raise
   Our thoughts to our Creator's praise,
   And neither sound nor language need.

3. Yet their divine instructions run
   Far as the journies of the sun
   And every nation knows their voice;
   The sun like some young bridegroom drest,
   Breaks from the chambers of the east,
   Rolls round and makes the earth rejoice.

X.

Gaelic Translations of the Psalms and Paraphrases, 1684-1826.

HE Scottish Metrical Psalms appear in the Gaelic language in six different Translations.

I. THE VERSION *by the* REV. ROBERT KIRK, *printed in* 1684.

On December 11, 1673, Kirk submitted a petition to the Privy Council, for liberty to print a translation of the Psalms into the Gaelic tongue. The matter was referred to the approbation of the Earl of Argyle, and conferences were appointed about it, to take place at Inveraray. The liberty sought was granted, and in due time a version appeared with the following title:—

"PSALMA DHAIBHIDH a nMeadrachd. Do reir an phriomhchanamain. Le Ma: Raibeard Kirk, Minisdir Shoisgeil Chriosd aig Balbhuidier. Maille re ughdarras. A bfuil neach gu dubhach inar measg? deanadh sè urnaidh; Abfuil neach ar bioth subhach? Sinnadh è Sailm. Ebisd: Sheum. Caibid. 5. Rainn. 13. Ar a ngcur a ngclò ann Dun-Edin le M. Sémus Kniblo, Iosua van Solingen agus Seòn Colmar, 1684." 18mo. Literally translated into English this title is:—

THE PSALMS OF DAVID in Metre, According to the original Language. By Mr. Robert Kirk, Minister of the Gospel of Christ at Balquidder. Along with Authority. Is any one sorrowful among you? let him make prayer; Is any one after being cheerful? Let him sing a Psalm. Epist. James. Chap. 5. ver. 13. Put in print in Edinburgh by M. James Kniblo, Joshua van Solingen, and John Colmar, 1684. 18mo.

This was the first *complete* copy of the Psalms that appeared in the Gaelic language. It bears a grant of " privelidge" from the Lords of the Privy Council, dated Edinburgh, 20th March, 1684, forbidding any person to interfere with the author's right to print it for eleven years. It contains also a lengthened address, by Kirk, "To the Potent and renowned Lord John Murray, Marquess of Athole, Earl of Tullibardin, Viscount of Balquidder, Lord Murray and Balvenny, Lord Keeper of his Majesty's Privy Seal, &c." There is also a Gaelic address to the reader. The 150 Psalms are followed by four Paraphrases.

The Rev. Robert Kirk, Minister of the Gospel at Balquidder—as he tells us in the title—was ordained to his charge by Episcopal authority, and at the Revolution, having qualified to the government, he was permitted to continue in his charge unmolested. His Translation of the Psalms was an important contribution to the means for establishing Protestant Christian worship in the Highlands. On account of the proficiency which he displayed in the Gaelic language, he was sent for to London to superintend the printing of the Irish Translation of the Bible, prepared under the direction of Bishop Bidell. During the time that he was engaged on the Psalter, he became aware of the intention of the Synod of Argyle to publish their translation; and such was his anxiety to have his completed first, that he sat up the greater part of the night for many months; and during this excessive labour, the method he adopted to keep himself awake was rather singular—he put a piece of lead in his mouth, and placed a basin of water in such a position that the lead dropped into it so soon as he fell asleep. And to limit the period of his repose, and secure his being aroused from sleep at a certain hour, he had recourse to another expedient—a contrivance very ingenious, though perhaps not so refined as that of our modern alarum-clocks. He suspended over his pillow a bowl, partially filled with water, and above the bowl an inverted bottle, filled with water, and loosely corked, so that at the pre-arranged time, the lower vessel having been filled by the gradual pouring of the water from that above, would overflow on the face and head of the sleeping Psalmodist, and effectually dispel his slumbers, and refresh him for renewed labours. He was thus obviously possessed of remarkable energy and perseverance. And that his mind was imbued with deep piety of feeling, is indicated by the opening paragraph of his preface, of which this is a translation:—" The Psalms are pleasant and profitable. A church resounding with sacred melody, is almost a little heaven full of angels. As the Garden of Eden, replenished with trees of life of potent efficacy, and with medicinal plants, so is this book of the psalms of David, which contains a remedy for all the diseases of the soul. The world, and every living creature it contains are the Harp; man is the Harper and Poet who sings the praise of the wonder working God; and David is one of the Company who are employed in sweetly and tunefully discoursing about the Almighty King."

" Little volume move boldly on ;
In pure godly strains awaken yonder people ;
Salute the hospitable land of the Fingalians,
The Highland regions, and the isles of Strangers" *(The Hebrides)*.

Kirk's Psalm Book has now become extremely rare. He died in 1692, and was buried in the churchyard of Aberfoyle, under a stone bearing this inscription:—" ROBERTUS KIRK, A.M., LINGUAE HIBERNIAE LUMEN."

II. THE PSALTER *by the* SYNOD OF ARGYLE, 1659-1715.

An incomplete edition of the Gaelic Psalms was issued under the authority of the Synod of Argyle, in 1659, with this title:—

"AN CEUD CHAOGAD DO SHALMAIBH DHAIBHIDH. Ar a dtarring as an Eabhra, a Meadar Dhàna Gaoidhilg, Le Seanadh Earraghaoidheal. Neoch a dorduigh an scinn a Neaglaisaibh, agus a Dteaghlichaibh, a ghnathuigheas an chanamhain sin is na criochaibh ceudna. (Gallic quotation from Col: 3: 16.) Do chuireadh so a gclo a Nglasgo, le Aindra Ainderson n' Mbliadhanna ar Dtighearna, 1659." Translated thus:—

"'THE FIRST FIFTY OF THE PSALMS OF DAVID. Drawn from the Hebrew in the metre of Gaelic Poems, By the Synod of Argyle. Parties who ordained them to be sung in Churches and in Families, who practise that language in the said districts (scrip. quotation.) This was printed in Glasgow by Andrew Anderson in the year of our Lord 1659."

This version is now very rare. Ten years after the publication of Kirk's Translation, the version of the Synod of Argyle was completed—the remaining 100 Psalms having been printed in 1694, in terms of an enactment by the Assembly, 11th November, 1690,—" that it be recommended to the ministers concerned in the Highlands to despatch the whole Paraphrase of the Irish Psalms to the press." On the 8th of March of that year (1694) an Order was issued by the Lords of the Privy Council, forbidding any one except the Synod of Argyle to print this version for the space of nineteen years. And on the 17th of April of the same year, (1694,), the General Assembly of the Church of Scotland, met at Edinburgh, ordained the following :—

"ACT ANENT THE IRISH PSALMS :—The General Assembly of this National Church, taking into consideration that there is a complete paraphrase of the whole Psalms in Irish metre, approven and emitted by the Synod of Argyle, who understand the Irish language, conform to an Act of the General Assembly, 1690, together with a translation of the Shorter Catechism of this Church, in Irish, bound with the said Psalms in one volume; and the General Assembly, understanding that in some parts of the National Church, where preaching and prayer are used in Irish, the Psalms are sung at the same diet in a different language, whereby an uniformity in the worship of God is marred, and many of the people deprived of the benefit of praising God in a known tongue: Therefore, as the General Assembly doth hereby appoint that this incongruous way of worshipping God shall be hereafter forborne, so they do recommend to all congregations and families who worship God in the Irish language, to make use of the said paraphrase therein; and also to make use of the foresaid translation of the Shorter Catechism, as an uniform mean of catechising the people."

The following is the title of this Version as it appeared in 1715 :—

" SAILM DHAIBHIDH a Meadar Dhàna Gaoidheilg, do reir na Heabhra: Agus na Translasioin is fearr a Mbèarla agus Nlaidin, do thionnsgnadh le Seanadh Earraghaoidheal san bhliadhna 1659, agus anois air a ntabhairt gu crich, do chum gu dèanta an seinm a Neaglaisaibh agus a dteaghlachaibh a ghnathuigheas an chànamhain sin, Col. 3. 16. Biodh focal Chriosd na chomhnuidhe ionnuibh gu saidhbhir sa nuile ghliocas ar dteagasg, agus ar munadh dhaoibh a cheile a Salmaibh, agus a bhfonnaibh molta Dè, agus a gcainticaibh Spioradalta, ag dèanamh ciuil don Tighearna le gràs ann bhur gcroidheadhaibh. Le ùghdarras. Do chuireadh so a ngclò a Navn (Daun?) Edin le Oighreachaibh Aindra Ainderson a Mbliadhna ar Dtighearna, 1715." 12mo. p.p. 260.

In English :—" THE PSALMS OF DAVID in the Metre of Gaelic Poems, according to the Hebrew: and the best translations in English and Latin, designed by the Synod of Argyle in the year 1659, and now brought to a conclusion that they may be sung in Churches and in families who practice that language (Col. &c.). With authority. This was printed in Edinburgh by the Heirs of Andrew Anderson in the year of our Lord 1715."

Editions of this version were subsequently printed in Glasgow by James Duncan in 1738, and 1751.

III. MACFARLANE'S PSALTER, 1753.

This Psalter is an amended and altered version of the Translation authorised by the Synod of Argyle. Macfarlane excludes many of the Irishisms, and adds forty five of the Paraphrases. It was first printed in 1753—Title:—

"SAILM DHAIDHIDH ann dan Gaoidhealach do reir na Heabhra, agus an eidir-theangachaidh a's fearr ann Laidin, an Gaoidheilg, 's ann Gaillbhearla. Do thionnsgnadh le Seneadh Earra-Ghaoidheal s a' Bhliadhna, 1659, agus do chriochnaigheadh s an, 1694, r'an seinn ann Eaglaisibh an Teaghlaichibh Gaoidhealach.

Agus do ghlanadh anois Mhearachduibh lionmhor clodh-bhualaidh, air iarrtas agus do reir Seolaidh an t'seanaidh cheadna. Le ughdarras. *Entered in Stationers' Hall.* Clodhbhuailt' agus r'an Reic le Ioin Orr, Leabhairreiceadoir. Ann Glascho. 1753." 12mo. p p. 302.

English:—" The Psalms of David in Gaelic verse according to the Hebrew, the best translations in Latin, in Gaelic, and in English. Designed by the Synod of Argyle in the year 1659, and finished in 1694, to be sung in churches [and] in Gaelic Families.

And now purged of many errors of printing, at the command and direction of the said Synod. By Authority. Entered, &c. Printed and sold by John Orr, Bookseller. In Glasgow. 1753."

The title of the Forty-five Paraphrases attached to this version is:—

" Laoidhe eidir-theangaicht agus eidir-mhinicht o chuimh-reannaibh eagsamhail do'n Scrioptur naomhtha. Comh-chruinnicht' agus deasaichte le Buidheann ainmnichte de Airdsheanadh Eaglais Alba. Agus a chuireadh le Reachd Airdsheanaidh, 1745, fa Bhreitheamhnas nan sinsir r'an sqrudadh. Agus iompoicht anois, gu Gaoidheilg Albannaich; air iarrtus Seanaidh Earra-Ghaoidheal: chum leas coitcheann Gaoidhealtachd Alba: le Alastoir Macpharlain, M.A. Ministeir an t soisgeil ann Cill Mheile airt 's an Cill an Inbhir. *Entered in Stationers' Hall.* Clodh-bhuailt' agus r'an Reic le Join Orr, Leabhair reiceadoir. Ann Glas-cho. 1753." p.p. 56.

English:—" Hymns translated and explained from parallel verses of the holy

Scriptures. Collected and prepared by a famed number of the General Assembly of the Church of Scotland. And put by the act of the General Assembly of 1745, under the judgement of the Elders for revision. And converted now to Albanic Gaelic; at the desire of the Synod of Argyle: for the general welfare of the Gaeldom of Scotland: by Alexander Macfarlane, M.A. Minister of the gospel in Kil-Melfort and Kil-ninver. Entered &c. Printed and sold by John Orr, Bookseller. In Glasgow, 1753."

The following Act of the Synod of Argyle shews the Authority on which Macfarlane executed this translation of the Paraphrases:—

"AT INVERARY, the Fifth Day of August, One Thousand Seven Hundred and Fifty one Years: SEDERUNT, the Provincial Synod of *Argyle. Sessio quinta, hora decima ante meridiem*, after Prayer, Roll called and marked;—The Synod having last year recommended to Mr. Alexander MacFarlain to translate into SCOTTISH GALLIC, the SCRIPTURE SONGS lately offered to the consideration of Presbyteries, by the General Assembly of this Church; and he having at a former Sederunt, laid before them a copy of the said Translation; they appointed a Committee to revise the same. And having now heard and considered the Report of the said Committee, and being very well satisfied therewith; They appoint the Moderator, in their name, to thank Mr. MacFarlain for the great pains he has taken in making out so just, exact, and beautiful a Translation; and being convinced, that as the Performance itself is excellently adapted to excite Devotion, the publication thereof will be of great Use in the several Corners of this Church where the SCOTS GALLIC is spoken; Therefore they earnestly recommend to Mr. MacFarlain to prepare a Copy for the Press with all convenient speed; and the rather because they judge his so doing to be a step towards introducing the said SCRIPTURE SONGS into our public Worship in the *Highlands*, whenever the Church shall approve of and authorise the same; which this Synod do unanimously wish may soon be the case." Extracted by JAMES SMITH, *Clk. Dept.*

Editions of this version were repeatedly issued from the press in Glasgow, Perth, Edinburgh, and Inverness. It acquired much more popularity in the North Highlands than in the West; and on the appearance of the version by Smith—which falls next to be noticed—it was almost entirely discarded in the West Highlands. All the editions appear to have the Shorter Catechism attached to them.

IV. Smith's Translation of the Psalms and Paraphrases.

The following is the title of a new version by Dr. John Smith, Minister of the first charge of Campbelton. It appeared in 1787.

"Sailm Dhaibhidh, maille ri Laoidhean o'n Scrioptur naomha; chum bhi air an sein ann an aora' Dhia. Air an leasachadh, agus air an cur amach do reir sealaidh, iartais, agus ughdarais Seanaidh Earra-Ghaeil. Le. J. Smith, D.D.. Duneideann, air son C. Elliot, Leabhar-reiceadair, 1787." 12mo. pp. 396.

English:—"The Psalms of David, along with Hymns from the holy Scriptures; to be sung in the worship of God. Improved and published according to the direction, request, and authority of the Synod of Argyle. By J. Smith, D.D. Edinburgh, for C. Elliot, Bookseller. 1787"

This version is considerably altered from any that formerly appeared—all the North country words and Irishisms are excluded, and the metre adapted to the West country dialect. It contains, in addition to the 150 Psalms, the full complement of Paraphrases and Hymns used in the Church of Scotland; besides the Creed, the Lord's Prayer, and the Ten Commandments in metre. The first edition contained 15 Psalm Tunes, which were not reprinted. This Translation has proved very popular, and has had a much more extensive circulation than any of its predecessors—about 35 or 40 editions having appeared up till 1830.

The Rev. John Smith, D.D., by whom this version was produced, was an eminent antiquarian and Celtic scholar. He was born at Glenorchy, in Argyleshire, in the year 1747. He attended the usual curriculum of studies for the ministry at the University of St. Andrews; and in 1774 was appointed assistant and successor in the parish of Kilbrandon, Lorn, where he laboured for seven years. During this period he translated for the Society for Propagating Christian Knowledge, "Allein's Alarm to the Unconverted." He was at this time in the prime of life, with a powerful and commanding voice, and most energetic action. He made his services in translating this stirring work subservient to his pulpit labours—preaching it to his people as he carried on the translation—aud thereby occasioned probably the first Protestant revival that ever occurred in the Highlands; which was designated in the district the "Creadamh Mor" or *The Big Faith.* In 1781 he became Minister of the first charge of Campbelton. Soon after his settlement in this charge, he published his Essay on "Gaelic Antiquities;" "A Dissertation on the Authenticity of the Poems of Ossian;" "A Collection of Ancient Poems translated from the Gaelic;" and a version of the originals of these translations. About 1783 he was associated with Dr. Stewart, Minister of Luss, in translating the Scriptures into Gaelic, and he wrote besides, a "Summary View and Explanation of the Writings of the Prophets." In 1787—the year in which his version of the Psalms was issued—he published the "Life of St. Columba, the Apostle of the Highlands," and he was the author of "A View of the Last Judgment." Besides his unwearied labours for the spiritual welfare of his people, he was eager to introduce among them an improved system of husbandry; and with this view, wrote many Essays on the subject, frequently obtaining prizes from the Highland Society. He died 1807, aged 60. His thrilling appeals, and fearless, thundering denunciations, rendered his pulpit ministrations peculiarly affecting and acceptable to the masses. His admirers amongst the people of his old flock in Kilbrandon greatly lamented his loss when he removed to Campbelton; and not satisfied with the services of any of the clergy of the Establishment around them, they made application to be received into the fellowship of the Reformed Presbyterian Church. Their application was successful, and they exist at the present time as a congregation in that communion.

V. Ross' Psalter, 1807.

"Sailm Dhaibhidh ann an Dan Gaidhealach do reir na Heabhra agus an eadar-theangaichaidh a's fearr an Laidin, an Gaidhlig, 's an Gaillbheurla, Do thiomsgnadh le Seanadh Earra-Ghaidheall sa' Bliadhna, 1659, agus do criochnaicheadh san 1694, 'r' an seinn am Eaglaisibh's ann an Teaghlaichibh Gaidhealach. Air an glanadh a nis o mhearachdaibh lionmhor a' Chlodh-bhualaidh, agus air an a tharrachadh, le ro bheag caochladh air na briathribh, do reir gne sgriobhaidh an t-seann Tiomnaidh agus an Tiomnaidh Nuaidh le Tomas Ros, A.M.. Dunedin Clodh-bhuailte le Tearloch Steuart; agus r'an reic le Ogle agus Aikman, an Dunedin; le M. Ogle, an Glascho; agus le R. Ogle, 295 Holborn an Lunnain, 1807." 18mo. pp. 356.

English:—"The Psalms of David in Gaelic Poetry according to the Hebrew and the best translations in Latin, in Gaelic, and in English, devised by the Synod of Argyle in the year 1659, and completed in 1694, to be sung in Churches and in Gaelic Families. Now purged from numerous errors of printing, and altered with little change of words, after the manner of the writing of the Old and New Testament, by Thomas Ross, A.M. Edinburgh, printed by Charles Steuart, and sold by Ogle and Aikman in Edinburgh; by M. Ogle in Glasgow; and by R. Ogle 295 Holburn, in London. 1807"

Only three Editions of this version appear to have been issued, and the circulation has been confined almost entirely to the North Highlands. It is merely an amended edition of Macfarlane's version, with the spelling so altered as to bring it more into conformity with the orthography of the Bible. The Irish words and phrases as they occur, are usually explained in foot-notes, by synonymous Gaelic vocables peculiar to Scotland; and which, being of the same number of syllables as those for which they are substituted, may be sung in their stead at the pleasure of the worshipper. The Paraphrases were not comprehended in this edition, but they appeared in the edition of 1820, with the same title as that under which they were given by Macfarlane in 1753.

The Rev. Thomas Ross, A.M., had at one time the ministerial charge of one of the Scottish Churches in Holland. When the French invaded that country, and the British subjects were compelled to evacuate it, Ross returned to his native land, and was appointed minister of the parish of Loch-Broom. He was a gifted and able scholar, and of high literary tastes and habits.

VI. THE ASSEMBLY'S PSALTER, 1826.

The first Edition of the Gaelic Psalms, issued with the authority of the General Assembly, appeared in 1826. It was carefully revised from the preceding editions, and printed in 4to. and 8vo. to adapt it for being bound with Bibles of these respective sizes. The following is its title:—

"SAILM DHAIBHIDH; maille ri Laoidhibh air an tarruing o'na Scrioptuiribh Naomha chum bhi air an seinn, ann an aoradh Dhe. Air an Leasachadh, agus air an cur a mach le h-ùghdarras Ardsheanaidh Eaglais na h-Alba. Air iarrtus agus costus na cuideachd urramaich a ta chum eolas Criosdaidh a sgaoileadh air feadh Gaeltachd agus Eileana na h-Alba. Duneidin; Clodh-bhuailte le Donncha Stionsan, 1826" The Paraphrases had a short separate title, similar to that under which they are referred to in the general title of the book—viz.,

"Laoidhean air an tarruing o na Scrioptuiribh Naomha, chum bhi air an seinn an aoradh Dhe."

English:—" The Psalms of David; along with the Hymns drawn from the holy Scriptures, to be sung in the worship of God. Improved and published by authority of the General Assembly of the Church of Scotland at the command and expense of the Honourable Society for propagating Christian Knowledge through Gaeldom, and the Islands of Scotland. Edinburgh: Printed by Duncan Stevenson, 1826."

In 1801 a version was published with the title:—

"SAILM DHAIBHIDH air an deana' nìs iomchuidh arson aora' Chriostuidhean. *A new Gaelic Version of the Psalms of David, more adapted to Christian Worship, and to the Capacity of plain and illiterate persons, by John Smith, D.D.. Glasgow; Printed by Niven, Napier, & Khull, and Sold by J. and J. Duncan, Booksellers, Trongate*, 1801."

This was a new version of the Psalms, more free than that in common use, and formed very much after the model of Watt's Paraphrases of the Psalms. The verse was rendered shorter, and as it was believed more assimilated to bardic composition than the measure of the common version.

XI.

Paraphrases, 1648 till 1781.

UNDER the impression that it will be deemed an appropriate supplement to our notices of the Psalms proper, we propose now to direct attention to the "Translations and Paraphrases of several passages of Scripture," which are usually appended to the Psalter for the purpose of being used in divine worship. The proposal of enlarging the Psalmody by annexing sacred songs and paraphrases of other portions of scripture, seems to have engaged the attention of the Assembly at an early date, and to have been frequently brought under their notice at various intervals. Indeed, the old versions of the Psalter usually contain a number of sacred pieces besides the Psalms, such as, "Veni Creator," "The Song of Simeon," &c. And it may have been observed from the preceding notices that the Assembly, whilst carefully superintending the preparation of the present version, were at the same time taking steps to provide the Church with additional matter for praise. Thus we find them, on 28th August, 1647, "recommending that Mr Zachary Boyd be at the pains to translate the other scriptural songs."

In accordance with this recommendation Boyd produced a work in the following year, along with his version of the Psalms, viz:—"THE SONGS OF THE OLD AND NEW TESTAMENT IN MEETER: By M. ZACHARY BOYD, Preacher of God's Word. Ephes. 5. 18. 19.—Glasgow: Printed by the Heirs of GEORGE ANDERSON, Anno. 1648." The work contains 17 pieces, viz.:—"The Song of Songs;" "The Song of Moses at the Red Sea;" "The Song of Moses a little before his death;" "The Song of Deborah;" "The Song of Hannah;" "David's lamentation for Saul and Jonathan;" "The Song of David at the promise of Messias;" "The Song of Isaiah concerning the vineyard;" "Isaiah's Song of thanks for God's mercies;" "Isaiah's Song, inciting to confidence in God;" "The Song of Hezekiah;" "The lamentations of Jeremiah;" "The Song of Jonah;" "The Song of Habakkuk;" "The Song of Marie;" "The Song of Zacharias," "The Song of Simeon." Prefixed is an Epistle in the following terms: "To the

The Scottish Metrical Psalms.

Right Reverend the faithful Ministers of GOD's work of the Church of SCOTLAND. RIGHT REVEREND, it pleased you in the Generall Assembly at Edinburgh anno 1647, to take to your consideration the great utility the church of GOD may have by the Songs contained in holy scriptures; after due deliberation, it pleased you to ordain that I should labour in that work; In obedience unto you, I have endeavoured to come as neer to the Text as was possible for me to do; and those my labours I in all humility offer to be considered by the most learned and most judicious brethren, that the Church having the use thereof may in obedience to the Apostle's precept, Ephes., 5, 18, in Psalmes and Hymnes and Spirituall Songs make melody in their heart to the Lord—Whom I entreat in all humility to direct you in all things by his holy Spirit: So I remain—From Glasgow, the 27 of February 1648, your humble Servant in the LORD, M. ZACHARY BOYD." The following is Boyd's version of

THE SONG OF SIMEON, LUKE 2. VERSE 2.

Now in thy mercy lettest thou
   thine own servant O Lord
At last by death in peace depart
   according to thy word.

2. For thy salvation mine eyes
   have seen for great and small,
3. Which thou prepared hast before
   the face of people all.

4. A precious light to lighten all
   the Gentiles far and neer
And als the glory of ISR'L
   that is thy people dear.

On the 25th of February, 1648, Mr. John Adamson was instructed by the Commission to "revise Mr. David Leitch's papers of poecie." MR. ADAMSON was Principal of Edinburgh University from 1623 till his death in November, 1653. MR. DAVID LEITCH was minister in Ellon, in Aberdeenshire; and to countenance and encourage him in this work, the Commission, at their meeting in Edinburgh, 5th April, 1648, ordered a letter to be written to the Presbytery of Ellon in the following terms:—"Right Reverend and welbeloved brethren,—These are to show you that our brother, Mr David Leich, being employed in paraphrasing the songs of the Old and New Testament, has been in this town some tyme, and forasmuch as he yet is appointed to continue in that employment, our earnest desyre is that yow endevour your selves, jointly for his further encouragement in that work, provided that it be no hindrance to him in his present charge." On the 10th of August, 1648, Messrs. John Adamson and Thomas Craufurd were instructed by the Assembly "to revise the labours ef Mr Zachary Boyd, upon the other Scripturall Songs." At Edinb., on 1st January, 1650, the Commission returned their "heartie thanks to Messrs John Adamson, Zachary Boyd and Robert Lowrie, for their paines and usefull labours in the translation of the Psalms and other Scriptural Songs in meeter." And at Edinburgh, 22nd Febry., 1650— "The Commission understanding that Mr. Robert Lowrie has taken some pains in putting the Scripturall Songs in meeter, they therefore desire him to present his labours therein to the Commission at their next meeting." MR. ROBERT LOWRIE was one of the ministers of Edinburgh. Having conformed at the Restoration, he was appointed Dean of Edinburgh, and in 1671 he was advanced to be Bishop of Brechin. He died in 1677.

MR. LEITCH, before he became minister of Ellon, had been a Professor in King's College, Aberdeen. He pronounced a funeral oration, in Latin, 9th April, 1635, on the death of Bishop Patrick Forbes. He was the author of several learned poems, and was one of the Chaplains to King Charles II., and also of the army that went into England. Of MR. THOMAS CRAWFORD there seems no biographical information. He is believed to have been the author of a work entitled "SPIRITUAL SONGS, OR HOLY POEMS, *a Garden of true Delight*, containing all the *Scripture Songs* that are not in the Book of *Psalms*, together with several sweet Prophetical and Evangelical Scriptures, meet to be composed into SONGS: *Translated into English Meeter*, and fitted to be sung with any of the common tunes of the Psalms. Done at first for the Author's own Recreation, But since Published, (before in part but now more compleat) to be as a Supplement to the Book of *Psalms*, out of the same rich Store-house, a further Help to the Spiritual Solace of his Christian Friends, and digested into SIX BOOKS, according to the Order and Distinction of the Books of "Scripture" &c.— Edinburgh: Printed by the Heir of Andrew Anderson, Printer to His most Sacred Majesty, for *John Gibson*, Merchant in Glasgow, *Anno* DOM. 1686." In "*The Preface to the Reader*" the Poet says, "he hath allowed himself no greater libertie than that hath been used in our latest Paraphrase of the Psalms, which he took for his model, as questionless, (complexly taken) for smoothness with closeness to the Text (which was mainly designed in the composure), the best he had seen extant in our Tongue, and with much diligence revised, ere it came the length of publick approbation." And further, "When it shall be thought fit (as was intended) by this Church, to adjoin the rest of the *Scriptural Songs* to the Book of *Psalms* for Publick use, and an approved Paraphrase shall be framed or pitched on for that purpose, it may be considered how many are to be reckoned of that number, which he will not take upon him to determine."

It does not appear that any of these Scriptural Songs were ever authoritatively given to the public—no further notice is taken of them in the minutes of the Commission. The project seems to have gone to rest for nearly half-a-century. At length deliberations were resumed. Some progress must have been made in the work prior to 1706. On April 8th of that year we have the following "Act and recommendation concerning the Scripture Songs:"—"The General Assembly having heard and considered an overture transmitted to them from the Committee for Overtures, to whom it was remitted to consider the reference of the Commission of the late General Assembly in relation to the Scriptural Songs, they did and hereby do recommend it to the several Presbyteries of the Church to endeavour to promote the use of these songs in private families within their bounds, according to the recommendation of the late Assembly; and for facilitating the Assembly's work in preparing the said songs for public use, the Assembly hereby do recommend it to Presbyteries to buy up copies of the said songs that are printed and to be sold here at Edinburgh, and ordain the report of the committees appointed by the Commission of the late Assembly to revise these songs, with the amendments made thereupon by the Committee that met at Glasgow, to be printed and transmitted to the several Presbyteries, that they may consider the same and compare them with the book itself; and the General Assembly recommends it to the said Presbyteries also diligently to compare these songs with the original texts, and to make what further amendments they shall see needful upon the said printed copies of these songs, both as to the translation and metre, keeping always to the original text."

1707, April, 21.—"*Act concerning the Scriptural Songs.*—The General Assembly, upon report of their Committee for Overtures who were appointed to receive the report of those named to put in order the remarks of Presbyteries upon the version of the Scriptural Songs, finding that but very few Presbyteries have sent in their remarks upon these songs, and that even those who have made any remarks upon them judge the said version not yet fit for public use—do therefore recommend it to the several Presbyteries to be careful yet to revise the said songs, and transmit their opinion thereanent to the next Assembly; and in the meantime appoints those who were nominated by the Commission of the late General Assembly to revise these songs at Edinburgh, yet to meet, and again revise the same, and report to the next General Assembly; and adds Mr. John M'Bryde to that Committee."

1708, April 27.—"*Act and Reference concerning the Publishing a Version of the Scriptural Songs.*—The General Assembly do instruct and appoint their Commission maturely to consider the printed version of the Scripture Songs, with the remarks of Presbyteries thereupon; and after examination thereof they are hereby authorised and empowered to conclude and establish that version, and to publish and emit it for the public use of the Church, as was formerly done of the like occasion, and when our version of the Psalms was published in the year 1649; and seeing there are many copies of the said version lying on the author's hand, it is recommended to ministers and others to buy the same for private use in the meantime."

We are not aware that any practical result followed this enactment. The printed minutes of the Assembly contain no reference to the subject until the meeting in May, 1745, when it seems that the services of versifiers and paraphrasts had been made available—services which have resulted in the collection now in use.

1745, May 18.—"*Act and Overture about some Pieces of Sacred Poesy.*—The General Assembly had laid before them, by their committee, some pieces of sacred poesy, under the title of Translations and Paraphrases of several passages of sacred Scripture, composed by private persons; and though the Assembly have not sufficient time to consider these poems maturely, so as to approve or disapprove of them, yet they judge the same may be printed; and do remit the consideration of them to the several Presbyteries, in order to their transmitting their observations to the next General Assembly, that they or any subsequent Assembly may give such orders about the whole affair as they shall judge for edification; and the Assembly appoint this their resolution to be prefixed to the impression."

1747, May 15.—"*Overture about the Psalmody.*—The General Assembly, considering the overture with respect to the Translations and Paraphrases of several pieces of sacred Scripture, did agree to appoint the committee which formerly had this affair under consideration, to meet at the times in which they were in use to meet before, viz., in the Society Hall, upon Tuesday before each quarterly meeting of the Commission, at ten o'clock, forenoon, and at other times and places as they see cause; and appoint that all instructions relating to it that have been sent up to the Assembly shall be laid before them, and that the Presbyteries shall send up what further instructions they think proper to the said committee, who shall report the same with their opinion to the next Assembly."

On May 21, 1748, the Committee for Overtures reported, and the Assembly remitted the Paraphrases, with proposed amendments, to the committee appointed by preceding Assemblies, adding Mr George Blackwell to their number.

On May 19, 1749, it was ascertained that several Presbyteries had proposed amendments of the Translations and Paraphrases, but that the greatest number had sent up no opinion; and that, in consequence of the confusion of the late rebellion, many Presbyteries had lost their copies. The matter was accordingly again remitted to the committee, with instructions to consider the amendments suggested; and if approved, to have a new impression printed, and copies forwarded to Presbyteries.

May 21, 1750.—The collection of Paraphrases, &c., having been reprinted with amendments, the Assembly ordered its transmission to the several Presbyteries.

1751, May 20.—"*Overture anent the Psalmody.*—The General Assembly finding that several of the Presbyteries have not sent up any opinion to this Assembly concerning the Psalmody, notwithstanding a new edition with amendments of the Translations and Paraphrases of Sacred Scripture was transmitted to them, do again transmit the same, requiring such Presbyteries as have hitherto been deficient to send up their opinions to the next Assembly; and in the meantime, the Assembly recommends the said Psalmody to be used in private families, and that the Presbyteries be careful to have a sufficient number of copies of the said last edition thereof, within their bounds."

After protracted and careful investigation into the merits of a great many selected pieces of sacred poetry, not a few of which had been considerably altered and amended, the collection was published in 1781, under this title:—

"*Translations and Paraphrases in Verse, of several Passages of Sacred Scripture.*— Collected and prepared by a Committee of the General Assembly of the Church of Scotland, in order to be sung in Churches. (Design of the burning bush). *Nec tamen consumebatur.* Edinburgh: Printed and sold by J. Dickson, printer to the Church of Scotland." Prefixed to the work is the following Act of Assembly:—

"At Edinburgh, 1st June, 1781.—Sess. 8.—There was produced, read, and agreed to by the General Assembly, the Report of the Committee concerning the "Translations and Paraphrases, in verse, of several Passages of Sacred Scripture," which had been prepared by a committee of a former Assembly; and the General Assembly, in terms of said report, did and hereby do appoint these "Translations and Paraphrases" to be transmitted to the several Presbyteries of this Church, in order that they may report their opinion concerning them to the ensuing General Assembly; and in the meantime, they allow this collection of sacred poems to be used in public worship in congregations where the minister finds it for edification. The General Assembly likewise renew the appointment of the Committee, with power to judge of any corrections or alterations of these poems that may be suggested previous to their transmission, and with direction to cause a proper number of copies, with such corrections as they may approve, to be printed, for the consideration of Presbyteries and for public use. They ordain the expense already incurred by printing this collection for the inspection of the members of this Assembly to be defrayed out of the public funds of the Church. And in order to prevent it from being afterwards printed in a careless and incorrect manner, they authorise and appoint the printer to the Church to print and publish it for sale, under the direction of the committee. And that he may be enabled to sell the copies at a moderate price, the General Assembly did and hereby do grant to him the exclusive privilege of printing and publishing this collection of Translations and Paraphrases for the term of five years." Extracted by John Drysdale, Cl. Ecc., Scot. (By an Act in the year 1786, the General Assembly renewed this exclusive privilege to the printer to the Church, for nine years from that date).

The following advertisement is appended to the collection:—"As it has been the general sentiment of devout persons that it would be of advantage to enlarge the Psalmody in public worship, by joining with the Psalms of David some other passages of Scripture, both from the Old and New Testaments, this design has been at several times under the deliberation of the Church of Scotland. In consequence of an Act of the General Assembly, appointing a committee to prepare some Paraphrases of sacred writ in verse for this purpose, a collection of such Paraphrases was published in the year 1745, and has been used in several churches in public worship.

"It having been represented to the General Assembly, in the year 1775, that it was proper this collection should be revised and some additions made to it, a committee was appointed, with instructions to receive and consider any corrections or additional materials that might be laid before them.

"By this Committee the collection now published has been prepared. All the Translations and Paraphrases which had appeared in the former publication are in substance retained, but they have been revised with care. Many alterations, and it is hoped improvements, are made upon them. A considerable number of new Paraphrases are added. They are all now arranged according to the order in which the several passages of Scripture lie in the Bible, and a few hymns are subjoined."

It is believed that the following list will be deemed interesting and valuable, as a record of the names of those to whose pious labours the Church is indebted for the portion of its Psalmody known as the "Paraphrases." These labours have been long gratefully appreciated, and will not soon be forgotten.

Paraphrases.	Authors.
1. "Let heav'n arise, let earth appear, said the Almighty Lord:"	Watts; altered by Cameron.
2. "O God of Bethel! by whose hand thy people still are fed;"	Doddridge; altered by Logan.
3. "Naked as from the earth we came, and enter'd life at first;"	Watts; altered by Cameron.
4. "How still and peaceful is the grave! where, life's vain tumults past,"	Blair; some alterations by Cameron.
5. "Though trouble springs not from the dust, nor sorrow from the ground;"	Watts; much altered.
6. "The rush may rise where waters flow, and flags beside the stream;"	Author unknown; ascribed to Watts without sufficient data.
7. "How shall the sons of Adam's race be pure before their God?"	Watts; slightly altered by Cameron.
8. "Few are thy days, and full of woe, O man, of woman born!"	Logan. *(App. XII.)*.
9. "Who can resist th' Almighty arm that made the starry sky?"	Logan.
10. "In streets, and op'nings of the gates, where pours the busy crowd,"	Logan.

Paraphrases, 1781.

PARAPHRASES.	AUTHORS.
11. "O happy is the man who hears instruction's warning voice;"	Logan.
12. "Ye indolent and slothful! rise, View the ant's labours, and be wise;"	Dr. Martin.
13. "Keep silence, all ye sons of men, and hear with rev'rence due;"	Watts; greatly altered.
14. "While others crowd the house of mirth, and haunt the gaudy show,"	Cameron.
15. "As long as life its term extends, Hope's blest dominion never ends;"	Watts; slightly altered.
16. "In life's gay morn, when sprightly youth with vital ardour glows,"	Dr. Blacklock.
17. "Rulers of Sodom! hear the voice of heav'n's eternal Lord;"	Cameron.
18. "Behold! the mountain of the Lord in latter days shall rise"	Logan.
19. "The race that long in darkness pin'd have seen a glorious light;"	Dr. John Morrison.
20. "How glorious Sion's courts appear, the city of our God!"	Watts; slightly altered by Blair.
21. "Attend, ye tribes that dwell remote, ye tribes at hand, give ear;"	Morrison.
22. "Why pour'st thou forth thine anxious plaint, despairing of relief,"	Watts; considerably altered.
23. "Behold my Servant! see him rise exalted in my might!"	Anonymous; altered by Logan.
24. "Ye heav'ns send forth your song of praise! earth, raise your voice below!"	Watts; greatly altered.
25. "How few receive with cordial faith the tidings which we bring?"	Rev. William Robertson.
26. "Ho! ye that thirst, approach the spring where living waters flow:"	Anonymous; altered by Cameron.
27. "Thus speaks the high and lofty One; ye tribes of earth, give ear;"	Morrison and Logan.
28. "Attend, and mark the solemn fast which to the Lord is dear;"	Morrison and Logan.

PARAPHRASES.	AUTHORS.
29. "Amidst the mighty, where is he who saith, and it is done?"	MORRISON.
30. "Come, let us to the Lord our God with contrite hearts return;"	MORRISON.
31. "Thus speaks the heathen: How shall man the Pow'r Supreme adore?"	LOGAN.
32. "What though no flow'rs the fig-tree clothe, though vines their fruit deny,"	ANONYMOUS; altered by CAMERON.
33. "Father of all! we bow to thee, who dwell'st in heav'n ador'd;"	BLAIR.
34. "Thus spoke the Saviour of the world, and rais'd his eyes to heav'n:"	BLAIR; slightly altered by CAMERON.
35. "'Twas on that night, when doom'd to know The eager rage of ev'ry foe,"	MORRISON.
36. "My soul and spirit, fill'd with joy, my God and Saviour praise,"	ANONYMOUS; altered by CAMERON.
37. "While humble shepherds watch'd their flocks in Bethl'hms plains by night,"	ANONYMOUS.
38. "Just and devout old Simeon liv'd; to him it was reveal'd,"	Ascribed to LOGAN.
39. "Hark, the glad sound, the Saviour comes! the Saviour promis'd long;"	DODDRIDGE; slight alterations by CAMERON.
40. "The wretched prodigal behold in mis'ry lying low,"	WATTS; greatly altered by CAMERON.
41. "As when the Hebrew prophet rais'd the brazen serpent high,"	WATTS; greatly altered by CAMERON.
42. "Let not your hearts with anxious thoughts be troubled or dismay'd;"	ROBERTSON; much altered by CAMERON.
43. "You now must hear my voice no more; my Father calls me home;"	ROBERTSON; much altered by CAMERON.
44. "Behold the Saviour on the cross, a spectacle of woe!"	BLAIR.
45. "Ungrateful sinners! whence this scorn of God's long-suff'ring grace?"	BLAIR; altered by CAMERON.
46. "Vain are the hopes the sons of men upon their works have built;"	WATTS; altered by CAMERON.

Paraphrases.	Authors.
47. "And shall we then go on to sin, that grace may more abound?"	Watts; altered by Cameron.
48. "Let Christian faith and hope dispel the fears of guilt and woe;"	Logan.
49. "Though perfect eloquence adorn'd my sweet persuading tongue,"	Randall; slightly altered by Cameron.
50. "When the last trumpet's awful voice this rending earth shall shake,"	Anonymous; altered by Cameron.
51. "Soon shall this earthly frame, dissolv'd, in death and ruins lie;"	Watts; greatly altered by Cameron.
52. "Ye who the name of Jesus bear, his sacred steps pursue;"	Anonymous; altered by Cameron.
53. "Take comfort, Christians, when your friends in Jesus fall asleep;"	Logan.
54. "I'm not asham'd to own my Lord, or to defend his cause,"	Watts; slight alterations by Cameron.
55. "My race is run; my warfare's o'er; the solemn hour is nigh,"	Watts; considerably altered by Cameron.
56. "How wretched was our former state, when, slaves to Satan's sway,"	Watts; greatly altered by Cameron.
57. "Jesus, the Son of God, who once for us his life resign'd,"	Blair; altered by Cameron.
58. "Where high the heav'nly temple stands, The house of God not made with hands,"	Logan.
59. "Behold what witnesses unseen encompass us around;"	Anonymous; altered by Cameron.
60. "Father of peace, and God of love! we own thy pow'r to save,"	Supposed by Watts; altered by Cameron.
61. "Bless'd be the everlasting God, the Father of our Lord;"	Watts; slight alterations by Cameron.
62. "Lo! in the last of days behold a faithless race arise;"	Dr. John Ogilvie.
63. "Behold th' amazing gift of love the Father hath bestow'd"	Watts; much altered by Cameron.
64. "To him that lov'd the souls of men, and wash'd us in his blood,"	Anonymous.

PARAPHRASES.	AUTHORS.
65. "Behold the glories of the Lamb amidst his Father's throne;"	WATTS; enlarged and altered by CAMERON.
66. "How bright these glorious spirits shine! whence all their white array?"	WATTS; enlarged and re-modelled by CAMERON.
67. "Lo! what a glorious sight appears to our admiring eyes!"	Embracing two by WATTS; altered by CAMERON.

HYMNS.	
1. "When all thy mercies, O my God!"	ADDISON.
2. "The spacious firmament on high,"	ADDISON.
3. "When rising from the bed of death,"	ADDISON.
4. "Blest morning! whose first dawning rays"	WATTS; slightly altered, and doxology added.
5. "The hour of my departure's come;"	LOGAN.

A few particulars may be given of the individuals whose names occupy this honoured position. We have already briefly noticed DR. ISAAC WATTS, when directing attention to his elaborate version of the Psalms. By referring to the above list, it will be seen that twenty-three of the Paraphrases, besides one Hymn, originally emanated from his busy pen,—all, however, altered to a greater or less degree by other authors,—chiefly by Cameron.

REV. WILLIAM CAMERON was born in 1751. Having studied for the ministry in the Church of Scotland, he was in due time licensed to preach the Gospel, and in 1785 was ordained to the pastoral charge of the parish of Kirknewton, in the county of Linlithgow, where he laboured till his death, which took place in Kirknewton Manse, on the 17th of November, 1811, in the 60th year of his age, and the 26th of his ministry. His poetical talents were of no mean order. His first work, a "Collection of Poems," was printed at Edinburgh in 1781, and a posthumous volume appeared in 1813. His song on the restoration of the forfeited estates, 1784,—beginning, "As o'er the Highland hills I hied," and adapted to the fine old tune—"The Haughs o' Cromdale"—is excellent, and was enthusiastically received. Two of the Paraphrases are entirely his own composition, whilst thirty-one have been more or less altered by him.

PHILIP DODDRIDGE, D.D., a famous Nonconformist divine, was born in London in 1702, and was successively minister at Kirkworth, Market Harborough, and Northampton. Having repaired to Lisbon for the benefit of his health, he died there in 1751. He acquired a great and deserved reputation, which has been extended and perpetuated by his works, the principal of which are "The Family Expositor," "The Rise and Progress of Religion in the Soul," "The Life of Colonel Gardiner," and "Hymns." Two of the Paraphrases have been altered from his productions.

REV. JOHN LOGAN was born in 1748, at Soutra, parish of Fala, Mid-Lothian. He was the son of a small farmer, a member of the Burgher Communion, who intended him for the ministry of that religious sect, but he himself preferred taking orders in the Established Church. Having received an elementary education at the parish school of Gosford, in East-Lothian, he removed to the University of Edinburgh, where he completed his Theological course in 1768. After being licensed by the Presbytery of Edinburgh, he acquired considerable popularity as a preacher, and was ordained minister of the parish of South Leith in 1773. Having laboured in this charge for a considerable period, he removed to London, where he devoted himself to literary pursuits, and died after a lingering illness on December 28, 1788, in the 40th year of his age. Soon after entering the Edinburgh University he had contracted an intimacy with a fellow-student—the tender and ingenious Michael Bruce. Both these young men were warmly attached to the cultivation of poetry, and congeniality of feeling and similarity of pursuits, resulted in their close and familiar companionship. Bruce, who was of a delicate constitution was cut off by consumption, on July 6th, 1767, at the early age of 21. Soon after his death, his poems were revised and corrected by his friend Logan, who published them at Edinburgh in 1770, with a preface, inserting several poems of his own without specifying them. In 1781, Logan issued a volume of poetry, which attracted much attention. In this collection he reprinted several of the pieces which he had formerly given to the world, along with those of Bruce. A painful charge rests against his memory regarding the real authorship of some of these pieces, and also respecting the use he made of a copious manuscript of Bruce's poetry, intrusted to him after the publication of the first volume. The beautiful "Ode to the Cuckoo," the episode of "Levina" in the poem of "Loch Leven," the "Ode to Paoli," and the "Eclogue after the manner of Ossian," which, it is declared, are clearly ascertained to have been the composition of Bruce, were subsequently claimed by Logan's biographer as his. Logan himself appears to have put forth some pretensions to being the author of the "Ode to the Cuckoo," and in July, 1782, applied for an interdict in the Court of Session against John Robertson, printer in Edinburgh, and William Anderson, bookseller, and afterwards Provost of Stirling, who were about to bring out an edition of Bruce's works, containing the poems mentioned, which interdict was removed in the succeeding August, Logan not being able to substantiate his pleas. The entire authorship of ten of the Paraphrases and one Hymn is ascribed to Logan, besides the alteration of two of the Paraphrases, and the joint-authorship of other two along with Morrison. *(App. XII.).*

REV. ROBERT BLAIR was the eldest son of Rev. David Blair, one of the ministers of Edinburgh, and chaplain to the King, was born at Edinburgh in 1699, and studied for the Church at the University of his native city. On January 5, 1781, he was ordained minister at Athelstaneford, in East-Lothian, where he continued till his death, which occurred, through fever, on February 4th, 1746, in the 47th year of his age. Blair was the sole author of two of the Paraphrases, and of the groundwork of other four—alterations on which have been effected by Cameron. He also produced a variety of minor pieces. But his fame is chiefly associated with the beautiful poem, "The Grave," which is one of the standard classics of English literature.

REV. DR. MARTIN, the author of the 12th Paraphrase, was minister of Monimail, in Fifeshire.

THOMAS BLACKLOCK, D.D., the author of the 16th Paraphrase, was born at Annan, in Dumfriesshire, Nov. 10, 1721. In early infancy he had the misfortune to lose his eyesight through the smallpox. His father anxiously devoted his leisure time to his instruction, reading to him useful and interesting books, principally poetical. He manifested a taste for poetry at a very early age, and composed some pieces when only about twelve years old. In his 19th year his father was accidentally killed, shortly after which the young poet removed to Edinburgh, and attended the Grammar School and University, Dr. John Stevenson having kindly taken upon himself the charge of his education. In 1746, a volume of his verses was published in Glasgow; and another in Edinburgh in 1754. In 1759 he was licensed by the Presbytery of Dumfries, and speedily acquired high reputation as a pulpit orator. He was ordained minister of the parish of Kirkcudbright in 1762, but, on account of his blindness, the people of the parish refused to acknowledge him as their pastor. A lawsuit ensued, which, after two years, was compromised by Blacklock retiring on a moderate annuity. In 1764 he repaired to Edinburgh, where he received young boarders into his house, and superintended their education. He died from fever in 1791.

JOHN MORRISON, D.D., was a native of Aberdeenshire, born about the year 1748, and became minister of Canisby, in the county of Caithness. The Paraphrases written by him, 5 in number—besides two, the authorship of which he shares with Logan—are among the finest in the collection, and convey a favourable opinion of his poetical talents. Several effusions of his youthful muse appeared in the *Edinburgh Weekly Magazine*. After his settlement as a minister, he devoted himself exclusively to his ministerial work. He died on the 12th June, 1798, in the 49th year of his age, and 18th of his ministry.

REV. WILLIAM ROBERTSON was minister of the Old Greyfriars Church, Edinburgh, and father of Principal Robertson, the celebrated historian. He died in the year 1743. He was the sole author of the 25th Paraphrase; and other two, the 42nd and 43rd, were originally written by him, but in their present state were altered by Cameron.

RANDALL, of Stirling, father of the late Dr. Davidson, one of the ministers of Edinburgh, was the original author of the 49th Paraphrase, which has been altered by Cameron.

JOHN OGILVIE, D.D., was the son of the Rev. Mr. Ogilvie, one of the ministers of Edinburgh, where he was born about 1733. He received his education at the Marischal College of that city, which afterwards honoured him with the degree of doctor in divinity. In 1759 he was ordained minister of Midmar, Aberdeenshire, where he continued till his death, in 1814. He was the author of the 62nd Paraphrase, and a great variety of works, chiefly poetical—scarcely one of which is known to the general reader, even by name, at the present day.

JOSEPH ADDISON, the author of the first three hymns, and a celebrated essayist and miscellaneous writer, was born on May 1, 1672, at Milston, in Wiltshire—the son of Dr. Lancelot Addison. Besides publishing a variety of works, both in prose and poetry, he was a liberal contributor to the *Tatler*, *Spectator*, and *Guardian*. His poetry is now little read, but his prose works have a special charm and a lasting worth; and as the first and best examples of a new style, they hold a high place in the history of English literature.

We give the following as specimens of the alterations to which the Paraphrases by Dr. Watts have been subjected at the hand of Cameron :—

By Watts.	Altered by Cameron.
Hymn 40. (L.M.) *Book* 1.	Paraphrase 66.

1. "What happy men, or angels, these
   "That all their robes are spotless white?
   "Whence did this glorious troop arrive
   "At the pure realms of heavenly light?"
2. From tort'ring racks and burning fires,
   And seas of their own blood they came;
   But nobler blood has wash'd their robes,
   Flowing from Christ the dying Lamb.

3. Now they approach the Almighty throne,
   With loud hosannas night and day,
   Sweet anthems to the great Three One
   Measure their blest eternity.
4. No more shall hunger pain their souls,
   He bids their parching thirst be gone,
   And spreads the shadow of his wings
   To screen them from the scorching sun.

5. The Lamb that fills the middle throne
   Shall shed around his milder beams,
   There shall they feast on his rich love,
   And drink full joys from living streams.
6. Thus shall their mighty bliss renew
   Thro' the vast round of endless years,
   And the soft hand of sovereign grace
   Heals all their wounds and wipes their tears.

1. How bright these glorious spirits shine!
   whence all their white array?
   How came they to the blissful seats
   of everlasting day?
2. Lo! these are they from suff'rings great
   who came to realms of light,
   And in the blood of Christ have wash'd
   those robes which shine so bright.

3. Now, with triumphal palms they stand
   before the throne on high,
   And serve the God they love amidst
   the glories of the sky.
4. His presence fills each heart with joy
   tunes ev'ry mouth to sing;
   By day, by night, the sacred courts
   with glad hosannas ring.

5. Hunger and thirst are felt no more,
   nor suns with scorching ray;
   God is their sun, whose cheering beams
   diffuse eternal day.
6. The Lord which dwells amidst the throne
   shall o'er them still preside;
   Feed them with nourishment divine,
   and all their footsteps guide.

7. 'Mong pastures green he'll lead his flock
   where living streams appear;
   And God the Lord from ev'ry eye
   shall wipe off ev'ry tear.

Paraphrases, 1781.

By Watts.
Hymn 103. (C.M.) *Book* 1.

1. I'm not asham'd to own my Lord,
    Or to defend his cause,
    Maintain the honour of his word,
    The glory of his cross.
2. Jesus my God, I know his name,
    His name is all my trust,
    Nor will he put my soul to shame,
    Nor let my hope be lost.

3. Firm as his throne his promise stands,
    And he can well secure
    What I've committed to his hands,
    Till the decisive hour.
4. Then will he own my worthless name
    Before his Father's face,
    And in the new Jerusalem
    Appoint my soul a place.

Altered by Cameron.
Paraphrase 54.

1. I'm not ashamed to own my Lord,
    or to defend his cause,
    Maintain the glory of his cross,
    and honour all his laws.
2. Jesus my Lord! I know his name,
    his name is all my boast;
    Nor will he put my soul to shame,
    nor let my hope be lost.

3. I know that safe with him remains,
    protected by his power,
    What I've committed to his trust,
    till the decisive hour.
4. Then will he own his servant's name
    before his Father's face,
    And in the New Jerusalem
    appoint my soul a place.

XII.

Hymns.

BY the adoption of the collection of "Translations and Paraphrases," the Scottish Church became possessed of a manual of praise, consisting of 62 sacred songs, besides the 150 Psalms of David. Nevertheless the desire has long been cherished—increasing in intensity—to have this number still further augmented, and another selection, consisting of a greater variety of pieces, approved and adopted for use in the services of the sanctuary. Some of the Dissenters have taken the initiative in this matter. The large and influential body now known by the name of United Presbyterians, have for many years been possessed of a manual of selected Hymns, of acknowledged, though naturally of varied excellence—consisting of 468 pieces, besides 23 doxologies—all founded on, and expository of, special portions of sacred scripture. At their meeting last year, the U.P. Synod appointed a committee to take into their consideration the whole subject of the revision of the Hymn Book.

For a considerable period the General Assembly of the Church of Scotland have been aiming at something of the same kind; a large committee of their number, in every respect qualified for the undertaking, having been actively engaged in selecting and arranging a variety of Hymns for public worship. At the meeting of the Assembly three years ago, 1st June, 1868, it was ascertained that the committee had made good progress in this work—had, in fact, almost brought it to a satisfactory conclusion. The report of the committee was submitted and read by joint-convener, Rev. Dr. Boyd, of St. Andrews. The committee had designated their collection "The Scottish Hymnal," because "Hymnal" expresses in one word what Hymn Book does in two; and the adoption of this word would, at once, distinguish the book from all others in Scotland—the term being in frequent use in England; and the designation "Scottish Hymnal," would be in keeping with a national church. The compilers "intended and believed that no Hymn in this collection is in any way at variance with the doctrinal system or the common forms of worship in the

Church of Scotland,"—whilst at the same time the idea was that it should represent fairly all lawful and healthy diversity of opinion, feeling, and taste, in our National Church. The work consists of 200 Hymns, selected from a variety of sources. The Latin productions of *medieval* Christendom have supplied 13 pieces: 6 are of German origin; 11 are "versions of Psalms," generally valuable, not merely as presenting variety of metre, but also as intrinsically excellent in regard of poetic character in the rendering. There are also a few representatives of the old English class, the language of which is contemporary with the authorised version of the Holy Scriptures. Of 61, 12 are borrowed from Watts, 14 from Wesley, 9 from Cowper, 10 from Heber, 9 from Montgomery, and 7 from Lyte; and the whole are classified under the following heads:— "Creation and Providence;" "Our Lord;" "The Holy Spirit;" "Missions;" "The Holy Trinity;" "The Christian Life;" "Heaven;" "Natural and Sacred Seasons." The following was the deliverance of the Assembly on the report being read:—

"Continue the committee with instructions to prosecute their labours, and allow the committee to issue a print of 1000 copies of the volume now on the table as it now stands, or as it may be amended by the committee, and this at such a time as that the office-bearers of the church may have ample opportunity before next General Assembly of carefully considering the contents of the volume, and this with the view of enabling the General Assembly to sanction its use in public worship as they may determine, it being understood that it is not to be introduced into any congregation previous to next Assembly."

JOHN COOK, Cl. Eccl. Scot.

At the next meeting of Assembly—May 29th, 1869—the "Committee on Paraphrases and Hymns" reported that they had carried out the instructions of the court, and circulated 1000 copies of the Hymnal; that "the volume had been reviewed in a considerable number of newspapers, in every instance more or less favourably;" and that a copy had been "sent to each Presbytery clerk, accompanied by a circular containing a few changes made or suggested." The changes consisted of the omission of some entire Hymns and verses, the substitution of some verses for others, and the addition of some new verses. The classification of the whole was also re-arranged. After the report had been considered, it was moved and agreed to:—

The Scottish Metrical Psalms.

"That the General Assembly did, and hereby do appoint the Book of Hymns now laid upon the table, as amended by the Appendix, also submitted, to be transmitted to the Presbyteries of this church, in order that they may report their opinion regarding them to next General Assembly."

JOHN COOK, Cl. Eccl. Scot.

Next Assembly met in May, 1870, and on the 23rd day of that month the report of the committee on the Hymnal was called for and produced, when it was ascertained that the changes indicated had been effected on the volume, when it was forthwith sent down to Presbyteries, and that thirty-seven reports had been sent in by Presbyteries. As a condensation of these reports, the following facts were stated:—"That there is scarcely any Hymn of the whole 200 that has not been objected to by some Presbytery; but that when the measure of agreement in disapproval is considered, the formidableness of this disappears, for if the Hymns are struck out that are objected to by more than one-third, only three Hymns fall to be omitted, and those objected to by more than one-fourth are only ten. On the other hand, so many as twenty-two Presbyteries express general approval of the book. Only three Presbyteries express disapproval. No Hymn is objected to by a majority of the reporting Presbyteries." The alterations are thus indicated in an appendix to the report:—"A. Omit the Hymns objected to by one-third and upwards of reporting Presbyteries. B. Add the three following:—'Te Deum Laudamus.'—Old Latin. 'Creator, Spirit, by whose aid.'—Latin, translated by Dryden. 'Lord, pour thy spirit from on high.'—James Montgomery. C. Bring forward the series of 'Hymns of the Trinity' to the beginning of the book. D. Hymn commencing 'When our heads are bowed with fear,' restore as last line of each verse—'Jesus, son of Mary, hear.' E. Change Jesu to Jesus, and substitute other epithets for 'dear' and 'sweet,' as applied to our Lord. F. To facilitate return to the old rule of special music to each Psalm or Hymn, that a preparatory list of appropriate tunes be appended." The report having been considered by the Assembly, a motion and amendment were proposed. The amendment was to the effect that the collection of Hymns should be still further revised. The motion was carried by a majority of 119 against 65, and accordingly became the judgment of the House. It is as follows:—

"That the Assembly approve of the report, re-appoint the committee, with power to add to their number, and remit the Hymnal to the committee with orders to expunge therefrom the Hymns which have been objected to by more than one-third of the reporting Presbyteries, and to carry out the recommendations contained in the committee's report; and, in general, to diligently revise the book, giving careful consideration to all suggestions contained in the reports from Presbyteries, and thereafter to publish an edition for the use of such congregations as may wish to avail themselves of it."

When the report on the Hymnal was brought up at the meeting of Assembly on Monday, 29th May last, Mr. Edgar of Tongland moved—"That whereas in the collection of Hymns now published under the title of 'The Scottish Hymnal,' there are Hymns very unsuitable for public worship, and objectionable on account of their composition or language, the committee be re-appointed—Dr. Boyd, convener—with instructions to communicate with the Presbyteries of the church, so as to ascertain what amendments should be made."

Dr. Boyd said that "it was very unnecessary he should say more than that the committee was composed of many clergymen who had deeply studied the subject. The best proof of the popularity of the book would be found in the fact that since October, 124,000 and odd copies had been sold. He was very far indeed from considering that the Hymn Book was perfect—indeed he thought he could have made it a better one—but the committee had to pass a great many Hymns to please as great a variety of people as possible. The sale would even have been larger, but many of the people had been waiting till the book was published with music. Now, they had engaged the celebrated Dr. Monk as musical editor, and the Hymnal, with music, would appear in a few days. The Hymns had received the greatest consideration; and he thought that after the book going through four separate editions, it would be a pity to alter it just now—considering, too, all the labour which had been bestowed upon it. He thought they should at least have four years peace, and would recommend the Assembly to re-appoint the committee." Mr. Edgar withdrew his motion, and Dr. Boyd's report was agreed to.

The General Assembly of the Free Church have also had a "Committee on Paraphrases and Hymns" in active existence for a number of years, and who are still vigorously prosecuting their labours. The following brief notices of their more recent operations may serve to give some idea of the position in which this matter now stands in regard to this church. At the meeting of the Assembly in

1869, the committee were instructed to revise carefully the existing collection of Paraphrases and Hymns, to select a limited number of scriptural and standard Paraphrases and Hymns in addition to those that might be retained, and to make a more thorough examination of the versions of the Psalms formerly prepared and submitted by the psalmody committee.

At the meeting of the Assembly on May 28th, 1870, Mr. Adam, Glasgow, convener of the "Committee on Paraphrases and Hymns," submitted their report, from which it appeared that the committee, to the best of their ability, had carried out the instructions of the Assembly, devoting not a little time and labour to the work. With a rare measure of unanimity, they had selected seventy-five "New Paraphrases and Hymns," which were printed and laid on the table of court. They had carefully revised the existing collection of Paraphrases, and recommended that twenty-six should be omitted and certain changes made on a few of the others. The committee were not prepared to report so decisively as regards the versions of the Psalms. They recommended that the collection of Paraphrases and Hymns selected by them should be issued for the information of the church, and that all suggestions regarding them should be made to the committee before the month of March next, with the view of having a final report on the subject prepared for next General Assembly. The committee felt that they would be able to concentrate an amount of attention on the new version of the Psalms, which had not hitherto been practicable; and on this point they invited suggestions from the church at large, in the same way as had been proposed in the case of the Paraphrases and Hymns. Having tabled his report, Mr. Adam said that there was another matter to which he thought it necessary to refer, and he did so in no party spirit, and for no party purpose. They all desired to act in a kind and respectful manner to other churches. Since he came to the Assembly he had received an extract from the minutes of the United Presbyterian Synod, and he did not think he would be discharging his duty to this church or to the United Presbyterian Synod if he did not read it, viz:—"The Synod resolve to appoint a committee to take the whole subject of the revision of the Hymn Book into their consideration, with power to correspond with other churches, with a view to obtain a common Hymn Book for the Presbyterian Churches." After a lengthened discussion, the following motion by Dr. Rainey, slightly amended, was unanimously adopted:—

"The Assembly, in accordance with the suggestion contained in the report,

Hymns. 93

instruct the committee to issue the selection of Hymns prepared by them for the information of the church, and to receive such suggestions as may be sent to them before the month of March next, with the view of presenting a final report to next General Assembly. The Assembly do this on the understanding that before any steps are taken to sanction the public use of the collection now submitted, or any other, it shall be sent to Presbyteries, so that they may have an opportunity of expressing to a future Assembly their judgment on any question of principle or detail connected with this matter, which appears to them fit or necessary to be proposed and decided. The Assembly also instruct the committee to issue their new versions of the Psalms, for the information of the church, in the same way as has been proposed in the case of the Paraphrases and Hymns, and, at the same time, remit them to the committee to receive suggestions, and prepare a final report upon them also to the General Assembly."

The Assembly held its next meeting in May, 1871, and on the 25th day of that month, the "Committee on Paraphrases and Hymns" reported that they had carried out their instructions in having got the Hymns, and the new versions of the Psalms, printed together in a convenient form, and at a cheap price, and thus placed them within the reach of all interested in the matter. The collection had met with a large measure of acceptance—not a few having begun to use it in families, classes, and meetings, in preference to other Hymn Books. Very few suggestions had been transmitted to them, and those they had received did not appear, either in their number or nature, such as to call for, or justify, a revision and reprinting of the collection.

The following, as the deliverance of the Assembly, moved by Mr. Neilson, Greenock, seconded by Dr. Wilson, Bombay, was agreed to:—"The General Assembly having appointed a committee to prepare a collection of Hymns and Paraphrases, and to issue the same for the information of the church, which has been done; and the Assembly, having also resolved that the committee should receive suggestions on the understanding that, before any steps are taken to sanction the public use of the collection now submitted, or any other, it shall be sent to Presbyteries, so that they may have an opportunity of expressing to a future Assembly their judgment on any question of principle or detail connected with the matter, which appears to them fit or necessary to be proposed or decided. The attention of Presbyteries is hereby called to this deliverance in order that they may give the subject such consideration as they may deem fit, not later than the 15th January, 1872, and inasmuch as few suggestions have been received in terms of this deliverance, the committee is instructed to receive additional suggestions up to this date, so that a final report may be laid before the March Commission, and that next Assembly may be in a position to take such action thereanent as may seem to it most for edification with regard to the worship of the sanctuary. The Assembly direct the same course to be followed with regard to the new versions of the Psalms." *(App. XIII.)*.

XIII.

The Music of the Old Psalters.

IN bringing these notices of our metrical Psalms, Hymns, &c., to a conclusion, we shall briefly direct attention to the Music of the Old Psalters. In tracing their history, one is forcibly impressed with the conviction that in the early days of the Scottish Reformed Church, a knowledge of sacred music was much more prevalent—much more generally and intelligently cultivated, than it has been of more recent date. Indeed, instruction in the theory and practice of singing seems to have formed a chief element in ordinary education. And schools entirely devoted to vocal music were instituted at least in all the principal towns, and were warmly supported and patronised. (*App. XIV.*). The inhabitants of Edinburgh, on a certain remarkable occasion, gave emphatic evidence of their zeal and ability to express their feelings through the medium of sacred song. In 1582 John Durie, one of the ministers of that town, had incurred the displeasure of the civil powers in consequence of his stern faithfulness to the Presbyterian cause, and the maintenance of Ecclesiastical discipline, chiefly in the matter of the excommunication of Montgomery. He was accordingly deprived of his benefice, prohibited from preaching, and expelled from the capital. His banishment, however, was but of short duration; and on his return he was met at the Netherbow Port—one of the gates of the city—" by the haill toun"— the whole of the vast multitude marching up the High Street, with their heads uncovered, and with ringing voices and enthusiastic spirits, singing, in the four parts, the old version of the 124th Psalm. (See *Plate IX.*).

> " Now Israel may say, and that truley
> If that the LORD had not our cause maintaind,
> If that the LORD had not our right sustained,
> When all the world, against us furiouslie
> Made their uproares, and said we should all die."

This incident is thus graphically told by Calderwood :—" John Durie cometh to Leith at night the 3d of September (1582). Upon Tuesday the 4th of September, as he is coming to Edinburgh, there met him at the Gallowgreen 200, but ere he came to the Netherbow their number increased to 400; but they were no sooner entered but they encreased to 600 or 700, and within short space the whole street was replenished even to Saint Geiles Kirk; the number was esteemed to 2000. At the Netherbow they took up the 124th Psalme, 'Now Israel may say,' &c., and sung in such a pleasant tune in four parts, known to the most part of the people, that coming up the street, all bareheaded, till they entered in the Kirk, with such a great sound and majestie, that it moved both themselves and all the huge multitude of the beholders, looking out at the shots and over stairs, with admiration and astonishment; the Duke himself beheld, and reave his beard for anger; he was more affrayed of this sight than anie thing that ever he had seene before in Scotland. When they came to the Kirk, Mr. James Lowsone made a short exhortation in the Reader's place, to move the multitude to thankfulness. Thereafter a psalm being sung, they departed with great joy." The same occurrence is thus described by Melville:—"Going upe the streit with bear heads and loud voices, sung to the praise of God and testifeing of great joy and consolation . . . . till heavin and erthe resoundit. This noyes when the Duc, being in the town, hard and ludgit in the Hie-gat, luiked out and saw, he rave his berde for anger, and hasted him af the town."

The old Psalters which appeared previous to 1650—when the present version was adopted—were almost all accompanied with appropriate music notation. Thus in an edition by Day in 1563, the Psalms appeared "with apt notes to synge them withall," and containing "A shorte introduction into the Science of Musicke, made for such as are desirous to have the knowledge thereof, for the singing of the Psalmes." In the same year, and again in 1565, Day issued another edition, being "The Whole Psalmes in foure parts—Medius, Contra-tenor, Tenor, and Bassus—whiche may be song to al musicall instrumentes, set forth for the encrease of vertue and abolishyng of other vayne and triflyng ballades." And in Day's edition of 1576 the "apt notes" of the tunes are given in two styles of notation, which are thus explained in a brief address "To THE READER":—"Thou shalt vnderstand, (gentle Reader) that I haue (for the helpe of those that are desirous to learne to sing) caused a new Print of Note to be made wyth letters to be ioyned by euery Note; whereby thou mayst know how to call euery Note by his right name, so that with a very little diligence (as thou art taught in the Introduction Printed heretofore in the Psalmes) thou mayst the more easily by the vewing of these letters, come to the knowledge of perfect *Solfyng:* whereby thou mayst sing the Psalmes the more easlier. The letters be these. V. *for* Vt. R. *for* Re. M. *for* My. F. *for* Fa. S. *for* Sol. L. *for* La. Thus where thou seest any letter ioyned by the note; you may easily call him by his right name."

The honour is unquestionably due to Calvin, the distinguished Genevan Reformer, of having originated and matured a true and distinctive psalmody for congregational worship, as he was the first to provide a metrical version of the entire psalms for such worship, in the living language of the people; and in the one respect as well as in the other his instructions and example have been followed by the Reformers of the Scottish Church. On this subject, Calvin's memory has been thoroughly vindicated in an admirable Article on "Calvin and Church Song" in "The British and Foreign Evangelical Review" for October, 1870, by C. B.—the initials of COLIN BROWN, Esq., Euing Lecturer on Music in the Andersonian University of Glasgow. In that Article Mr. Brown exposes the gross ignorance and presumption of Hullah when he says (Lectures on Musical History, p. 73):—"Indeed Calvin seems never to have recognised music as a means of religious expression, scarcely even to have appreciated it as an aid to devotion, and the music of his followers has suffered accordingly;"—and the no less reckless assertion of the Rev. Henry Allon, (Exeter Hall Lectures, 1862, p. 286.)—"Calvin was utterly destitute of musical sensibility, as every page of his works and every element of his character indicate."

Calvin's Psalms, as has already been noticed, speedily attained the most extraordinary popularity amongst those for whom they were originally intended. They were committed to memory by all classes of the populace, and sung to all sorts of tunes, even the most profane—a proceeding which so grieved Calvin's heart and affected his "musical sensibility," that he applied to the first musicians in Europe to furnish him with tunes worthy of the sacred words. Accordingly the fifty Psalms by Marot were set to music by Guilleaume Franc, of Strasburg, in 1545. These tunes continue still in use among the Protestants of France and Holland; and among them appear for the first time the "Old Hundred," and many others of the finest tunes in the whole range of psalmody. After Franc's death, Calvin applied to Claude Goudimel of Rome, to have the music harmonised and the work completed. This was not accomplished till about the year 1561, when Calvin had laboured in the cause during twenty-three years of his life—and when the "fully harmonised psalter for use in public worship appeared." This "Psalter is a monument of beauty, which all succeeding ages have used as a mine and a model. The tunes are the common inheritance of the Protestant churches, and are familiarly known to all lovers of psalmody, as unsurpassed for simplicity, beauty, and grandeur, by the music of any country or of any age."

The GENEVAN PSALTER contains a remarkable Preface by Calvin, which gives a full and lucid explanation of his views of the nature and uses of Sacred song. It appeared prefixed to the first edition in 1543, and is found in all subsequent issues. The following Extract from it, kindly furnished by Mr. Brown, by whom it has been translated for the use of his class, will speak for itself. It exhibits as thorough, hearty, comprehensive, and exalted sentiments on the subject of Psalmody as have ever been expressed:—

"To all Christians, lovers of the Word of God, greeting.

"As it is a thing enjoined in Christianity, and amongst the most necessary, that every believer, in his own place, should observe and maintain the communion of the church, frequenting the assemblies which are held on Sabbaths and other days, to honour and serve God; so it is right and reasonable, that all should know and understand what is said and done in the place of worship, so as to draw from it advantage and edification."

"As for public prayers, there are two kinds of them—the one is expressed in words only, the other with song; and this is no recent invention, for from the first origin of the church, this has been the case, as appears in history. And even St. Paul does not speak of verbal prayer alone, but also of singing. And in truth, we know by experience that song has great force and power in moving and inflaming the heart of man to invoke and praise God with more vehement and ardent zeal.

"It should always be seen to that the song should not be light and frivolous, but that it have weight and majesty, as saith Saint Augustine; and also that there is a great difference between the music that is employed for the enjoyment of men at table, and in their houses, and the psalms which they sing in Church in the presence of God and his angels. But when the form here given is rightly judged of, we hope that it will be found holy and pure; seeing that it is simply constructed for the edification of which we have spoken, as well as that the use of singing may be greatly extended. So that even in the houses and in the fields, it may be to us an incitement and an instrument to praise God and raise our hearts to Him; and to console us in meditating on His power, goodness, wisdom, and justice, which is more necessary for us than we know how to express.

"For the first, it is not without cause that the Holy Spirit exhorts us so carefully, by the Holy Scripture, to rejoice ourselves in God, and that all our joy should rest there as its true end. For He knows how truly we are inclined to please ourselves in vanity. Thus while our nature draws and leads us to seek all manner of foolish and vicious enjoyment—on the contrary, our Lord, to separate and draw us from the allurements of the flesh and of the world, presents to us every possible means to fill us with that spiritual joy which he commends so much to us.

"But amongst other things which are suitable for the recreation of men, and for yielding them pleasure, music is either the first, or one of the chief, and we must esteem it a gift of God bestowed for that end. Therefore, by so much the more, we ought to see that it is not abused, for fear of soiling and contaminating it; turning that to our condemnation which was given for our profit and good. Even were there no other consideration than this alone, it ought to move us to regulate the use of music, so as to make it subservient to all good morals, and that it should not give occasion for loosing the bridle of dissoluteness, that it should not lead to voluptuousness, nor be the instrument of immodesty and impurity.

"But further, there is scarcely anything in this world which can more powerfully turn or bend hither and thither the manners of men, as Plato has wisely remarked. And in fact we experimentally feel that it has a secret and incredible power over our hearts to move them one way or other. Therefore we ought to be so much the more careful to regulate it in such a manner, that it may be useful to us, and in no ways pernicious. For this reason, the ancient doctors of the church often complained that the people of their time were addicted to disgraceful and immodest songs, which, not without cause, they esteemed and called a deadly and satanic poison for corrupting the world.

"But in speaking of music I include two parts, to wit, the words, or subject and matter; seeondly, the song or melody. It is true that all evil words, as saith St. Paul, corrupt good manners, but when melody is united to them, they much more powerfully pierce the heart, and enter in: just as when by a funnel wine is poured into a vessel, so poison and corruption is infused into the depth of the heart by the melody.

"What then is to be done? It is to have songs not only pure, but also holy, that they may be incitements to stir us up to pray to and praise God, and to meditate on His works, in order to love Him, fear Him, honour and glorify Him. But what Saint Augustine says is true, that none can sing things worthy of God but he who has received the power from Himself. Wherefore when we have sought all round, searching here and there, we shall find no songs better and more suitable for this end than the Psalms of David which the Holy Spirit dictated and gave to him. And therefore when we sing them, we are as certain that God has put words into our mouths as if He Himself sang within us to exalt His glory. Wherefore Chrysostom exhorts all men and women and little children to accustom themselves to sing them as a means of associating themselves with the company of angels; further, we must remember what St. Paul says, that spiritual songs cannot be sung well but with the heart; but the heart requires the understanding: and in that, saith St. Augustine, lies the difference between the song of man and that of birds, for a linnet, a nightingale, and a jay *(papegay)*, may sing well, but it will be without understanding.

"But the peculiar gift of man is to sing knowing what he says. Further, the understanding ought to accompany the heart and affections, which cannot be unless we have the song imprinted in our memory, that we may be ever singing it.

"This present book, for this cause, besides what otherwise has been said, ought to be particularly acceptable to every one who desires, without reproach, and according to God, to rejoice in seeing his own salvation, and the good of his neighbours; and thus has no need to be much recommended by me, as it carries in itself its own value and praise. Only let the world be well advised, that instead of songs partly vain and frivolous, partly foolish and dull, partly filthy and vile, and consequently wicked and hurtful, which it has hitherto used, it should accustom itself hereafter to sing these heavenly and divine songs, with good King David.

"Touching the music, it appeared best that it should be simple in the way we have put it, to carry weight and majesty suitable to the subject, and even to be fit to be sung in church as has been said.

"GENEVA, 10th JUNE, 1543."

EST'S PSALTER is favourably spoken of on account of the music by which the Psalms are accompanied, and although not properly a Scottish but an English manual, may be here briefly referred to. Its title is "THE WHOLE BOOKE OF PSALMES with the wonted tunes as they are song in Churches; composed into foure parts. All vvhich are so placed that foure may sing, ech one a seuerall part in this booke VVherein the Church tunes are carefully corrected, and thereunto added other short tunes usually song in London, and other places of this Realme. With a Table at the end of the booke of such tunes as are newly added &c. Compiled by sondry Authors. Imprinted at London by Thomas Est the Assignee of William Boyd. 1592."

The following is Est's Preface :—"Although I might have used the skill of some one learned Musition in the setting of these Psalmes in 4 partes, yet for varieties sake I have intreated the help of many, beeing such as I know to be expert in the Arte, and sufficient to answere such curious carping Musitions whose skill hath not been embloyed to the furthering of this work. And I haue not onely set downe in this booke, all the Tunes vsually printed heretofore with as much truth as I could possibly gather among diuers of our ordinary Psalme bookes, but also have added those which are commonly song now adayes, and not printed in our common Psalme bookes with the rest. And all this have I so orderly cast that the 4 partes lye always together in open sight. The which my trauayle as it hath been to the furtherance of Musicke in all godly sort, and to the comfort of all good Christians; as I pray thee to take it in good part, and vse it to the glory of God. T. E."

In his introduction to this Psalter, Dr. E. F. Rimbault has these interesting explanatory remarks :—"There is a peculiarity in the mode of harmonising the church tunes in the sixteenth and early part of the following century, which requires notice. The melody or 'plain song,' as it is sometimes called, is given to the *tenor* voice, and not as in the generality of modern music, to the *treble*. This mode of arrangement was derived from the Romish Church, where the *canto-fermo* or plain song is to this day sung by men's voices. It was, no doubt, intended that the congregation should sing the tune (which from its pitch and compass would suit any kind of voice), and that the accompanying parts should be sung by a choir of voices. The *cantus* or upper part is the work of the arranger, whilst the *tenor* (or line above the *bass*, for it is sometimes written in the alto cleff) is invariably that of the melody or 'old church tune.'"

The Scottish Metrical Psalms.

RAVENSCROFT'S edition of the Psalter is also a remarkable one, and merits more than merely passing notice, viz.:—THE WHOLE BOOKE OF PSALMES, with the Hymnes Evangelicall and Songs Spirituall, composed into 4 parts by Sundry Authors. Newly corrected and enlarged by Tho: Rauenscroft, Bachelor of Musicke. London 1621."

The following is the Index of Psalm Tunes usually sung in Cathedral Churches, Collegiats, Chappels, &c.:—

"*English Tunes:*—Bathe and Wels, or Glasenbury—Psalms 19, 63, 140: Bristoll, 16, 64: Cambridge, 2, 73, 106, 117, 128: Canterbury, 25; Chichester, 22, 53, 110: Christ's Hospitall, 72, 107: Ely, 21, 2nd part of 51: Exceter, 15, 65: Glocester, 10, 48, 143: Hereford, 11, 49, 144; Lincolne, 7, 56, 142: Lichfield and Couentry, 9, 58: London, 67: Norwich, 5, 55, 102: Oxford, 4, 74, 109, 129: Peterborough, 8, 57: Rochester, 24, 82, 139: Salisbury, 17, 54: Winchester, 23, 84, 98, 101, 116, 133, 150: Windsor, or Eaton, 62, 85, 108, 123: Woluerhampton, 26, 83.

"*Northerne Tunes:*—Yorke, 27, 66, 115, 138: Durham, 28, 76: Chester, 31, 80, 119, 146: Carleile, 29, 79: Southwell, 2nd part of 50, 70, 134: Manchester, 147.

"*Scottish Tunes*. King's, 32, 86: Duke's, 33, 87: Abby, 34, 88: Dumfermling, 35, 89: Dundy, 36, 90: Glascow, 37, 91: Martyrs, 39, 92, 99, 118.

"*Welch Tunes*, Landaph, 40, 93: Bangor, 42, 94: S. David's, 43, 95: S. Asaph or Wrixham, 96: Ludlow, 45.

" Low Dutch Tones, 12, 60, 114, 137. High Dutch Tones, 112, 125, 127. Italian Tones, 120. French Tones, 50, 100, 111, 113, 121, 122, 124, 126, 130, the 10 Commandements. English Tunes imitating the High Dutch, Italian, French, and Netherlandish Tones, 1, 3, 6, 14, 18, 21, 30, 38, 41, 44, 51, 52, 59, 61, 68, 69, 71, 77, 78, 103, 104, 119, 132, 136, 137, 141."

"The names of the Authors which Composed the Tunes of the Psalmes ino 4 parts:—

"Thomas Tallis, *A Psalm before morning prayer.* John Douland, Doctor of Musicke, *French Tune* (ps. 100. L M.) Thomas Morley, Bachelor of Musicke, *ps.* 1. &c. Gyles Farnaby, Bachelor of Musicke, *French Tune, &c.* Thomas Tomkins, Bachelor of Musicke, *VVorcester Tune, Dumfermling Tune.* John Tomkins, Bachelor of Musicke, *Glocester Tune.* Martin Pierson, Bachelor of Musicke, *Southwell Tune.* William Parsons, *The Lamentation.* Edmund Hooper,

George Kirby, Edward Blancks, *French & Dutch Tunes*. Richard Allison, *Rochester Tune*. John Farmer, Michael Cauendish, John Bennet, *Cheshire Tune*. Robert Palmer, John Milton, *Norwich Tune*, *Yorke Tune*. Simon Stubbs, *Martyrs Tune*. William Crauford, *Ely Tune*. William Harrison, *Lincolne Tune*. Thomas Ravenscroft, Bachelor of Musicke, *Cambridge Tune*. *Oxford Tune*, W. Cobbold, John Ward. E. Johnson."

Ravenscroft has a lengthy address—" To all That have *skill*, or *will*, vnto *Sacred Musicke*, I wish CONCORD among *themselves* with GOD and with their own CONSCIENCES." It commences in these terms:—

" Harmonicall Brethren, I have here undertaken with no small labour and charge, to bring the Tunes of the Psalmes, Hymnes Euangelicall, and Songs Spirituall (as they are usually sung throughout Great Brittaine) into one entire volume; which are so composed for the most part, that the unskilfull may, with little practice, be enabled to sing them in parts, after a plausible manner." The address closes thus:—

" I have therefore endeauoured for the fitting of every Heart to that Psalme, which it shall most affect, to place speciall Tunes proper to the nature of Each Psalme (not imitating Art so much as the naturall inclination, but joyning one with another) and am bold to admonish the singers that they observe three Rules.

" 1. That Psalmes of Tribulation be sung with a low voyce and long measure.

" 2. That Psalmes of Thanksgiving be sung with a voyce indifferent, neither too loud nor too soft, and with a measure neither too swift nor too slow.

" 3. That Psalmes of Reioycing be sung with a loud voyce, a swift and iocund measure.

" In all which, the obseruing of Time, Tune, and Eare, will produce a perfect Harmony.

" Accept kindly what I have laboured earnestly and use it to thy comfort. Thus I end, humbly wishing to all true Christian Hearts, that sweet consolation in singing prayers unto God here upon Earth, as may bring vs hereafter to beare a part with the Quire of Angels in the Heauens. Your well according and best wishing Brother.—THO. RAUENCROFT."

The version printed at Edinburgh, in 1635, by the Heirs of Andrew Hart, was considered one of the most important that had appeared up till that time. It contains 31 tunes, in full notation, viz.:—The Old Common Tune, King's Tune, Duke's, English, French, London, Stilt, Dumfermling, Dundie, Abbay, Cheshire, Glasgow, Culros, Martyrs, Glaston, Wigton, Innerness, Jedburgh, Couper, Glenluce, Irving, Newtoun, Galloway, Melros, Dumbar, Elgin, Monros, Maxtoun, Cathnes, Durhame, Winchester. All these have the four parts—tenor or church part, contra, treble, and bassus—arranged with much skill and care; and some of them, such as Dumfermling and Culros, have a fifth part, quintus, immediately preceding the bassus. It is worthy of remark that these tunes are given partly on one page, and the remainder inverted on the other—the tenor and contra having the other parts, treble and bassus, inverted on the page opposite—the object apparently being that all the four parts might be sung from the one book, the singers occupying places of twos opposite each other at a narrow table. Besides these there are a number of tunes "In Reports," and throughout the whole book appropriate music is prefixed to each Psalm. By the term "Report" in musical nomenclature is meant a short fugal passage. It may indicate either a *carrying back*—i.e., after a passage has been started by one harmonic part, it is taken back to the same point and started anew by another; or a *carrying again*—i.e., the passage is repeated by the parts in succession.

The editor, who has compiled and arranged this music, has obviously been at immense labour, and has shown considerable tact and judgment in his execution of the task. At the close of an address to the "Good and gentle Reader," he designates himself simply by the letters E. M., which are known to be the initials of an ardent lover of sacred music, Edward Miller, A.M., who resided in Edinburgh as a teacher of music, and who was one of the prebendaries of the Chapel-Royal. The address is written in a quaint and racy style. The following quotation from it will explain itself:—

"This book being to bee published in so fair a letter, and so fine paper to the intent that nothing should be lacking to the decoring thereof, there is added the sweet ornament of Music, in foure or mo parts throughout the whole Psalmes; Besides a great many Common Tunes, some grave, some light, fitting diverse dispositions; As also some Psalmes in Reports, for the further delight of qualified persons in the said Art. If you bee curious to know who hath undergone these paines for your benefite, I professe myself a Welwiller to Musick, who in love and paines for advancement thereof will yeeld to few, though in qualification to many: I have spent too much tyme, travell, and expense on that faculty, if my skill therein come short of this present task; *sed exitus acta probet*. The motives moving mee hereunto are chiefely GOD's glorie, the advancement of this Art, the saving of pains to teachers hereof; the incitation of others to greater acts of this kind, the earnest desire of some well affected, the imployment of my poor talent; together with an abuse observed in all Churches, where sundrie Tribles, Basses, and Counters, set by diverse Authors, being sung upon one and the same Tenor, do discordingly rub each upon another, offending both Musicall and rude ears, which never tasted of this Art, which unhappie fault I thought might happily bee helped, and the Church Music made more plausible by publishing this Booke. I acknowledge sincerely the whole compositions of the parts to belong to the primest Musicians that ever this kingdom had, as Deane John Angus, Blackhall, Smith, Peebles, Sharp, Black, Buchan, and others famous for their skill in this kind. I would bee most unwilling to wrong such Shyning lights of this Art, by obscuring their Names, and arrogating anything to myselfe, which any wayes might derogate from them. For (God is my witness) I affect not popular applause, knowing how little soliditie there is in that shadow-like seeming substance, studying to approve myself to God in a good conscience; which testimonie finding in my Sóul, I contemn all worldly approbation or opprobration. The first copies of these parts were doubtlesly right set down by these skilful Authors, but have been wronged and vitiat by unskilful copiers thereof, as all things are injured by tyme. And herein consisted a part of my paines, that collecting all the sets I could find on the Psalmes, after painfull triall thereof, I selected the best for this work according to my simple judgement."

The special characteristics of this old music, are very plainly and fully brought out in the "*Prefatory Remarks to Havergal's Old Church Psalmody*"—the following extracts from which cannot fail to be appreciated:—

"The distinctive character of Old Tunes has long been out of common recollection. Simple and easy in their phrases, and always syllabic in their partition, the commonest ears and least cultivated voices could master them. Grave, but cheerful, dignified and chaste, they are admirably adapted to meet a great variety of language, and to foster a calm and earnest devotion."

"The harmony to the old tunes was sometimes of the simplest sort. Generally speaking, however, the old harmonists were inclined to a little cleverness in counterpoint. The "Harmonised Psalter," published by John Day, 1635, abounds with modest ingenuities. The version of the 44th Psalm—

"Another of the same by R. Brimle" (appearing in Dibdin's Standard Psalm Tune Book,") is uncommonly beautiful. The close of it is a clever instance of writing "In Reports," i.e. *bringing back* some part of the tune and turning it into a short fugue. But whether simple or ingenious their harmony retained the following characteristics:—1. *Truthfulness of progression in all the parts.* 2. *Contrariety or obliquity of motion between the extreme parts.* 3. *Fulness of combination; fundamental chords being preferred to half chords.* 4. *Closeness, or fitting distribution of the parts as to relative distance.* 5. *Avoidance of certain chords and discords.* 6. *Frequent interchange of major and minor chords.*"

"The TIME and PITCH of tunes in older days, were not exactly as they now are. Singers formerly sang with good speed. A dozen verses, reduced to six by a double tune, formed a very moderate portion for one occasion. The modern drawl, which makes four single verses quite long enough, was most likely occasioned by innovations upon the syllabic style in the early part of the last century. The keys, or scales, in which the tunes were set, were no criterion as to the pitch in which they were sung. They were mostly set in only two or three keys to suit the convenience of the printer, as to leger lines, and accidental sharps or flats; but they were sung at any pitch which best suited the singers."

"It would be an omission not to mention the constant practice of beginning and ending each strain with a full chord: and the almost constant use of the *Tierce de Picardie,* or major third, at every close in a minor mode; as well as on the contrary the utter abhorrence of everything *appogiatural* in the melody. The old tunes contain no instance of that mawkish hanging upon the sixth or fourth which now so secularizes most modern tunes. They settle at once in a firm and masculine style on the fifth, or third." "Whenever a discord was used, it was sung in *suspension* and *held* till it was resolved. Modern practise discards this elegant custom; chiefly, it is probable, because it involves some little syncopation to which ordinary singers are not trained."

"The oldest tunes are remarkable for broken syncopated rhythm. They are not commonly composed of notes of equal length, in corresponding position; but comprise semibreves, and minims, rather capriciously disposed. The tunes in the old Genevan Psalter are famous specimens of this sort of irregularity. Ravenscroft, in 1621, seems to have delighted in it; for he actually printed melodies with more rhythmical syncopations than even older copies contained.

It was not till Playford's era—about 1670—that the old church-tunes began to be written with equalized notation."

"Another peculiarity is the early custom of assigning the tunes themselves to Tenor voices, and setting for Treble voices, a merely harmonic part above. The origin of the custom may be attributed to the circumstances of the times. Coeval with the Reformation, psalm-singing became so general that *thousands* of people singing together in massive *unison* was a common occurrence. To relieve the sternness and monotony of such singing, skilful musicians, even the best masters of the day, composed parts of the popular tunes in such manner as allowed them to be sung by all the people, without alteration or interruption, and yet with sufficient embellishment to please the lovers of harmony."

In the "PROCEEDINGS OF THE SOCIETY OF ANTIQUARIES OF SCOTLAND," Vol. VII., April, 1868, p. 445, a Paper appears of much importance in connection with the Church Music of the Reformation, entitled—" AN ACCOUNT OF THE SCOTTISH PSALTER of A.D. 1566, containing the PSALMS, CANTICLES, and HYMNS, set to music in four Parts, in the manuscripts of THOMAS WODE or WOOD, Vicar of Sanctandrous. By DAVID LAING, Esq., (now LL.D.) For. Sec. S. A. Scot." The following details, which doubtless will be received with all the interest they are so well fitted to excite, are gathered from that Paper. We are happy that we have succeeded in securing impressions of the admirable Plates with which it is illustrated, in *facsimile* of the manuscripts. They appear at the end of this volume, and are referred to throughout these notes.

The manuscripts of Wode, or Wood, consist of four volumes—devoted respectively to the four parts of the music—the First containing the Tenor, the Second the Treble, the Third the Contra-Tenor, and the Fourth the Bassus. Dr. Laing is the fortunate possessor of the First, Second, and Fourth volumes. The Third has disappeared; but it is hoped that it is not finally lost. A thin supplemental Fifth volume is preserved in Trinity College Library, Dublin, entitled by Wood—"'This is the Fyft Buke, addit to the four Psalme Bukkis, for Songis of four or fyue Pairtis, meit and apt for musitians to recreat thair spirittis when as they shall be ouercum with heuines or any kynd of sadnes, not only musitians, but also euen to the ignorant of a gentle nature, hearing shall be comforted, and be mirry with us. 1569."

VOLUME FIRST—TENOR.—(*Facsimile Plates*, I. II.).—The number of tunes is one hundred and two, with instructions to sing the other pieces in the printed Psalter, to one or other of these. The frontispiece contains a sketch of an elderly man in a long gown, holding an open book of music in his left hand, and a clarionet to his mouth in his right. Over his head is the word "TENNOWR;" and over this again these lines appear inscribed in a scroll:—

> "It may be knawin be my hewinly hew
> I am ane man of mekill modestie
> And yairfor synngis my part with notis most trew
> As it efteris unto my facultie."

The colophon to the Psalms is in these terms—(*Plate* VIII.):—"Endis ye Psalmès set furth in iiij partes, conforme to the tennour of ye Buke, 1566 (and followeth certain Canticles and first Veni Creator, &c.) Be ane honorable and singulare cunning man Dauid Pables in Sanctandrous, And Noted and Wreaten be me Thomas Wode."

These tunes were harmonised by DAVID PEEBLES at the request of LORD JAMES STEWART, afterwards Earl of Murray and Regent of Scotland. The following note appears towards the end of the volume, written after the Regent's death, in February, 1569-70:—

"I HAUE thought gude to make it knawin wha sett the thre pairtes to and agreable to the Tenor, or common pairt of the Psalme buke: the Mess and the Papisticall seruice abolished, and the preaching of the Euangell stablisit heir, into Sanct Androus, MY LORD JAMIS (wha efter was Erle of Murray and Regent) being at the Reformation, Pryour of Sanct Androus, causes ane of his channons, to name DAUID PABLES, being ane of the chieff musitians into this land, to set three pairtes to the Tenor; and my Lord commandit the said Dauid to leave the curiosity of musicke, and sa to make plaine and dulce, and sa he hes done: bot the said Dauid he was not earnest; bot I being cume to this Toune, to remain, I was ever requesting and solisting till they were all set; and the Canticles (like as *Veni Creator*, the *Song of Ambrose*, the *Song of Mary*, &c.) I oft did wreat to Maister Andro Blakehall, to Jhone Angus, and sum Andro Kempe set, sa I notit tenors, and send sum to Mussilbrough, and sum to Dunfarmling, and sa were done: God grant we use them all to his glory!—notwithstanding of this trauell I have taken, I cannot understand bot musike sall perish in this land alutterlye. . . . .

The Music of the Old Psalters. 109

To ane great man that hes bot ane resonable gripe of musike, thir Fyue Bukes were worthy thair wayght of gould."

VOLUME SECOND—TREBLE.—(*Plates* III. IV.).—The frontispiece of this volume exhibits a young man in a green dress, holding in his right hand a large music book, and pointing with his left to the word "TRIBBILL;" and at the top of the page there is a scroll with these lines:—

> "My gleistring collowr, glorius and grene
> betakinis zouth, vt glaid and mirry hart
> qlk ever dois vt courage frome ye spleine
> But preice or paine vt pleisor syng my part."

At the close of the Psalms in this volume we have *(Plate VIII.)*,—" Set in iiij partes Be ane honorable man Dauid Pables In Sanctandrous. And Noted and Wretin by me Thomas Wode, 5 of decembar, 1566."

The original copy of the volume contains Wood's explanation of his object in undertaking to write a duplicate set of the Four Parts:—

"THIR Bukis I begouth in the zeir of God J^m V^c lxij (1562) zeirs, and I rewlit and wes in purpose to haue first wreatin the first vearce of euerilk Psalme that hes ane tune; and sum that knew this my purpose and preparation, desyrit me to stay a quhyle, for the heall Psalmis wes printit in Geneua and wer to cum heame shortly, and so I held my hand till the heall Psalmis com hame, and I wreat the first vearce of euerilke Psalme that had ane tune put to it; and in lyk maner the Canticles and euer as I obteinit ony to be set, did put them in heir till I had gottin them all. Efter this four or fyve zeiris I tuk uther threscore throwghis of lumbert paper and X or XII, and wreat all thir Psalmis and Canticles and notit them better and farer nor thay ar heir, and thay lyand besyde me thir mony zeiris unbund, for layke of the Kynges armies drawing be maister Jhone Geddy; and seeing that maister Jhone forgettis and hes put me sa lang in houpe I purpose God willing to cause bind theme as shortly as I may."

The Canticle *Si quis diliget me* is given at the end of this volume, "set be Dauid Pables in Four partis in the year of God 1530, or thairby, and ane noueice callit Francy Heagy, and was this Dauid Pables awin dissyple, set the Fyft pairt, a lytill before Pinky (1547) and that uerray weell." In what follows we have an interesting allusion to the skill in music of King James the Fifth; besides a doleful expression of the author's fears regarding the fate of his favourite "science and craft":—

"Now zee knaw that this is the Fyft pairt (of *Si quis diliget*) maid to the Four, as Dauid Pables first set it, and presentit the sam to KYNG JAMIS THE FYFT, quha wes ane musitian himself; he had ane singular gud eir, and culd sing that he had neuer seine before, bot his voyce wes rawky and harske. I have said, in ane of thir bukis, that Musik will pereishe, and this buke will shaw zou sum resons quhy: We se be experiance that craft nor syence is not learnit bot to the end he may leiue be it quhen he has the craft or science; and if D^r· Farfax wer alyue in this cuntry he wald be contemnit, and pereise for layk of mentinance; and sa of neid force it man dikeay."

VOLUME THIRD—CONTRA TENOR—has not been recovered. A supposed copy in the College Library, has been found to be a duplicate of Vol. II., and without a Frontispiece.

VOLUME FOURTH—THE BASSUS—*(Plate V.)*, has no frontispiece. The Psalms close with—*(Plate VIII.)*, "Set in iiij partes Be ane honorable man Dauid Peables in S. Noted and Wreatin by me Thomas Wode, 5 of dembar, a^o· d^o· 1566." At the end of the 23rd Psalm in the duplicated copy of this volume we have—"Thir four buikkis wes only pennit be me Thomas Wod Vicar of Sanctandrous, 1578."

Plates VI., VII. contain the first and second verses of Ps. 137, "When as we sate in Babylon," the ornamental borders telling their own sad tale, as they exhibit a variety of musical instruments hanging from the willows, and captive Jews standing in sadness by Babel's streams.

In *Plates IX.-XII.* the music of the three parts, as they appear in the MS., is given, for the purpose of shewing at once both the tune and the harmony.

Appended to the Psalms there are a variety of Canticles or Church Hymns, somewhat similar to those which appear in the older editions of the English Psalm-Books of Sternhold and Hopkins, set to music in four or five parts. The following list contains their titles and opening words, with the names of the several composers, as supplied by Wood:—

LIST OF HYMNS AND CANTICLES IN WOOD'S MSS.

1. Veni Creator Spiritus.—KEMP.
   "Cum, Holy Ghost, Eternal God."

2. The humble Sute of a Synnar.—BLACKHALL.
   "O Lord, of whom I do depend."

3. The Song of Ambrose.—KEMP.
   "We praise thee, O God, we acknowledge thee."

4. The Song of the Thre Childring.—ANGUS.
   "O all ye workes of God the Lord, bless ye the Lord."

5. The Song of Zacharias.—ANGUS.
   "The onlye Lord of Israell be praised evermore."

6. The Sang of the Blessit Virgin.—ANGUS.
   "My soule doth magnific the Lord."

7. The Sang of Simeon, callit "*Nunc Dimitis.*"—ANGUS.
   "O Lord, because my heart's desire."

8. The Simboll or Creide of Athanasius.—ANGUS.
   "What man, socuer he be, saluation will attaine."

9. The Lamentation of a Sinnar.
   "O Lord, turne not away thy face."

10. The Lord's Prayer.
    "Our father which in heaven art."

11. The Ten Commands.
    "Harke, Israell, and what I say."

12. The Complaint of ane Sinner.—KEMP.
    "Where righteousness doth say, Lord."

13. The Ten Commands.—ANGUS.
    "Attend my people, and give eare."

14. The Sang of Simeon.—ANGUS.
    "Now suffer me, O Lord."

15. The Lord's Prayer (another version).—ANGUS.
"Our Father which in heaven art,
And mak'st us all one brotherhood."
16. The XII Articles of our Belieff.—ANGUS.
"All my belief and confidence."
17. Da pacem Domine.—ANGUS.
"Give peace in these our dayes, O Lord."
18. Robber (Robert) Wisdome; rather call this a prayer.—BLACKHALL.
"Preserue us Lord, by thy dere worde."

"Folloueth Sertan Godlye Songs, perfectly set in iiii. pairtis, and singular gude musike, which I haue put in heir amongs the rest, and first *Te Deum Laudamus* in prose, set by ANDRO KEMPT, 1566.—Wreattin and notit be me, Thomas Wod, vicar of Sanct Androus."

19. The Sang of Ambrose and of Augustine, in iv. pairtes.—KEMP.
"Te Deum," &c.—"We praise thee, O God," &c.
20. Psalm CI. Voluntarie. In v. pairtes. Quod M. Andro Blackhall, M.V^c.lxvj (corrected in one MS. to 1568).
"Of mercye and of judgement bothe."
21. Psalm CXXVII. Voluntarie. In v. pairtes.—BLACKHALL.
"Blessed art thou that fearis God."

Wood's portion of the Supplemental (the fifth) volume appears to extend only to page 33. The following is a summary of its contents:—

Page 1.—CI Psalme, v. pairtis. Be M. A. Blackhall (the secund tribble) *Of mercy and of judgemet*. Finis, quod Maister Andro Blakhall, in Halyrude Hous (now minister of Musselbrugh), 1569, giffin in propyne to the King.

Page 5.—*Aspice Domine*, in v. pairtis. quod ane Italian.

Page 7.—Psalme CXXVIII. Set and send be Blakhall to my L. Mar at his first marriage with my L. of Angus' Sister. Begins—"*Blessed art thou thou fearest God.*" v. pairtis. quod Blakhall.

Page 11.—O God abufe, &c. In iiij. pairtis, composit be Shir Jhone Futhy, bayth letter and not., &c.

Page 13.—*Donune in virtute tua letabitur Rex.* V. pairtes set in Ingland be ane baneist Scottis preist. At the end Wood had written—"Quod ane Inglisheman, and, as I have heard, he was blind quhen he set it." This is erased, and on the margin is added—"This was set in Ingland be ane Scottis preist baneist."

Page 18.—*Omnes Gentes Attendite.* V. pairtis, set in Ingland.

Page 19.—*Deus miseriatur nostri.* iiij. pairtis, at the end, Inglishe. Thomas Wod, Vicar of Sanct Androis, with my hand.

Page 22.—"Judge and revenge my cause, O Lord." xliii. Psalme, v. pairtis, Blackhall.

Page 25.—ffollowis sertain sangis vpon plaine sang of dyvers men, and to singular gude musike. iiij. pairtis, plaine sang and all.—*In Nomini.* Quod Talis, iiij. pairtis

Page 26.—Ane uther sang, callit *In Nomini.* iij. pairtis upon the plain sang.

Page 28.—*Qui Consolabitur.* V. pairtis. (On margin) "I layk ane pairt."

Page 29.--*Si quis diligit me.* V. pairtis. (At end) Quod Dauid Pables, sumtyme ane chanone in the Abbay of Sanct Androus, ane of the principall mussitians in all this land in his tyme. This sang was set about the zeir of God I^m V^c xxx (1530) zeirs.

Page 30.—*Descendi in hortum menm.* 4 pairtis. quod (name blank).

Page 31.—*Susane vnioure.* Italian. V. partis.

Page 32.—Followis ane mirry sang, iiij pairtis, callit *Vniour, finis, correctit.*

Thomas Wood, Wod, or Wode, has, by his skill and perseverance evinced in these volumes, laid the cause of sacred psalmody under deep and lasting obligation. We have no certain information of his early history. In 1562 he had commenced his labours on the music adapted to the Metrical Psalms, and in course of four years his work in four books had been completed. Laing remarks:—" Not being aware of any difference in date of the duplicate volumes, or that explanatory notes were added at various times, I fell into the common mistake of supposing him to have held the office of Vicar. for some years previous to 1566. At that period it was not unusual for one person to hold an office, while another enjoyed the teinds or emoluments; but the office itself of Vicar ceased to be recognised in the Presbyterian Church, although the vicarage teinds were assigned by special grant from the Crown, as a stipend to Ministers or Readers. There is little doubt that Wood acted as Reader in one or other of the churches in Fife before he obtained a special grant of the Vicarage of St. Andrews, in 1576, by virtue of which he assumed the title of Vicar of St. Andrews. During a vacancy at St. Andrews, in the Register of the Thirds of Benifices, for 1574, the stipend is entered as being "The haill fruites of the vicarage, vacand by deceis of umquhill Mr. Adam Heriot," (minister of Aberdeen, who died in 1574). From the Register of the Privy Seal, we further learn that on the 21st March, 1575-6, Thomas Wood having obtained from " My Lord Regentis Grace a presentation to the Vicarage of Sanct Androis, Mr. John Wynrame, superintendent of Fyfe, was charged to admit him to the said vicarage."

ROBERT FAIRFAX was an eminent English composer during the reigns of Henry VII. and Henry VIII. He was of a Yorkshire family, and took the degree of Mus. D. in the University of Cambridge, in the year 1504, and was incorporated at Oxford in 1511. His MS. collection of the most ancient English songs, to which music has been preserved, is well-known to musical antiquarians. He was organist of the Abbey Church of St. Alban's, where he lies interred.

DEAN JOHN ANGUS was born about the year 1515, and became one of the conventual brethren of the Abbey of Dunfermline. Shortly after 1543, he embraced the Protestant faith, and obtained a pension, and also a living in connection with the Chapel Royal of Stirling. He died before the 2nd of March, 1596-7. Wood speaks of him in affectionate terms as " gude Angus, gude and meike John Angus."

MR. ANDREW BLACKHALL was a canon of the Abbey of Holyrood House at the time of the Reformation. He also denounced Popery, and was first settled as a Protestant minister at Ormiston, in East Lothian, in 1567. In 1574 he was translated to the large and important parish of Inveresk or Musselburgh, where he continued till his death on the 31st January, 1609. When the old church at Inveresk was pulled down and rebuilt in 1806, a large slab was fixed on the outer wall near the south porch, bearing an inscription in memory of the Rev. John Williamson, who died in 1740. Above this inscription, it is recorded that his predecessor, Blackhall, was 73 when he died on 31st January, 1609. There is probably a mistake of ten years in regard to his age, as otherwise, in October, 1593, he would have been only 57 when he applied to the Synod, *" in respect of his age,* and the greatness of the congregation," for a helper, or a second minister to the parish.

SIR JOHN FUTHIE, a priest, celebrated as an organist, returned to Scotland in

1532. Wood tells us that he was still living in 1592, when he must have attained a very advanced age. "O God abufe, &c., was composit by Sir Jhone Futhy, bayth letter and note. This man wes the first Organeist that euer brought into Scotland the curius new fingering and playing on Organs, and yit it is mair nor threscore yeiris since he com hame. This is wreatin Jm. Vc. fourscore and xij. (1592)."

ANDREW KEMP was master of the sang or music school at Aberdeen in 1570. To one of the additional airs Wood adds—"Quod Kemp, and noted be his awin hand and not myne."

DAVID PEBLIS OR PEEBLES was one of the conventual brethren of the Abbey Church of St. Andrews. He died in December, 1579. Wood calls him "ane honorable and singulare cunning man—ane of the principall musitians in all this land in his tyme."

It was by Peebles that these tunes were harmonised according to the desire of Lord James Stewart, then Prior of St. Andrews, who was created Earl of Murray, and became Regent of Scotland. His instructions were to avoid the intricacies or "curiosity" of musical composition, and to adopt a plain and sweet style best suited for general use. In this desire to have the ordinary Psalm tunes—the "Church part"—accompanied with simple and easy harmonies, Lord James was doubtless in some degree influenced by his own experience of the gratifying effects of the psalmody so conducted among the French Hugenots, and in other Protestant churches abroad. Among the Reformed Churches of the Continent, this department of public worship was reckoned a special favourite, and engaged in by the whole assembly. For many centuries Popery had defrauded the Congregation of worshippers of its rights in this as in everything else. At the end of the sixth century, Pope Gregory condemned the people to sit in silence, and assigned the service of song to a choir, who alone should conduct it, believing that he was thus effecting a great improvement in the psalmody of the Church. The more ancient and scriptural custom of singing was restored at the Reformation. And as the Metrical Psalms were introduced into the service of the Scottish Church, and set to music in simple and appropriate harmony, they were eagerly embraced by the people; and the sacred song by the entire congregation, formed a very prominent and exhilarating part of public worship.

We have said that in these old days public schools existed for education in the "craft and syence of musike," and we have referred to the enthusiastic strains of psalmody with which the "hail toun" of Edinburgh marched in triumphal procession with Durie on his return from exile. We are also told by James Melville that John Erskine of Dun, among his other services in the cause of the Reformation, "of his charity entertained a blind man who had a singular good voice. Him he caused the doctor (teacher) of our school teach the Psalms in metre with the tunes thereof, and sing them in the kirk, by hearing of whom I was so delighted that I learned many of the Psalms and tunes thereof in metre, quhilk I have thought ever syn syne a great blessing and comfort." And Dr. M'Crie, speaking of the method in which public worship was conducted in Scotland about 1638, says—"Prayer being ended, the congregation joined in singing a portion of the Psalms, a part of the service in which they took great delight, and in which they were so well instructed that many of them could sing without the aid of a Psalm-book."

Nevertheless, the result has proved that it was not without some degree of reasonable foundation that fear was entertained by Thomas Wood, "bot musike," the 'craft and syence' in which he took such delight, "sall perish in this land alutterlye." Sacred music, both scientifically and practically, was much appreciated, and for a time—longer perhaps than Wood anticipated—was zealously cultivated as a branch of study, and a special and precious department of divine worship, by all classes of the community. It did not long continue so, and very certainly it is not so now. The Church, somehow, fell into a state of criminal indifference and callousness in this as in other respects. The subject did not continue to receive the countenance and attention demanded by the vast importance of its claims. Notwithstanding the great progress that has been made in many attainments during the last two centuries, congregational psalmody has not kept pace with the onward march; on the contrary, it has in very many instances, and we fear as a rule, sadly fallen from the high position it occupied in these old times. Could Thomas Wood, or Dr. Fairfax, or Edward Miller, come forth from his tomb, with all his musical tastes and sympathies, and take his place amongst his fellowmen in some of our worshipping assemblies, and listen to the manner in which the sacred service of song is rendered—and that only by part of the congregation—we suspect he would be thrown into the condition which the Earl of Rochester felt assured would have been that of King David, had he heard one of his Psalms as translated by Sternhold and Hopkins, sung on a certain occasion —"'twould make him mad." (*App. XV.*).

It is gratifying, however, to know that a reaction in this matter has commenced —that an improvement in the Church's psalmody has been inaugurated and is going on—that steps have been taken, short as yet perhaps, and tortoise-like, still steps in the right direction, and therefore to be permitted to entertain the hope that at a day not very far distant, the position of the Church, as regards the service of praise, shall be raised to its proper level. It may not happen that public schools shall exist again as they did of yore, for the special purpose of imparting instruction in music; but music is gradually receiving increasing attention, and assuming a more important place in the general work of our ordinary public schools. The Church is becoming every day more alive to the importance of the subject, and in her various branches psalmody committees have for some years been in existence, devising and applying means for the accomplishment of the end in view. The Established Church has issued a manual, "The Church of Scotland Psalm and Hymn Tune-Book," which, according to a recent report of the committee, is increasing in popularity, and tending to the dissemination of pure ecclesiastical tunes, and the exclusion of tunes deemed objectionable. The committee are meanwhile making certain improvements in the work, under the editorship of Mr. H. Monk of London, whose wide-spread musical reputation is a sufficient guarantee for its character. The Free Church has also issued a manual, which has been before the public for a number of years, designated "The Scottish Psalmody." The report submitted by the committee to the Assembly in May last, indicated as results effected:—(1.) A general discontinuance of such tunes as Walmer, Violet Grove, New Lydia, &c., and the disuse of repeating tunes. (2.) The extended use and increased popularity of the syllabic style of tune, and the revival of tunes of the early times. (3.) Heightened interest in church music; increased teaching, practising, part-singing, and study of musical notation, together with elevated qualifications of precentors. (4.) Greater uniformity in tunes employed, rates of speed, adjusting of tunes to passages sung and harmonic arrangements. (5.) Increased use of varieties of metre, greater help afforded in congregational singing by the upper classes of society, and greatly extended sale of collections of church tunes. The Committee were instructed to carry on their work, and the attention of the Education Committee was directed to the need of adequate provision for musical instruction in the schools of the country. (*App. XVI.*).

We have thus endeavoured to trace from its starting point the development of the Scottish Metrical Psalms, supplementing our notices by some historical details of additional materials for praise that have been adopted by the Church; and we would now simply invite attention to the divine injunction frequently reiterated—"Sing praises, sing praises, God is King of all the earth: sing ye praises with understanding." Paul knew that the service of praise in the sanctuary was an express ordinance of Jehovah, and he declared his determination to obey the injunction when he said—"I will sing with the spirit, and I will sing with the understanding also." The command is remarkably plain and significant, and we are not at liberty to obey it or not as we please. It is at our peril if we disobey. Well, we are to sing, that is, we are to give vocal expression to the matter for praise that is brought before us—not to sit silent listening to the voices of a choir, or the sounds of an organ, a harmonium, or a fiddle! A performance on a musical instrument, however exquisite and thrilling may be its effect, is not singing, and no more is it singing simply to listen to it; moreover, we are to sing with the spirit and with the understanding—that is heartily, feelingly, intelligently, skilfully. We should understand what we are to do, and how we are to do it. What are we to do? To praise Jehovah, King of all the earth, implying an intelligent acquaintance with Him as such, with our dependence on Him, and the exceeding riches of His providence and grace toward us. And how? To sing intelligently and skilfully—knowing the import and significancy of the song in which we express our praise—giving utterance to that song with all the emotion it is fitted to awaken in the heart, and with all the musical skill we possess, or of which we can be made capable by means of competent instruction. Were the members of our Christian congregations thus familiarly acquainted with the "Psalms and Hymns, and Spiritual Songs," in spirit as well as in letter—were they thoroughly trained in the principles and practice of sacred music, and able to take the parts of the song for which their voices are best adapted, and carry it out in full harmony—how much more pleasant and attractive would the whole services of public worship be?

APPENDIX.

APPENDIX.

No. I.

The Version of 1556—"*One and Fiftie Psalmes.*"

PREFATORY REMARKS BY WHITTINGHAM.

HERE is a peculiar interest associated with this version, arising from the fact that all the Psalms, and 42 of the tunes contained in it were latterly incorporated in the Scottish Psalter. The volume contains a preface, written apparently by Whyttingham, which is valuable as indicating the principles on which the Psalmody of the Genevan Church was moulded, and which were afterwards more fully developed in the Psalter of the Church of Scotland. The following is a portion of it:—

"But because prayers are after two maner of sortes, that is, either in wordes only, or els with songe joyned thereunto; and thys latter part, as well for lack of the true use thereof, as due consideration of the same, is called by many into dout, whether it may be used in a reformed church: it is expedient that we note briefly a few thinges perteyning therunto. S. Paul geving a rule how men shulde singe, first saith. 'I will singe in voice, and I will singe with understanding.' . . . . And as musike or singinge is naturall unto us, and therefore every man deliteth therein; so our mercifull God setteth before our eyes, how we may rejoyce and sing to the glorie of his name, recreation of our spirits and profit of ourselves.

"But as ther is no gift of god so precious or excellent that Satan hath not after a sort drawen to himself and corrupt, so hath he most impudentlye abused this notable gift of singinge, chiefly by the papistes his ministers, in disfiguring it, partly by strange language that can not edifie, and partly by a curious wanton sort, hyringe men to tickle the ears and flatter the phantasies, not esteminge it as a gifte approved by the worde of god, profitable for the churche, and confirmed by all antiquitie. As, besides other places, is most manifest by the words of Plinius, called the younger, who when he was depute in Aisia unto the Emperour Trajan, and had receyved charge to enquire out the Christians to put them to deathe, writ emongs other thinges, touchinge the Christians, 'That their maners were to singe verses, or psalmes early in the morninge to Christ their God.' . . . . Seinge therefore god's woorde dothe approve it, antiquitie beareth witenes thereof, and best reformed churches have receyved the same, no man can reprove it, except he will contemne Gods worde, despice Antiquitie, and utterlie condemne the godlie reformed Churches.

"And there are no songes more meete than the Psalmes of the Prophete David, which the holy ghoste hath framed to the same use, and commended to the churche, as conteininge the effect of the whole scriptures, that hereby our heartes might be more lyvelie touched, as appereth by Moses, Ezechias, Judith, Deborah, Marie, Zacharie, and others, who by songs and metre, rather than in their commune speache and prose, gave thankes to god for suche comfort as he sent them."

No. II.

Royal Licences to Printers. "Cum privilegio," &c.

IT will be observed that one or other of the co-significant phrases—"*Cum privilegio;* "*Cum privilegio regio;* "*Cum privilegio regali;* "*Cum privilegio regiae majestatis;* "*Cum privilegio ad imprimendum solum;*"—usually appears on the title page of these old Psalters, as indicating the authority under which the work has been issued from the press. The authorisation which it bespeaks is not confined to the Bible, or the Psalms, or any of the books of Scripture. Its sanction is conferred on acts of parliament, books of customs' rates, "the haill four pairtis of gramer according to Sebaustiane, the dialogues of Corderius, the celect and familiar epissillis of Cecero, the seawen seages, the ballat buik, the second rudimentis of Dumbar, the feabillis of Esope, Gray, Steill," &c. Nor does the phrase denote any privilege peculiar to the printer working under "Royal letters patent." For example—we have the Psalms printed at Edinburgh in 1578 by Thomas Bassandyne, dwelling at the Nether Bow—*cum privilegio.* In 1579, we have "The Bible and holy Scriptures contained in the Old and Newe Testaments Printed at Edinburgh be Alexander Arbuthnot, Printer to the Kings Majestie dwelling at the Kirk of Field, 1579, "*Cum gratia et privilegio regiae Majestatis.*" In the same year we have "Responsio ad Archib. Hamiltonii Apostatae Diologum. Thoma Smetonio Scoto Auctore. Edinburgi, apud Johannem Rosseum, pro Henrico Charteris, Anno Do. 1579. *Cum privilegio regali.*" In 1588, a work by King James (ane fruitful Meditation on Rev: xx. &c.) and in 1589, another (an Exposition of 1 Chron. xv. 25, &c.) were printed by Henry Charteris, *cum privilegio regali,* though he was never one of his Majesty's printers. Almost all the books of that period, by whomsoever printed, were printed *cum privilegio regio,* or *cum privilegio regali.* It seems to have been as necessary for the King's printer, as for any other, to use this formula on the title page of every book. The same practice prevailed in England. Thus we find Bullinger's "*Fiftie Godlie and Learned Sermons,* imprinted at London by Ralph Newberie, dwelling in Fleet Street, a little above the Conduit, who hath store of those bookes for those that want both in Latine and English, *Cum gratia et priulegio Regiae Maiestatis,* 1587."

It is not very easy to perceive what was the value of the privilege implied in the office of King's Printer in those old days. Lekprevick, as "our Soveraine Lordis Imprentar had full power to print all works in Latin or English for the weill and commoditie of this realm and lieges thereof, and all sic things as tends to the glorie of God, induring all the space and terms of twenty years." He was constituted King's Printer in 1567, and in the same year he was licensed to print the translation commonly called the Geneva Bible. Why was not his original licence itself sufficient? He printed Queen Mary's Acts in 1565, and the Acts of the first five Jameses and Queen Mary in 1566. Yet, in less than six years after his nomination as King's Printer, viz., in 1573, "The King's Majesties proclamation" concerning the incoming of the English forces, &c., was printed *cum privilegio regio* by Thomas Bassandyne, who was never one of his Majesty's printers. In the course of the year 1573, Lekprevick printed at St. Andrews the Acts of Parliament 1571. But the Acts of Parliament of 1567, which had been printed by him in 1568, were reprinted by John Ross in 1575—and Ross was not King's Printer. It is true that Lekprevick incurred the displeasure of the government in 1574, and was confined for some time in Edinburgh Castle, for having printed, without licence, "ane dialogue or mutuall talking betwixt a clerk and a courteour, concerning four parische kirks till ane minister, collectit out of thair mouthis and put into verse be a young man quha did then forgather with thame in his jornay," to the reproach and slander of our Sovereign Lords Regent, &c. But if he was understood to forfeit office on this occasion it is certain that he was not exposed to the penalties of the Act 1551, against unlicensed printing, for we find him continuing to print in Edinburgh nearly twenty years afterwards. One of his well-known works is "Catechismus Latino carmine redditus, et in libros quatuor digestus. Patricii Adamsoni Scoti poetae elegantissimi, opera atque industria," Edin. 1581. Dedicated to James VI.

Again:—John Gibson, bookbinder to his Majesty, purchased from Gilbert Masterton, burgess in Edinburgh, a gift, which had been disposed and assigned to him by Mr. George Young, Archdeacon of St. Andrews, in 1587, and which Young had received from the King on the 20th of September, 1585. This gift was confirmed to John Gibson by his Majesty, 20th June, 1589, for printing within the realm, or causing to be printed within or without the same, "The Bible in our vulgar tongue with the Psalm Book, the double and single Catechise," and generally all books specified in the license granted to Alexander Arbuthnot. By a subsequent gift, dated 13th May, 1590, Gibson was empowered to print the Bible, and various other works. Nevertheless, in that same year,

Appendix.

Robert Waldegrave was constituted by Royal gift, Our Sovereign Lord's printer for life—a gift which conferred on him, and on no other, power to print all acts of parliament, &c., as also all and sundry books, volumes, works, and writs which shall be seen, allowed, and approved by his Majesty, or the presbytery or session of Edinburgh. And yet farther, within three weeks after this grant to Waldegrave—viz., on 28th of October, 1590—a Letter under the Privy Seal conferred on Mr. Zachary Pont full liberty, freedom and license to exercise by himself, his servants and deputies, the office of chief printer within this realm, and to imprint all kinds of books set forth in any kind of tongue or language not forbidden by the statutes and laws of his Majesty's realm. This subject is fully discussed in Dr. Lee's able and exhaustive work, "Memorial for Bible Societies," to which we refer the reader who is curious on the question. We leave it by giving the sentiments of Mr. Solicitor-General Yorke, as expressed in the case of *Baskett* against *the University of Cambridge*. He holds that the King has no power at common law over the art of printing. On the exclusive right to print works said to be incident to and inherent in the office of King's Printer, he says, "The law knows no such officer by prescription nor by Act of Parliament; it will not therefore protect him, and say that the King (who made him) shall not grant the same concurrent privilege to another. Supposing Printership to be an office, the King may name as many printers as he pleases."

We append three specimens of these Licences.

Licence to Robert Lekprevik, Imprentar in Edinburgh, Jan: 14, 1567.

Ane Letter maid with awise and consent of my Lord Regent makand mentioun That thai understanding that it is not onlie neidfull in commoun welthis to have the commoun lawis quhilkis ar the rule of the subjectis in civile thingis imprentit alsweile for the commoditie of this present aige as of the posteritie tocum But alsua all sic godlie werkis and volumis as tendis to the glorie of God Thairfore Licencand and gevand to Robert Lekprevik Imprentar in Edinburgh privelige and full powir to imprent all and quhatsumever actis workis valumes and utheris necessaris alsweile in latine as in inglische for the weill and commoditie of this realme and the liegis thairof And als all sic thingis as tendis to the glorie of God Induring all the space and termes of tuenty zeiris nixt following the dait heirof chairgeing all and sindrie Imprentaris writtaris and utheris liegis within this realme

That thai nor nane of thaime take upon hand to imprent or caus be imprentit be quhatsumevir persoun or personis outhir within this realme or outwith the samyn in ony tyme heireftir during the said space the workis volumes and buikis underwrittin or caus bring hither the same out of uthir cuntreis except onlie the said Robert Lekprevik quha salbe nominat during the said space our Soverane Lordis Imprentar That is to say the buikis callit Donatus pro pueris Rudimentis of Pelisso The actis of parliamentis maid or to be maid (except the actis of his hienes last parliament) The croniklis of this realme The buik callit Regia Majestas The psalmes of David with the inglis and latine catechismes les and mair The buik callit the Omeleyis for reidaris in kirkis Togidder with the grammer to be set furth callit the generall grammer to be usit within the scolis of this realme for erudition of the youth And that under the painis of confiscatioun of the same workis and buikis that salhappin to be imprentit and payment of the sowme of two hundreth pundis money of this realme With command and charge to all and sindrie provestis baillies and officiaris of his hienes burrowis to serche and seik the contravenaris heirof and cause thir presentis to be put to the dew executioun conforme to the tennour thairof in all pointis during the space foirsaid And be thir presentis Our said Soverane with advice and consent foirsaid Ratifeis and apprevis the gift gevin and grantit be his umquhile derrest fader and his hienes moder under their prive seill to the said Robert for imprenting of the Actis of Parliament and psalmes ellis imprentit be him conforme to the tennour of the samin in all pointis of the dait the viij day of februar The zieir of God I^m v^c lxv zeiris And gif ony of our said Soveranis liegis tak upoun hand to imprent within this realme or cause be imprentit outwith the samein ony of the foirsaidis workis volumes and buikis specialie abone expressit except only the said Robert during the said space Ordains the samin to be confiscat and becum under eschete and the persone contravenand the samin to pay the said sowme of twa hundreth pundis money foirsaid That is to say The ane half to our soveranes use and the uther half to the said Robertis use frelie quietlie &c But ony revocation &c At Edinburgh the xiiij day of Januare The zeir of God I^m V^c lxvij zeiris

Per Signaturam.

[This appears to be a renewal or ratification of a licence given to Lekprevik two years previously. On the 14th of April, 1568, he was awarded "full licence privelege and power To imprent all and haill ane buke callit the Inglis bybil imprentit of before at Geneva."]

Gift under the Privy Seal to Maister Robert Charteris Prentar, Dec. 8, 1603
 [Reg. Sec. Sig. lxiv. 143.]

Ane letter maid makand constituand and ordinand Maister Robert Charteris printer to our Soverane Lord and gevand to him the privilege thairof for all the dayis of his lyfetyme With power to the said Mr Robert (and nane utheris) be himselff and his servandis for quhome he salbe haldin to ansuer To imprent and caus be imprentit all and sindrie actis of parliament uther actis statutes proclamationes letteris and charges concerning his Majestie and his estait As alsua all and sindrie buikis volumes werkis and writtis quhilkis salbe seine allowed and approved be his Majestie the presbiterie or Sessioun of Edinburgh and thairupone to sell and dispone at his pleasure   And to the effect that the said Mr Robert may the mair frielie use and exercise this present priviledge his hiens hes alswa takin and be thir presentis takis the said Mr Robert under his Majesties speciall protectioun mantenance defense and saulfgairde &c. . . . . . At Striviling the aucht day of December I^m Vj^c and thre yeiris.

Per Signaturam.

Licence to Sir William Alexander for the space of 31 years, to print the Psalms of King David, translated by King James Dec. 28, 1627. [Registrum Secreti Sigilli, c. 1627-1628, fol. 305.]

Ane lettre maid makand mentiown that oure Soueraine Lord considering how it pleised his late Royal father king James the sext of worthie memorie for many zeires togidder to have taken grit paynes in translating of the Psalmes of King David in meeter and in conferring thairof with the most approved Hebrue translatoris vpone that subject having in his said lyftyme brocht that work to gud perfectioun   And His Majestie well knowing how gud and comfortable the said wark will prove to all his hiens subjects by having those psalmes translated according to the trew meining and delyverie of that holy and princely authour and withall esteiming nothing more deir to him than to performe this said late royall fatheris intentioun for publishing the same that thairby his royal verkies and graces may still be the more recent with the posteritie of all his royall successores and loving subjectis   And his Majestie lykewayes considering the great paynes already taken and to be taken by his hienes right trusty and weill beloved counsellour Sir William Alexander knycht his Majesties principall secretarie for his kingdome of Scotland to quhais cair his Majestie hath speciallie entrusted the said work in collecting and reviewing of the same, and in seeing the first impressioun thairof to be carefullie and weill done and withall being gratiouslie pleased that he sould reape the benefite of his travellis thairin Thairfore his henes with advice and consent of his counsell and exchequer of his said kingdome Ordaines a Letre ro be maid vnder the Previe Seall thareof in dew forme Geving and granting Lykas his Majestie with advyce and consent foirsaid gevis and grantis to the said Sir William Alexander his aires assignais pairtneris and associatis thair servantis and workmen in thair name and to nane ellis full power libertie and sole licence during the space of threttie ane zeires nixt and immediatlie following the dait heirof to print and caus print the said wark of the psalmes to be entituled the Psalmes of King David translated by King James With power to him and the said Sir William Alexander and his forsaids (gif neid be) to erect and establish work houses in any part of the said kingdomes as they sall think maist expedient and to provyd all things requisite for that purpose and to print the said psalmes in quhat number they sall please during the said heall tearme of zeires And to sell barter and dispose thairvpone at quhat rait and after quhat forme thay sall think meitt throughout the haill kingdome and everie pairt thairof and that without any let trouble or molestatioun to be used against thame or any of thame be any of his Majesties subjectis or otheris quhatsomever and that during the space afoirsaid Prohibiting and discharging Lykas his Majestie by these presents speciallie prohibits and discharges during the said space of threttie ane zeires all and quhatsomever persones within the said kingdome als weill natives as forrayneris other than the said Sir William and his foirsaidis from printing selling and bartering thairin of the saidis buikis entituled the Psalmes of King David translated by King James without the speciall power and lieence gevin to thame by the said Sir William or his foirsaidis and that vnder the pane of confiscatioun not onlie of the haill workis tooles and instrumentis maid for that purpose but lykewayes of the said bookes thameselffis so to be printed sold and bartered by thame or any of thame within the said kingdome the ane half of the benefite thairof to come to his Majesties vse and the other half to the vse of the said Sir William and his foirsaids And the pairties contraveneris to be censured fyned or imprisoned at the seicht of his Majesties said Privie Counsell With speciall command to thame of his hienes said Privie Counsall and Exchequer for the tyme being to give out warrantis from tyme to tyme as they sall be requyred by the said Sir William or his foirsaidis to all Scherreffis Justices of Peace Provestis

Bayliffs Constables and otheris his Majesties officeris to be ayding and assisting to find apprehend and sais vpone the said workes tooles and others necessaries for printing As lykwayes vpon the said bookes thamselffis and vpon the bodies of the transgressoures the goodes and bookes to be furth cumming to the use afoirsaid .And the saidis persones to be censured in maner above-writtin And that the said Letre be further extended in the best forme with all clauses neidfull Gewin At Quhythall the twenty aught day of December the zeir of God I^m vj^c and tuentie sevin zeires.

III.

The duty of possessing a Bible and Psalm book rigidly enforced.

IN course of the year 1579 an Act of Parliament was passed ordaining every householder worth 300 merks of yearly rent, and every yeoman or burgess worth £500 stock to have a bible and psalm book, in vulgar language, in their houses, under the penalty of ten pounds. A *searcher* was appointed to visit every householder described in the Act; and it appears from the records of the Privy Council that he was not idle. In the year 1580, the Magistrates and Town Council of Edinburgh issued a proclamation commanding all the householders to have Bibles, "under the pains contained in the Act of parliament, and advertising them that the Bibles are to be sauld in the merchant buith of Andrew Williamson, on the north side of this burgh, besyde the Meill Mercat." On the 11th of Nov., 1580, "Alex. Clerk of Balberry, provost, &c., ordanis the haill nytbors of this burt to be callit in before the bailies be their quarters for not keeping of the said act, to be adjugeit in the unlaw therein contenit, and for eschewing of all fraude ordains sic as sall bring their bybills and psalm buiks to hafe their names written and subscryvit be the clerk; and therefter the buiks deliverit to them." On the 16th of Nov. there was an order to pursue all persons "that has incurrit the payne of the act for not having ane bybill or psalm buik." Andro Sclater and Thomas Aikinheid, masters of the hospital, were appointed "Collectors of the paynes." Two years afterwards, John Williamson, "general searcheour throughout the haill boundis of this his hienes realm," obtained decreet in the Privy Council against Andro Ballingall and John Weland, Sheriffs-depute of Fife, for not concurring, fortifying, defending, and assisting him in the execution of his duty. *Dr. Lees Memorial.*

IV.

The Authorship of the Old Psalms, 1549-1564.

THE following tables, with prefatory explanation, are transferred from Livingstone's edition of the Scottish Metrical Psalter of 1635. They are interesting as showing at one view the names of the Versifiers of those old Psalms, and the special work performed by each.

The sources of information concerning the authorship of the psalms are the intimations attached to them in the early publications. Regarding the 37 by Sternhold and 7 by Hopkins in 1549, there are express statements, and in 1556 abbreviations of these names are prefixed to their respective Psalms. The new psalms under the latter year are anonymous, but the authors both of these and of the additions in 1560 are given in the publication of 1561, which thus verifies columns 1, 2, 3, and 4 of the table. Column 5 is drawn from the 1562 edition of the English Psalter, so far as concerns the psalms then first published. The preceding columns also are confirmed by that edition. There are, however, some discrepancies which require to be noticed. I. In edition 1561 (1.) The 100th Psalm is ascribed to Sternhold, but as Kethe furnished all the other editions of that year, it can hardly be doubted that this also is his. There is no reason to think that the Genevan exiles had intercourse with those who obtained possession of the few psalms by Sternhold, which seem to have been discovered subsequently to his death. The rhyming of lines first and third is a feature found in none of Sternhold's pieces. And another edition of the same year ascribes the psalm to Kethe. (2.) The 111th is reckoned to Kethe, but is, in 1562, ranked as Norton's. The former must be held as correct. The former reason under last case applies to this, and Norton makes no other contribution before 1562. II. Under 1562 there are the following: (1.) Psalm 28th to Hopkins, but it is included among Sternhold's in 1549. (2.) Psalm 66th to Sternhold, but the rhyming of first and third lines determine it to Hopkins, to whom it is ascribed in 1565. (3.) Psalm 102nd to Hopkins, but other editions to Norton. The rhyme and the position of each in regard to the last 50 psalms decide for the latter. (4.) Psalm 128th has T. T. attached, which must be a mistake for T. S., this psalm being one of the original 44. (5.) Psalm 129th is marked W. W.,

The Scottish Metrical Psalms.

but Whittingham's version is one of the rejected, and in 1565 the new version is given to Norton. The authors of the new Psalms, in the volume of 1560, are taken from the volume itself, except that of Psalm 95, which it leaves blank.

The first 17 psalms in regular order belong equally to each of the following dates, and are therefore omitted; all these were by Sternhold.

1549.	1556.	1560.	1561.	1562.	1564.
44 Psalms.	51 Psalms.	65 Psalms.	87 Psalms.	Complete English.	Comp. Scot.
Ps.	Ps.	Ps.	Ps.	Ps.	Ps.
...	...	...	...	18 St.	St.
19 St.	St.	St.	St.	St.	St.
20 St.	St.	St.	St.	St.	St.
21 St.	St.	St.	St.	St.	St.
...	...	...	...	22 St.	St.
...	23 Wh.	Wh.	Wh.	23 St.	Wh.
...	...	...	...	24 Hop.	24 Cr.
25 St.	St.	St.	St.	St.	St.
...	...	...	...	26 Hop.	Hop.
...	...	...	27 Ke.	27 Hop.	Ke.
28 St.	St.	St.	St.	St.	St.
29 St.	St.	St.	St.	St.	St.
30 Hop.	Hop.	Hop.	Hop.	Hop.	Hop.
...	...	...	...	31 Hop.	Hop.
32 St.	St.	St.	St.	St.	St.
33 Hop.	Hop.	Hop.	Hop.	Hop.	Hop.
34 St.	St.	St.	St.	St.	St.
...	...	...	...	35 Hop.	Hop.
...	...	...	36 Ke.	36 Hop.	Ke.
...	...	37 Wh.	Wh.	Wh.	Wh.
...	...	...	...	38 Hop.	Hop.
...	...	...	...	39 Hop.	Hop.
...	...	...	...	40 Hop.	Hop.
41 St.	St.	St.	St.	St.	St.
42 Hop.	Hop.	Hop.	Hop.	Hop.	Hop.

Appendix.

1549.	1556.	1560.	1561.	1562.	1564.
44 Psalms.	51 Psalms.	65 Psalms.	87 Psalms.	Complete English.	Comp. Scot.
Ps.	Ps.	Ps.	Ps.	Ps.	Ps.
43 St.	St.	St.	St.	St.	St.
44 St.	St.	St.	St.	St.	St.
...	...	...	...	45 Hop.	Hop.
...	...	...	...	46 Hop.	Hop.
...	...	...	47 Ke.	47 Hop.	Ke.
...	...	...	...	48 Hop.	Hop.
49 St.	St.	St.	St.	St.	St.
...	...	50 Wh.	Wh.	50 Hop.	Wh.
...	51 Wh.	Wh.	Wh.	Wh.	Wh.
...	...	...	...	51 Nor.	...
52 Hop.	Hop.	Hop.	Hop.	Hop.	Hop.
...	...	...	...	53 Nor.	Nor.
...	...	...	54 Ke.	54 Hop.	Ke.
...	...	...	...	55 Hop.	Hop.
...	...	...	...	56 Hop.	56 Cr.
...	...	...	...	57 Hop.	57 Po.
...	...	...	58 Ke.	58 Hop.	Ke.
...	...	...	...	59 Hop.	59 Po.
...	...	...	...	60 Hop.	Hop.
...	...	...	...	61 Hop.	Hop.
...	...	...	62 Ke.	62 Hop.	Ke.
63 St.	St.	St.	St.	St.	St.
...	...	...	...	64 Hop,	Hop.
...	...	...	...	65 Hop.	Hop.
...	...	...	...	66 Hop.	Hop.
...	...	67 Wisdom	...	...	...
...	...	67 Wh.	Wh.	67 Hop.	Wh.
68 St.	St.	St.	St.	St.	St.
...	...	...	...	69 Hop.	Hop.
...	...	...	70 Ke.	70 Hop.	Ke.
...	...	71 Wh.	Wh.	71 Hop.	Wh.

1549.	1556.	1560.	1561.	1562.	1564.
44 Psalms.	51 Psalms.	65 Psalms.	87 Psalms.	Complete English.	Comp. Scot.
Ps.	Ps.	Ps.	Ps.	Ps.	Ps.
...	...	...	...	72 Hop.	Hop.
73 St.	St.	St.	St.	St.	St.
...	...	...	...	74 Hop.	Hop.
...	...	...	...	75 Nor.	75 Cr.
...	...	...	...	76 Hop.	76 Po.
...	...	...	...	77 Hop.	Hop.
78 St.	St.	St.	St.	St.	St.
79 Hop.	Hop.	Hop.	Hop.	Hop.	Hop.
...	...	...	...	80 Hop.	Po.
...	...	...	...	81 Hop.	81 Po.
82 Hop.	Hop.	Hop.	Hop.	Hop.	Hop.
...	...	...	...	83 Hop.	83 Po.
...	...	...	...	84 Hop.	Hop.
...	...	...	85 Ke.	85 Hop.	Ke.
...	...	...	...	86 Hop.	Hop.
...	...	...	...	87 Hop.	Hop.
...	...	...	88 Ke.	88 Hop.	Ke.
...	...	...	...	89 Hop.	Hop.
...	...	...	90 Ke.	90 Hop.	Ke.
...	...	...	91 Ke.	91 Hop.	Ke.
...	...	...	...	92 Hop.	Hop.
...	...	...	...	93 Hop.	Hop.
...	...	...	94 Ke.	94 Hop.	Ke.
...	...	95 ...	...	95 Hop.	Hop.
...	...	...	...	96 Hop.	Hop.
...	...	...	...	97 Hop.	Hop.
...	...	...	...	98 Hop.	Hop.
...	...	...	...	99 Hop.	Hop.
...	...	...	100 Ke.	100	Ke.
...	...	...	101 Ke.	101 Nor.	Ke.
...	...	...	...	102 Nor.	102 Cr.

Appendix.

1549.	1556.	1560.	1561.	1562.	1564.
44 Psalms.	51 Psalms.	65 Psalms.	87 Psalms.	Complete English.	Comp. Scot.
Ps.	Ps.	Ps.	Ps.	Ps.	Ps.
103 St.	St.	St.	St.	St.	St.
...	...	...	104 Ke.	Ke.	Ke.
...	...	...	...	105 Nor.	105 Cr.
...	...	...	...	106 Nor.	Nor.
...	...	...	107 Ke.	Ke.	Ke.
...	...	...	...	108 Nor.	108 Cr.
...	...	...	...	109 Nor.	Nor.
...	...	...	...	110 Nor.	110 Cr.
...	...	...	111 Ke.	Ke.	Ke.
...	...	...	112 Ke.	Ke.	Ke.
...	...	...	113 Ke.	Ke.	Ke.
...	114 Wh.	Wh.	Wh.	Wh.	Wh.
...	115 Wh.	Wh.	Wh.	115 Nor.	Wh.
...	...	...	...	116 Nor.	Nor.
...	...	...	...	117 Nor.	117 Cr.
...	...	...	...	118 Mar.	118 Cr.
...	...	119 Wh.	Wh.	Wh.	Wh.
120 St.	St.	St.	St.	St.	St.
...	...	121 Wh.	Wh.	Wh.	Wh.
...	...	...	122 Ke.	Ke.	Ke.
123 St.	St.	St.	St.	St.	St.
...	...	124 Wh.	Wh.	Wh.	Wh.
...	...	125 Wis.	125 Ke.	Ke.	Ke.
...	...	...	126 Ke.	Ke.	Ke.
...	...	127 Wh.	Wh.	Wh.	Wh.
128 St.	St.	St.	St.	St.	St.
...	...	129 Wh.	Wh.	129 Nor.	Wh.
...	130 Wh.	Wh.	Wh.	Wh.	Wh.
...	...	...	...	131 M[arkant]	Mar.
...	...	...	...	132 Mar.	132 Cr.
...	133 Wh.	Wh.	Wh.	Wh.	Wh.

The Scottish Metrical Psalms.

1549. 44 Psalms. Ps.	1556. 51 Psalms. Ps.	1560. 65 Psalms. Ps.	1561. 87 Psalms. Ps.	1562. Complete English. Ps.	1564. Comp. Scot. Ps.
...	...	...	134 Ke.	Ke.	Ke.
...	...	...	...	135 Mar.	Mar.
...	...	...	...	136 Nor.	136 Cr.
...	137 Wh.	Wh.	Wh.	Wh.	Wh.
...	...	...	138 Ke.	138 Nor.	Ke.
...	...	...	...	139 Nor.	Nor.
...	...	...	...	140 Nor.	140 Cr.
...	...	...	...	141 Nor.	141 Cr.
...	...	...	142 Ke.	142 Nor.	Ke.
...	...	...	...	143 Nor.	143 Cr.
...	...	...	...	144 Nor.	Nor.
...	...	...	...	145 Nor.	145 Cr.
146 Hop.	Hop.	Hop.	Hop.	Hop.	Hop.
...	...	...	...	147 Nor.	Nor.
...	...	148 Pul.	Pul.	Pul.	Pul.
...	...	149 Pul.	Pul.	149 Nor.	Pul.
...	...	...	...	150 Nor.	Nor.

Appendix.

V.

The "Conclusions," with specimens of Prayers. Edit. 1595.

IN the edition of the Psalms, printed by Charteris, Edinburgh, in 1595, thirty-two Conclusions, or renderings of the Gloria Patri are given, being one for each variety of metre, so that one might be sung at the close of each psalm, or part of a psalm. They appear here in the full set for the first time. One, only, is given in the edition of 1575. Some of the later editions have part of them, some the whole, and some none; but the use of the Gloria Patri in some or in all the metres was universal in 1638. Baillie speaks of it as the "constant practice of our church." Somewhat similar versions of this formula are still printed at the end of the Psalms in the English Book of Common Prayer. They are here given in full:—

CONCLUSION TO PSALM I. *Common Metre.*

There are two varieties, and to these the numerous psalms in common measure are referred:

(1st) Thy people and thy Heritage
    Lord blis, guide and preserue:
    Incres them, Lord, and reule thair hartis,
    That they may neuer suerue.

(2nd) O Lord thou art the readie help
    Of them that traistis in thae
    Saif and defend thy chosen flock
    That now distressed be.

    Gloir to the Father, and the Sone,
    And to the halie Gaist,
    As it was in the beginning
    Is novv, and ay sall last.

Up to the 84th Psalm all the psalms in common metre are simply referred to these conclusions, whilst from the 84th forward, the conclusions are printed anew.

TO PSALM XXV. *Short Metre.*

O Lord the strenth and rock,
    of all that traist in thee:
Saif and defend thy chosen flock,
    from all calamitie.

Gloir to the Father be
    the Sonne and halie Gaist:
As it hes bene continuallie
    is novv and euer shall last.

To Psalm XXVII. *Long Metre.*

All pepill on the eirth reioyce
In God of maist misericorde:
With invvard mynde, and outvvard voice,
Let vs give laude vnto the Lord.

To God bə Gloir interminabill
And his Sonne Christ, baith God and man,
And halie Gaist inseparabill
As vvas ay sen the vvarld bəgan.

To Psalm XXXVI.

Gloir bə to God allanerlie,
And to his Sonne eternallie:
And to the halie Paraclite.

Three persons in ane Dəitie
In Warld of Warldis infinite.

To Psalm XLVII.

And gif him all glorie
In psalmes most svveit
And to his Sonne Christ
And blist Paracleit.

Quhilk from the beginning
Did ever extend
And so shall continevv
Warld vvithout end.

To Psalm L.

Honour and glorie
  Vnto the Father bee:
And to his Sonne
  Quhilk is in heuin sa hie
And right also
  Vnto the holie Spreit.

Of troubled heartes
  The comforter most svveit
As it vvas euer
  Before in the beginning
Is novv and shall
  Be Warld vvithout ending.

To Psalm LXII.

To God therefore
  let vs vvith bəsie cure
Giue laude and glore
  As feruentlie as vve can.

As vvas bəfore
  ay sen the vvarld bəgan:
Quhilk euermore
  but cessing shall indure.

In the case of this Psalm, and of the 47th, the eight lines of the "Gloria," added to the last four of the Psalm make up the number necessary for the tune.

To Psalm LXVII.

To God our Father
  And to his deir sone
  And to the halie Gaist
Quhilk three are all one:

Be gloir as it vvas
  In all tymes bygone:
  Is novv, and sall bə
Quhen tyme sall be none.

To Psalm LXX.

To God be gloire interminabill
And his sone verie God and man:
And halie Gaist inseparabill,
As vvas ay sen the vvarld began.

To Psalm LXXVI.

To God alone of michtis most
Be laud, praise, gloir and dignitie:
The Father, sonne, and holy Ghost,
Thre persons in Divinitie:
As ay hes bene in tymes before,
Is novv, and shal be euermore
Throu sea and land in ilk degre.

To Psalm LXXX.

To our Father bening,
   that made vs of nocht,
To Christ our Lord and King,
   from deith that vs bocht.
And the halie spreit
   That faild vs neuer
Be glorie infinite
   for novv and for euer.

To Psalm LXXXI.

Laude, honour, praise, and gloir immortall,
To our Father quhilk art in Heuin:
And to the Sonne in Godheid equall,
And hailie Gaist lyke laud be geuin.
Quhilk ay vvas obserued,
And onelie reserued,
To his Maiestie:
Euen sen the beginning,
And zit still continuing,
Perpetuallie.

To Psalm LXXXIII.

Worship and glore
   Vnto the Trinitie:
The Father, Sone,
   And blessit Paraclite.
Eternall God
   Essentiall Veritie:
Three personnes
In one substance vnite
   All of povver
and vvisedome infinite
   Quhilk neuer had
beginning, nor ending:
   Our hope on them
sall euer be depending.

To Psalm LXXXV.

Gloir to the Father of michtis maist,
Vnto the Sonne and halie Gaist,
One God in persons three:
Coequall and als Coeterne
Thy faithfull flock gyde and gouerne
To thy felicitie.

To Psalm CIIII.

From sleuth, and from sin
  gude Lord vprais vs:
That vve may conuene,
  to vvorship thy Name,
For that is the chief thing,
  gretlie suld pleis vs.
Gif vve vnto thy vvill,
  our lyfis do frame.

Thy meiknes hath made
  much for to mease vs
Thairfoir let vs giue
  praise, honour, and glore
To God our deir Father,
  and to his Sonne Iesus:
And to the halie Gaist
  Novv and euermore.

To Psalm CX.

Onelie to God of povver infinite,
And to the promisit seid Emmanuell:

And als mot be vnto the halie Spreit,
Honour, vvorship and gloir perpetuall.

To Psalm CXI.

To our gret God be gloir
And his Sone euermore,
And Spreit quhilk they vs send,

As was in the beginning,
And shall be continving,
Euen to the vvarldis end.

To Psalm CXII.

To vvorship God let vs make haist,
And be not slavv to giue him glore:
To Father, Sone, and halie Gaist,

As vvas, and sall be euermore:
From grie to grie, and stage to stage,
From tyme to tyme, and age to age.

To Psalm CXIII.

Eternall God Omnipotent,
Quha fabricate the Firmament,
And euerie thing thairin conteind:
Grant vnto vs that vvee alvvaies,
May vvorship thee vvith detfull praise,
Quhilk in thy Name ar heir conueind.

Giue praise and honour vnto God,
Quha chastises vs vvith his soft rod,
Of Fatherlie correctioun;
To quhome be gloir, and to no mo,
As vvas, and is, and shall be so,
For, euer, but defectioun.

To Psalm CXVIII.

The mercifull God of Israell,
Quha maid the heuin, earth, and se:
The blessed Sone Emmanuel,
Our promisit Saviour for to be:

And to the Spreit of veritie,
(All thre of might equiualent:)
Be gloir and honour incessantlie
And vvorship indeficient.

To Psalm CXXI.

To God quha is in euerie place,
Beneth, and als aboue,
The Father, and the Sone,

And to the halie Spreit of grace,
Be vvorship ineffabill,
With voices incessabill.

To Psalm CXXII.

Cum let vs forgather
To praise God the Father:
Euerilk morning of the day:
Sing Psalmes in sueit sound,
Let our voces redound
From eirth, unto heuin: and say

To God our Creatour
And Christ our Saluatour,
And the Paraclyte maist holie,
Our gyde and counsellour,
Be laude, gloir, and honour,
For euermore continuallie.

To Psalm CXXIIII.

Let us reioyce
  be all meinis externall,
And invvard heart,
  and let us praise the Lord:
Quha creat all

the haill vvarld be his vvord:
The Father, Sonne,
  and the Spreit Supernall:
Quha vvas, and is,
  and shall be Eternall.

To Psalm CXXV.

To God, quha leuis and reignis ay,
And to his promeist Sone sa deir,
And to the Spreit send be thame heir,

Give praise and honour night and day:
As it was ay befoir,
And sall be evermore.

To Psalm CXXVI.

Kingdome, Empyre,
  power, triumph and victorie:
Be to our God,
  quha creat the vvarld of nocht:
Father Eterne,
  and his Sone the King of glorie:

And halie Spreit
  that knavves and reulis mannis thocht.
As vvas ay sen
  the vvarldis foundatioun:
From age to age,
  in all generatioun.

To Psalm CXXVII.

Praise to the Godheid infinite
The Omnipotent Trinitie
Thre persons in Divinitie.

The Father, Sone, and halie Spreit.
To praise them make us readie boun
Fra the sone ryse till it ga doun.

To Psalm CXXIX.

To the Father,
  our onelie Lord and King:
And to his Sone,
  and holie Spreit give vve,

Honour, and praise,
  as in the beginning
Wes, and novv is:
  and so euermore shall be.

To Psalm CXXX.

O gude God maist mercifull,
  The Father of our Lord,
Thy Sone baith gude and pitifull
  From deith that vs restored.

To quhome vvith the halie Spreit,
  Be honour, laud, and gloir,
In vvarld of vvarlds infinite,
  As it vvas ay before.

To Psalm CXXXII.

To our Father Celestiall,
And his deir Son and holie Spreit:
Thre distinct persons, coequall

In one Godheid, vvhole, and compleit,
Be praise, and gloir, perpetuall.

To Psalm CXXXVI.

Gloir to the Father be,
And to the Sone maist sweit:
The samin gloir give vve,
Vnto the halie Spreit.

As vvas before
God create all,
Is novv, and shall
Be euermore.

To Psalm CXLII.

To our Father
  in heuinnis sa hie:
And to his Sone
  be gloir condigne
With equal praise,
  and laude vvorship vve,

The halie Gaist,
  in Vnite Trinitie
As it vves in
  the beginning,
And sall be but ending.

To Psalm CXLIII.

Our God of michtis most
To praise, let vs applaude:
The Sone, and holie Ghoist,
To quhome be gloir and laude,

As it vvas lang before,
The Warld tuke beginning:
And so sall euermore,
Abyde without ending.

To Psalm CXLIX.

To our Father abone,
And to his deir Sonne,
And the halie Gaist:

Be honour and gloir,
As it was before,
And for ay shall laste.

Besides these Conclusions, this version contains also a full complement of Prayers "upon" the Psalmes—one Prayer following each Psalm. It is believed that this is the only Scottish version of the Psalter which contains such Prayers. Similar appendages, however, appear under the name of "Collectes"—one attached to each Psalm—in Archbishop Parker's Version, printed about 35 years previously—1560—and which in all probability was taken as an example, and imitated in the Scottish version. The following are from each of these collections:—

SPECIMENS OF PARKER'S COLLECTES, 1560.

Collecte for Psalm LII.

Almighty God, which in thy power and fearfull wrath beatest down all the vanitie of the worlde and spite of man's pride, graunt vs so to florish as fruitfull Olyve trees in the house and congregation of thy people that by trust of thy name we may be delivered from the curse and malediction of thy wrath through &c.

Collecte for Psalm XCII.

Almighty God, which art the contynuall ioye and perpetuall felicitye of all thy saynts, whom thou doost inwardly water with the dew of thy heauenly grace, whereby thou makest them to floryshe like the Palme tree in the celestiall courts of thy church: we beseech thee that thou would so discusse from vs the burdenous weight of sinne, that we may enioye their fellowship. Through Christ.

Collecte for Psalm CVIII.

Graunt to al such as feare thy name O Lord, perpetual prosperity in the state of their lyues: referring all their actes and dedes to the glorification of the same, through Christ.

SPECIMENS OF PRAYERS IN SCOTTISH VERSION, 1595.

A Prayer vpon the I Psalme.

O Mercifull and heauenly Father that hes creatit us vnto blissitnes and soueraigne felicitie, and hes giuen vnto vs thy halie Lavv, to be the only reule and squair, quhairby vve suld liue vveill and godlie, make vs be thy gude grace to renunce our avvin carnall and fleschlie desires, and all euill company, escheuand the vvay of sinners, that vvee may bring furth sic fruites of the spirit, that beand alvvayis vnder thy halie protectioun, vvee may haue perfite assurance and cōfidence, that quhen thy Sone Iesus Christ shall appeir to deuyde the gaitis from the sheip, vvee may be accoūted amangis the number of them that are redemit be his blude. So be it.

A Prayer vpon the VIII Psalme.

Eternall God that by thy mightie Providence governis all creaturis; vve humblie beseik thee, that it vvald pleis the to visite vs be thy Son Iesus Christ, and restore us to that honour, from quhilk vvee vvere castin dovvne, be the sinne of our forefatheris; and that vve may in rememberance of thy great benefites tovvardis vs, celebrate thy meruelous povver, baith novv and euer mair. So be it.

A Prayer vpon the XIX Psalme.

O God Creator of all things, grant that We may acknouledge and magnifie thy great strength and pour that declaris the self in the conseruing and gyding of this vvarld: suffer nocht that vve vvander any quhit from thy halie Lavv, quhilk is pure and perfect: bot takand delyte thairin, vve may haillie be sa gouernit be it, that in the end vve may be participant of the heueulie saluatioun through Iesus Christ. So be it.

A Prayer vpon the XXII Psalme.

Albeit, (O God of al consolatioun and comfort) thou suffer vs for a littill seasoun to bee afflictit diverse vvayes: and makis vs (as it vver) to be the outcastis of the vvarld; zit for sa mekill as vve haif our onelie traist in thy gudenes, vve beseik three to assist vs, and delyuer vs of all thir troubillis that distressis vs, that in the

Appendix. 145

middest of thy halie Congregatioun, vvee may rander thee hartie praises and thanks, through Iesus Christ thy onelie Sonne. So be it.

A Prayer vpon the XXIII Psalme.

Eternall and everlasting Father, fountaine of all felicitie; vve rander thee prayses and thanks for that thou hes declarit vnto vs our Pastour and defender quha sall delyuer vs from the povver of our adversaries. Grant vnto vs, that vve castand avvay all feir and terrour of deith, may embrace and confesse thy trueth, quhilk it hes plesit the to reueill to vs by thy sone our Lord and soueraigne Maister, Christ Iesus. So be it.

A Prayer vpon XLII Psalme.

Celestiall Father, that at all tymes exercyses thy pure flock vvith diuerse afflictiounis: Assist vs, and delyuer vs from the troubillis that are fallin on vs that the vvickit and proud contemners haif na caus to think, that in vaine vvee depend vpon thee: but that they may be cempellit to vnderstand, that thou art the strenth and fortresse of all them that luiffis and honors thee, in thy Sonne Iessus Christ. So be it.

A Prayer vpon the LI Psalme.

Father of all mercies, that delytis nocht in the deith of ane sinner; Extend thy compassioun vpon us, and vvesch us from all our sinnes, that vve haif committed agains thy halie Maiestie, sen the tyme vve first enterit in this vvarld. Creat in vs ane clene hart, and strenthen vs continuallie vvith the povver of thy haly Spreit, that we beand haillie consecrate to thy seruice may set furth thy praises, through Iesus Christ our Saviour. So be it.

A Prayer vpon LXVII Psalme.

Eternall God, the Father of all lichts, vvithout the knavvledge of quhome, vve are mair miserabill then the verray brute beistis: Extend thy blessing ouer us, and make that thy maist hailie Name may be knavvin throughout the haill earth, and may be vvorshipped of all pepill and nations; to the intent, that all men feiling thy mercifull benediction, may vvalk in thy feir, as vve are teachit be Iesus Christ, thy Sonne. So be it.

A Prayer vpon LXXIV Psalme.

Father of mercie, for sa mekill as thou hes iust occasioun to punish vs in respect vvee haue not made our profite of thir benefites, quhilk thou hes povvered furth ō vs euer vnto this present hour: Zit haif regaird to the glorie of thy haly Name, quhilk is blasphemit be proud contempners and despysers thereof. Withdravv not thy fauour from vs; but remember on the couenant made vvith our auld Fathers, and strenthen vs be thy adoptioun, ratefyit in vs through Iesus Christ, thy Sonne. So be it.

A Prayer vpon LXXIX Psalme.

O Lord, the protectour and defender of the pure and oppressit, although the rage and furie of our enemies bee sic, that they neuer ceise from continuall tormenting of vs all maner of vvayis, and seikis na thing bot our vtter destructioun. Zit vvee beseik thee for to assist vs and turne avvay thine anger that hings ouer vs vpon them that blasphemis thee, that all the vvarld may vnderstand that thou despysis not the complaints and sobbis of them that callis vpon thee in treuth and veritie, in the name of Iesus Christ, thy Sonne. So be it.

A Prayer vpon LXXXIV Psalme.

Maist mercifull and heauenlie Father, vvithout the knavvledge of quhome, vvee can na vvayis attein to lyfe euerlasting or eternall saluation; Seeing that it hes plesit thee of thy mercie, (gude and gratious God) to grant vs libertie to conuene ourseluis togeather, to inuocate and call vpon thy maist halie Name, and to heire and embrace healthsome and sound doctrine, as out of thy avvin mouth. Continevv (of thy avvin gudedes) according to thy vvonted mercie, this thy heauenlie fauour tovvardes vs and our posteritie; and defend the cause of all them that vvalkes befoir thy halie Maiestie in innocencie and cleannes of lyfe, that vve may bee encouraged dailie mair to put our haill traist and confidence in thee, and that through the merites of Iesus Christ, thy deir and onelie Sonne, our Saviour. So be it.

A Prayer vpon XCIII Psalme.

Maist potent King of Kings, and Lord of Lords, quhais glorie is incomprehensibill, quhais Maiestie is infinite, and quhais povver is incomparabill: Mainteine thy seruands in quyetnes: and grant that vve may be sua settillit on the certaintie of thy promises, that quhat sumeuir thing cum vpon vs, vve may abyde firme in thy faith, and may leif vprightlie and vvith out reproch in the midis of the Kirk quhilk Iesus Christ thy Sonne hes bocht vvith his precious blude. So be it.

A Prayer vpon C Psalme.

O Lord, the plentifull heip of all happines, sen it hes plesit the of thy free mercie and gudenesse to chuse vs for thy avvin heritage, and to regener vs spiritually Entertaine vs vnder thy vvings vnto the end; and grant that vve may dailie grovve in the knavvledge of thy gudenesse, trouth, and mercie, quhilkis thou hes manifested vnto vs, through our Redeemer, and Sauiour Iesus Christ. So be it.

A Prayer vpon CIII Psalme.

Celestiall Father, that at all tymes hes shavvin thy singular fauour and gudenesse tovvardis all them that feir the: Luke not vpon the multitude of our iniquities, quhairvvith vve offend thee, seeing the great fragilitie and bruckilnesse quhilk is in vs. But remember the Coueunaunt that thou hes made vvith our Fathers, and ratifeit in thy Sonne Christ Iesus: that be the vertevv thairof, vve may assure ourseluis of the eternall saluatioun, that vve vvith thy angels may praise and glorifie the for euer and euer. So be it.

A Prayer vpon CX Psalme.

Eternall God, quhilk hes appointit thy onelie Sone, for our King and Priest, that vve micht be sanctified be the Sacrifice of his bodie vpon the Croce. Grant that vve may in sic sort be participant of his benefites that vve may renounce our avvin selfis, and serve him in all haliness, and puritie of lyfe: and may offer vp Spirituall sacrifices that may be pleasant and acceptable vnto the, through the self same Iesus Christ. So be it.

A Prayer vpon CXXX Psalme.

Pitifull Father, quha is full of mercie, that neuer reiectes the Prayers of them that callis upon thee in treuth and veritie: Haif mercie vpon vs, and destroy the multitude of our iniquities, according to the treuth of thy promises, quhilkis thou hes promisit vnto vs, and quhairin vvee repose our haill confidence, according as vve are teichit be thy Word of thy Sonne our onelie Sauiour. So be it.

A Prayer vpon CXXXII Psalme.

O louing Father, quha be thy aith hes promisit vnto vs, ane Saviour Jesus Christ, thy Sone: thou hes not deceuit vs, bot hes giuen him vnto vs, as thy Word hes declarit, and be thy Sacramentis thou hes confirmit. Yea, he hes further promisit vnto vs, that he vvill abyde vvith vs vntill the consummatioun of the vvarlde. Thairfoir, deir Father, vve beseik thee, that thou vvill blesse vs in all our turnis, gouerne vs, and replenish vs vvith ioy. Let thy Crovvn and Kingdome abyde aboue vs, and preserue vs in peice, through the same Iesus Christ, thy Sone. So be it.

A Prayer vpon CXLIV Psalme.

Pvissant God of Armies, that knavvis our brukkilnesse, and infirmities to be sa great, that be our selfis vve are not abill to stand vp ane moment befoir our adversaries, gif thy michtie povver did not uphald vs. Bovv doun thy self out of the heauens, and stretch furth thy strong hand; that they that seikis our ruyne may see thou our protectour and defender. Gif vs sic prosperous succes, that all the vvarld may se, they are nocht miserabill that depends on thee, and acclaimes the to be thair God, trouch Iesus Christ, our Sauiour. So be it.

A Prayer vpon CXLV Psalme.

Thy mercies (Lord) are aboue all thy vvarkes, faithfull art thou in all thy promisis, and iust in all thy doings. Be ane mercifull Father vnto vs, for Christ Iesus thy Sones saik. Gouern our vvayis, for vve are vvaike: Strenthen vs for vve are failzeit: Refresh vs for vve are famischit; and plentiffullie bestovv thy gud giftis vpon vs. Defend vs from the snairis of Satan, our auld enemie, that he tempt vs not out of the richt vvay bot that vve may euermair be reddie to praise and glorifie thy halie name, through Iesus Christ. So be it.

A Prayer vpon CL Psalme.

Maist vvorthie art thou, (O gude and gracious God) of all praises, euin for thy avvin saik quha surmountis all thingis in halinesse. Be thee onelie, vve are maid halie and sanctifyit. We prais thee for our glorious Redemption, purchasit to vs in thy deirlie belouit Sonne Christ Iesus, as our devvtie continuallie biddis vs: Give vs thairfoir thy haly Spirite to gouerne vs. And grant, that all things quhilk brethis vvith lyfe, may praise thee, as the true lyfe of all creatures, through the sam Iesus Christ, our Lord, quha reignis vvith thee and the halie Gaist, on God, for euer and euer. So be it.

VI.

Baillie defending the use of the "Gloria Patri."

HE use of the "Gloria Patri," or Conclusion to the Psalms, is defended by the celebrated Baillie, in the following interesting and graphic paper. It occurs among his unpublished MSS., and bears no date, but was probably written about 1643. He designates it :—
"*The summe of my conference yesterday with three or four yeomen of my flock who refused to sing the Conclusion.*

"Consider 1. If it be not a rashnesse in yow, who ar fullie persuadit by long experience of my great respect and love towards yow, to give over anie part of the publict worship of God without ever acquainting me or anie other person of the reasons that moved your minde to mak such a change in God's service. Will not this be found a neglect of that duetie whilk yow ought in conscience towards my ministrie, which yow say, and I beleeve you, is verie dear to you?

" 2. If yow so readilie have embraced the scruples which privat men and strangers have cast in your minde about this one point, bewar that this dispose not your hearts to embrace more of there evill seed. I forewarne yow, the rejecting of the conclusion is one of the first linkes of the whole chaine of Brunisme. We have oft seene, from this beginning, seducers, in this land, have drawne on there followers to scunder at and reject our whole Psalmes in meeter, and then to refuse our prayers, then our Sacrements, then our preaching, then at last our church, our covenant, and all. Everie erroneous way hath an evill spirit that leads on people from one point to another: and whom it finds inclinable to walk in that way, it lets them not rest till it hath drawne them to the uttermost end of the errour. Yow doubt not but it was so in Poperie and Arminianisme. Be assured the spirit of Brunisme is of the same nature. Wherefor as yow would be loath to cast away your whole psalmes, as yow would be loath to give over your prayers, sacraments, preaching, as yow would not forsak whollie our church, and your sworne covenant, and drink down all the errors of Brunisme, tak head to your spirit, whilk yow find so readie to learne the first lessons of these seducers.

" 3. Consider that while yow enquire the ground of this conclusion, that it is not eneuch for these seducers to tempt simple people to give to them the resson of everie part of the publict worship, or without farder to cast them away. It became them who require yow to forsake the constant practise of our church to give you clear Scripturall and particular ressons against it. But we are content here to dispense with the pains, and give yow some of these ressons quhilk we have for that practise. The matter of that conclusion is nothing but the paraphrase in meeter of this one sentence. Glory be to God for ever. There is onlie two words paraphrased into it. COD, and EVER. That the Father, Son, and Holy Ghost, is a good paraphrase of the word GOD, none will doubt but hereticks, who denie the Trinitie. That the naturall paraphrase of EVER is, what was in the beginning, what is now, and what shall be, even these hereticks doubt not, nor anie other who have wit to conceive of Eternitie. Or, if anie should doubt of this, yet Revel. 1. 8, would resolve them, which expresses the eternitie of Christ in this paraphrase, who is, and who was, and who is to come. I grant some of the Brunists reject all paraphrase and all meetering of Scripture, and so our whole Psalme book, but yow, I know, abhorre all such follie. So then the matter of the controverted conclusion being alone Glory to God for ever, the ground of it will be a number of Scriptures both in Old and New Testament: Psalmes XLI. 13.; XLV. 1, 2: Gal. 1. 5: Phil. IV. 18: 1 Tim. 1. 17: 2 Tim. IV. 18: 1 Pet. IV. 11; V. 11; Heb, XIII. 21; 2 Cor. XI. 31; Revel. 1. 6. These, and many moe Scriptures, are good grounds for all the matter which is in the Conclusion. As for the putting of that matter in the end of a Psalme, the Church, which hath power to order the parts of Gods worship, 1 Cor. XIV. 40, hath good reason for it, for Christ, in that paterne of all prayers and praises, teaches us to conclude for thine is glorie for ever.

"As for the frequent repetition of it, we have it but once almost in one spirituall song, for everie portion of the Psalme which is right divided, is a full spirituall hymne to ws. That it is lawfull to conclude everie prayer with the matter of this conclusion, none of yow doubts, for it is your dailie practise, according to Christs paterne. Now it is strange if a praise which yow say is lawfull and pleases God, should be unlawfull when it is sung at the back of our praises. The matter is the same; the saying and singing are but diverse wayes of expressing it. If it be convenient to mak this matter a conclusion of our prayers, it must be als, if not more convenient to mak it a conclusion of our praises; for it being a formal praise aggrees more, and is in nature sibber to praises than to supplications and prayers.

"4. Consider the weight of the objections against it. It is an humane Popish invention. We denie it to be so; for we have given good scripturall grounds for it. We grant it is a part of the Liturgie and Mass Book too. But this proves it not to be anie worse than the Lord's Prayer and the Beleefe, which are both in these evill books. True, the Brunists will teach yow to scunder at both; yet they will grant that manie things in the Liturgie and Mass Book also, as the whole book of Psalmes, much of the Old and New Testament, is no more the worse for the standing in these evill places, then the sun beams for shining on a dunghill.

"It is objected againe, that they challenge not the lawfullnesse of the use of it, but its frequent repitition. 1. This objection seemes to be fashionall, for pose your minds if you can use it although never so rarelie, yow will find it is the lawfulnesse of the thing itself you denie, and not the frequent repitition of it onlie. 2. It is not oft repeated, since at most it is but once in one song. 3. There is so much instruction and edification and comfort in this short phrase, so clear expressions of the honour of the three persons, so evident demonstration of eternitie, that the churches frequent repitition of it hath not onlie the example of the Holy Ghost, who repeats the like weightie sentences, as the binding word of the Psalmes. So in Psal. 107, the same close is repeated four times; in the 118, the same words ar repeated five times; in the 136 Psalme the same is repeated 26 times; not only I say the like sentences are repeated oft by the Spirit of God, but the same sentence we are speaking of is, in the alleagit places, by the Apostles and Psalmist, verie oft repeated, whiles in the mids, whils in the end of the discourse.

"They object 3. They may not be tyed to the use of a thing indifferent. 1. This maxime may not be granted except it be weill limitet. 2. Will they have it a thing indifferent to give eternall glorie to God? 3. There is no ty laid on yow for the practise; but when it is left free to be used sometimes, and omitted sometimes, you to yourself with a perpetuall abstinence, and with a superstitious fear of sin, whether the matter is lawfull and not sinfull, refuse ever that peece of worship as polluted. But there is too much said of this matter. I earnestlie exhort you in the name of God not to slight these things I have said, but as you would not continue to be an evill example to my flock, as yow would not contemn the truth of God in my mouth, as yow would not open the doore of your hearts to manie and dangerous novelties, return to your former practice and chearfullie joine with me, your pastor, and the rest of the flock, to ascribe to the Father, Son, O Holie Ghost, that eternall praise which is dew to his name."

The Brownists, to whom Baillie alludes in this paper, were a religious sect so called from the name of their founder, Robert Brown, who was descended of a good family, and received a liberal education at Cambridge. Bitterly opposed to the forms of discipline and government of the English Church, and charging the Presbyterian forms also with corruption, he organized a separate Society at Norwich, about 1580. Their articles of faith do not appear to have differed much from those of the Establishment; but their tenets in regard to church government were dissimilar, and approximated to those of Congregationalism, or Independency, and are regarded in fact as having formed the germ of that system. The Brownists were exposed to severe persecution—often even to the death—at the hands of the Church party. Brown himself declared on his deathbed that he had been in thirty-two different prisons; in some of which he could not see his hand at noon-day. He ended his days in Northampton jail in the year 1630, aged 80 years. It is alleged, however, that the cause of his incarceration was an assault.

In calling these yeomen of his flock to account in the matter of the "Gloria Patri," Baillie was acting in entire accordance with the sentiments of such leading men as Henderson, Dickson, Rutherford, Gillespie, and Blair, who quite approved of, and defended the use of the Doxology; whilst the conduct of the innovators complained of attracted the attention of the courts of the Church, and called forth public action. For some years previous to this time, the church had been agitated about the use of this formula, besides some other features of public worship as then conducted. The Commissioners of Assembly of 1642 wrote to some Presbyteries of the Synod of Glasgow and Ayr, to beware of innovations, condemning those who scrupled at the usual ceremonies and forms of the Church as favourers of Brownism. Bishop Burnet in his "Conferences" gives the following account of this letter:—"When some designers for popularity in the western parts of that kirk did begin to disuse *the Lord's Prayer in worship*, and the singing of the *Conclusion* or *Doxology* after the *Psalm*, and *the Minister's kneeling for private devotion* when he entered the pulpit, the *General Assembly* took this in very ill part, and in a letter they wrote to the Presbyteries complained sadly, Of a spirit of innovation was beginning to get into the Kirk, and to throw these laudable practices out of it, mentioning the three I named, which are commanded to be still practised; and such as refused obedience are appointed to be conferred with in order to the giving of them satisfaction; and if they continued untractable, the Presbyteries were to proceed against them, as they should be answerable to the next General Assembly. This letter I can produce authentically attested."*

* Burnet's Vindication of Church and State of Scotland, p. 182. Glas: 1673.

The subject came again under the consideration of the Assembly of the following year—1643—when, in the prospect of speedily being possessed of a "Directory for Public Worship," it was thought sufficient to pass an Act forbidding disputation and "condemning one of another in such lawful things as have been universally received, and by perpetuall custome practised by the most faithful ministers of the Gospell, and opposers of corruptions in this Kirk since the first beginning of reformation to these times." The result was, however, the exclusion of the formula from the Directory for Worship—the Scottish Covenanters conceding the point in question to the English Puritans, for the sake of peace and uniformity. In his description of the proceedings of the Westminster Assembly in preparing the Directory for Worship, Baillie wrote on April 25, 1645, in the following terms:—"Also about the Conclusion of the Psalme we [the Scottish Commissioners] had no debate with them [the English Divines]: with scruple the Independents and all sung it, so far as I know, when it was printed at the end of two or three psalms. But in the new translation of the Psalmes, resolving to keep punctuallie to the original text, without any addition, we and they were content to omitt that whereupon we saw both the Popish and Prelaticall partie did so much dote, as to put it to the end of the most of their lessons and all their psalmes."

VII.

Knox's Liturgy described, with The Spiritual Songs in full.

THE version of the Psalms, with appendages, printed in Edinburgh by the Heirs of And: Hart, in 1635, is popularly known as KNOX'S LITURGY, or KNOX'S PSALTER. It is simply a matured form of the Genevan Version, developed from the earliest issues of Sternhold and Hopkins; and first authoritatively adopted by the Church of Scotland in 1564. The name of the great reformer has become associated with the Psalter, as it has become associated with the entire work of the Scottish Reformation, and with all its chief characteristics. Knox constituted as it were, the connecting link between the Scottish Protestants and the English exiles in Geneva, between whom a remarkable harmony of religious sentiment existed. In 1554 he felt it expedient to leave his native country, where the cause of Protestantism was suffering violence under the tyranny of Mary. He chose Geneva as the place of his exile, where many of his reforming brethren had already taken refuge, and here he was received by Calvin with the most cordial affection. In all important points of faith and discipline these great reformers were perfectly agreed; and their practice was entirely harmonious in respect to forms of public worship. Knox was quite enraptured with the purity of religion as established under Calvin, and wrote to a friend at home in regard to it, in these unqualified terms:—"In my heart I could have wished, yea and cannot cease to wish, that it might please GOD to conduct and guide yourself to this place; where, I neither fear nor eshame to say, is the most perfect School of CHRIST that ever was in the earth since the days of the apostles. In other places, I confess CHRIST to be truly preached; but manners and religion to be so sincerely reformed, I have not yet seen in any other place beside."*

Towards the close of this year—1554—Knox repaired to Frankfort, in compliance with an urgent invitation from the English exiles there, to become their minister. Here, in co-operation with "Maister Whittingham, Maister Gilby, Maister Fox, and Maister T. Cole," he drew up an Order of Worship, closely

---

* M'CRIE's Life of Knox. Period V.

modelled upon the Genevan Service, the Order of which had been in existence about ten years. His residence in Frankfort was, however, very brief; and after visiting his endeared Calvin, he returned to his native country. In the meantime Whittingham, who was closely associated with Knox in all these movements, accompanied with a number of the Frankfort refugees, removed to Geneva, where, in 1555 an English congregation was organised, who made choice of Knox and Goodman as co-pastors; and Knox, in compliance with their invitation, returned to Geneva in September, 1556. The work which we have described in the text—"The Forme of Prayers and Ministration of Sacraments, &c. vsed in the Englishe Congregation at Geneua . . . . . M.D.LVI." was immediately issued for the use of this Congregation, and under the auspices of its leaders.* The design of its publication was not simply to supply the wants of the Congregation at Geneva; but rather, as we are informed in the Preface, with a view to its extensive use both in England and Scotland. Upon the return of Knox to Scotland he obtained for it the general sanction of the Scottish churches. So early as 1560 it was adopted by Act of the General Assembly, and it was repeatedly approved in subsequent years as the established form of worship.

The following is a minute analysis of this work as it appeared in 1635—a version enlarged and matured from that of 1556—with the Spiritual Songs given in full:—

THE TITLE—which is quoted in the text—then;—
1. A TABLE of the moveable Feasts, Golden number, Epact, &c. for xxv yeeres to come, with an exact Kalendar. 13 p.p.
2. AN ADMONITION for the better understanding of this preceding Kalendar. 1 p.
3. THE CONTENTS of this Booke. 2 p.p.
4. THE CONFESSION of FAITH used in the English Congregation at Geneva; received and approved by the Church of Scotland. 6 p.p.
5. Of MINISTERS ELDERS and DEACONS, their election, office, and duties. 4 p.p.
6. The WEEKLY ASSEMBLY of the Ministers, Elders and Deacons. 2 p.
7. The FORME and ORDER of the Election of the Superintendent, which may serve in electing of all other Ministers; at Edinburgh the 9. of March 1560—Iohn Knox being Moderator. 9 p.p.

* The title of this book as subsequently reprinted—1600—was "The Book of Common Order, or the Order of the English Kirk at Geneva, whereof John Knox was minister: Approved by the famous and learned man John Calvin. Received and used by the Reformed Kirk of Scotland, and ordinarily prefixed to the Psalmes in metre" DUNLOP's Confessions, ii. 383.

8. The ORDER of ECCLESIASTICAL DISCIPLINE. (The necessity and manner of it) 4 p.p.
9. The ORDER of EXCOMMUNICATION, and of public repentance, used in the Church of Scotland, and commanded to bee printed by the generall Assembly of the same, in the Moneth of June 1571.—comprising—

1. What Crimes bee worthie of excommunication, &c.
2. Confession of the penitent.
3. Offences that deserve publick repentance, and order to proceed therein.
4. The Forme and Order of publick repentance.
5. An admonition to the Church.
6. The Forme of Excommunication.
7. A Prayer for and dealings with the obstinate.
8. Sentence of Excommunication, with invocation of the name of Christ.
9. The Order to receave the Excommunicate againe to the Societie of the Church.
10. The Forme of Absolution—In all 42 p.p.

These Orders are closed by the following:—" ROM. 16. *Soli Sapienti* DEO per IESUM CHRISTUM *gloria in perpetuum*, AMEN. This Book is thought necessarie and profitable for the Church, and commanded to bee printed by the generall Assembly. Set foorth by IOHN KNOX, Minister, and sighted by us whose names follow, as wee are appointed by the said general Assembly. Iohn Willok. M. Iohn Craig. Robert Pont. Iohn Row. David Lindsay. Gulielmus Christisonus. Iames Craig, &c."

10. THE VISITATION OF THE SICK, with a prayer for the sick and the manner of burial. 9 p.p.
11. THE CONFESSION *of our sins.* 1 p.
12. Another CONFESSION and PRAYER, commonly used in the Church of Edinburgh on the day of Common Prayer. 3 p.
13. A CONFESSION OF SINS to be used before the Sermon. 2 p.
14. A CONFESSION OF SIN, and Petitions made unto God, in the time of our extreme troubles, and yet commonly used in the Churches of Scotland before the Sermon. 2 p.p.
15. PRAYER after Sermon for the whole Estate of Christ's Church. 4 p.p.
"These Prayers following are used in the French Church of Geneva:

The first serveth for Sunday after the Sermon, and the other that followeth is said upon Wednesday which is the day of Common prayer."

16. ANOTHER MANER of PRAYER after the Sermon. 6 p.p.
17. PRAYER used after Sermon on day appointed for Common prayer. 6 p.p.
18. A PRAYER used in the Churches of Scotland, in the time of persecution by the Frenchmen; but principally when the Lord's Table is to be ministered. 6 p.p.
19. A THANKSGIVING unto God, after our deliverance from the tyranny of the Frenchmen, with prayers made for the continuance of the peace between the realms of Scotland and England. 2 p.p.
20. A PRAYER used in the Assemblies of the Church, as well particular as generall. 2 p.p.
21. A PRAYER to be used when God threateneth his judgement. 4 p.p.
22. A PRAYER in time of affliction. 3 p.p.
23. A PRAYER for the King and Queenes Majestie, with their royall of-spring. 1. p.
24. THE MANER of the Administration of the Lords Supper. 8 p.p.
25. THE FORME of MARRIAGE. 5 p.p.
26. THE ORDER of BAPTISME. 15 p.p.
27. A TREATISE of FASTING (46 p.p.) With the Confession that shall goe before the reading of the Law, and before every Exercise, The Exercise of the whole week, and Three causes of this public Fast. 12. p.p.
28. THESE (three) CONCLUSIONS may be sung after any Psalme, which hath eight Syllabes in the first line, and sixe in the second. (These are given in full:—) 1 p.

<table>
<tr><td>1st</td><td>2nd</td></tr>
<tr><td>O God thou art the strength and rock
Of all that trust in thee:
Save and defend thy chosen flock,
That now in danger bee.</td><td>Thy People and thine Heritage
LORD blesse, guide, and preserve:
Increase them LORD, and rule their hearts,
That they may never swerve.</td></tr>
</table>

3rd
Glorie to the FATHER, to the SON
And to the holy GHOST
As it was in the beginning,
Is now, and ay shall last.

29. HEERE FOLLOW THE COMMON TUNES in foure partes, diligently revised and amended—With some Psalmes in Reports—29 p.p.

30. THE MUSICAL EDITOR'S ADDRESS to the Gentle Reader. 3 p.p.
31. THE PSALMS OF DAVID, with Music throughout, and Prose Psalms on Margin.
32. FOURTEEN SPIRITUALL SONGS. (See below.) 35 p.p.
33. TABLE of The whole PSALMS and SONGS. 2. p.p.
34. A FORME of PRAYERS to be used in private houses everie morning and evening. 6. p.p.
35. A COMPLAINT of the tyrannie used against the Saints of God, conteining a Confession of our Sins, and a prayer for the delyverance and preservation of the Church and confusion of the enemies. 6 p.p.
36. A PRAYER necessarie for all men   2. p.p.
37. A GODLY PRAYER to be said at all tymes   2 p.p.
38. A THANKSGIVING to be said before meate
39. A THANKSGIVING to be said after meate

The whole concluding with this prayer :—

  O GOD keepe thy Church, our KING and
  QUEENE, with their royall Children, together with the whole bodie of the land:
  and give us peace through CHRIST
    IESUS our LORD, Amen.

FINIS

THE SPIRITUAL SONGS, 1635.

THE TEN COMMANDEMENTS of Almightie GOD.

EXODUS XX.

Sing this as the 51. Psalme.

  Attend my people and give ear,
  Of ferlie things I will thee tell:
  See that my words in minde thou bear,
  And to my precepts listen well
I. I am thy Soveraigne LORD and GOD,
  Who have thee brought from careful thral
  And eke reclaimed from Pharaoh's rod,
  Make thee no gods on them to call.

II. Nor fashioned form of any thing
  In Heaven or Earth to worship it:
  For I thy God by revenging
  With grievous plagues this sin will smite.
III. Take not in vaine his holy name,
  Abuse it not after thy will:
  For so thou mightst soon purchase blame,
  And in his wrath hee would thee spill.

IV. The Lord from work the seventh day
    ceast
    And brought all things to perfect end:
    So thou and thine that day take rest,
    That to Gods Hestes yee may attend.
V. Unto thy Parents honour give,
    As Gods commandements do pretend:
    That thou long dayes and good mayst
        live
    In earth where God a place doth lend.

VI. Beware of murther and cruel hate
VII. All filthie fornication feare:
VIII. See thou steale not in any rate,
IX. False witnesse against no man beare.
X. Thy neighbours house wish not to
    have,
    His wife, or ought that hee calles
        mine:
    His field, his oxe, his asse, his slave,
    Or any thing which is not thine.

A Prayer.

Sing this as the 27 *Psalme.*

The Spirit of grace grant us, O Lord
To keep these Lawes our hearts restore:
And cause us all with one accord
To magnifie thy Name therefore.

For of our selves no strength wee have,
To keep these Lawes after thy will:
Thy might therefore, O Christ wee crave,
That wee in thee may them fulfill.

Lord, for thy Names sake grant us this,
Thou art our strength, O Saviour Christ:
Of thee to speed how should wee misse,
In whom our treasure doth consist.

To thee for evermore bee praise,
With the Father in each respect,
And with thy holy Spirit alwayes,
The Comforter of thine Elect.

The Lords Prayer.

Sing this as the 112. *Psalme.*

Our Father which in Heaven art,
And makes us all one brotherhood:
Wee call upon thee with our heart,
Our heavenly Father and our God:
    Grant wee pray not with lips alone,
    But with the hearts deep sigh and grone.

Thy blessed Name bee sanctified,
Thine holy Word mought us inflame:
In holy life for to abide,
To magnifie thine holy Name:
    From all errours defend and keep,
    The little flock of thy poor sheep.

Thy Kingdome come even at this houre
And hencefoorth everlastingly:
Thine holy Ghost into us powre,
With all his gifts most plenteously:
    From Sathans rage and filthy band
    Defend us with thy mighty hand.

Thy will bee done with diligence,
Like as in heaven in earth also:
In trouble grant us patience,
Thee to obey in wealth and wo:
    Let not flesh, blood, nor any ill
    Prevaile against thine holy will.

Give us this day our dayly bread,
And all other good gifts of thine:
Keep us from war, and from blood sheed,
Also from sicknesse, dearth and pine:
  That we may live in quyetnesse.
  Without all greedie carefulnesse.

Forgive us our offences all,
Relieve our carefull conscience:
As wee forgive both great and small,
Who unto us have done offence:
  Prepare us LORD for to serve thee
  In perfect love and unitie.

O LORD, into temptation
Lead us not when the fiend doth rage,
To withstand his invasion
Give power, and strength to every age.
  Arme and make strong thy feeble host
  With faith and with the holy Ghost.

O Lord, from evill delyer us,
The dayes and times are dangerous:
From everlasting death save us,
And in our last end comfort us:
  A blessed end to us bequeath,
  Into thine hands our Soules receive.

For thou O LORD, art King of kings,
And thou hast power over all:
Thy glory shyneth in all things,
In the wid world universall:
  Amen, let it bee done O LORD,
  That wee have praid with one accord.

VENI CREATOR

Sing this as the 95. Psalme.

Come holy Ghost, Eternall God,
  proceeding from above:
Both from the Father and the Son,
  the God of peace and love.
Visite our minds, and into us
  thine Heavenly Grace inspire.
That in all truth and godlinesse
  Wee may have true desire.

Thou art the very Comforter
  in all wo and distresse:
The heavenly gift of GOD, most High,
  Which no tongue can expresse.

The fountain and the lively spring
  of joy celestiall:
The fire so bright, the loue so clear,
  And unction spirituall.

Thou in thy gifts are manifold:
  whereby Christs Church doth stand:
In faithfull hearts writing thy law
  the finger of GODS hand.
According to thy promise made,
  thou gavest speech of grace,
That through thine help the praise of GOD
  may stand in every place.

O holy Ghost! into our wits
  send down thine heavenly light:
Kindle our hearts with fervent love,
  to serve God day and night.
Strengthen and stablish our weaknesse,
  so feeble and so fraile,
That neither flesh, the world, nor devill
  against us do prevaile.

Put back our enemies far from us,
  and grant us to obteine
Peace in our hearts with God and man
  without grudge or disdaine.
And grant, O Lord, that thou beeing
  our leader and our guide,
We may eschew the snares of sin
  and from thee never slide.

To us such plentie of thy grace
  good Lord grant wee thee pray:
That thou may bee our Comforter
  at the last dreadfull day.

Of all strife and dissension,
  O Lord, dissolve the bands:
And make the knots of peace and love
  throughout all Christian lands.

Grant us, O Lord through thee to know
  the Father of all might,
That of his dear beloved Son
  wee may attaine the sight.
And that with perfect faith also
  wee may acknowledge thee:
The Spirit of them both alway,
  one God in persons three.

Laude and praise bee to the Father,
  and to the Son equall,
And to the holy Sprite also,
  one God coeternall.
And wee pray that the only Son
  vouchsafe his Sprite to send
To all that do professe his Name
  unto the worlds end.

THE SONG OF SIMEON

Sing this as the 19. *Psalme.*

O Lord, because mine hearts desire
  hath wished long to see
Mine only Lord and Saviour
  thy Son before I die
The joy and health of all mankind
  desired long before,
Who now is come into the world
  of mercie bringing store.

Thou sufferest thy servant now
  in peace for to depart,
According to thine holy word,
  which lighteneth mine heart.

Because mine eyes which thou hast made
  to give my bodie light
Have now beheld thy saving health,
  which is the Lord of might.

Whom thou mercifully hast set
  of thine abundant grace,
In open sight and visible
  before all peoples face.
The Gentiles to illuminate
  and Sathan overquell:
And eke to be the glory of
  thy people Israel.

Appendix.

THE XII ARTICLES OF THE CHRISTIAN BELIEFE

Sing this as the 61. *Psalme.*

All my beliefe and confidence,
   is in the LORD of might:
The Father who all things hath made,
   the day and eke the night.
The Heavens and the Firmament,
   and also many a Star:
The earth and all that is therein,
   which passe mans reason far.

And in like manner I believe
   in Christ, our Lord, his Son:
Coequall with the Deitie,
   and man in flesh and bone.
Conceived by the holy Ghost,
   his word doth make mee sure,
And of his Mother Mary born,
   yet shee a Virgin pure.

Because mankind to Sathan was
   for sin in bond and thrall:
Hee came, and offered up himself
   to death to save us all.
And suffering most grievous pain,
   then Pilate beeing judge,
Was crucified upon the crosse,
   and thereat did not grudge.

He thold the last assault of death,
   which did lifes torments end;
Thereafter was hee buried,
   and did to hell descend.
And in the third day of his death
   Hee rose to life again
To the end hee might be glorified
   out of all grief and pain.

Ascending to the Heavens high,
   to sit in glorie still
On Gods right hand his Father dear
   according to his will.
Until the day of judgment come,
   when hee shall come again:
With Angels power (yea of that day
   wee all are uncertain)

To judge all people righteouslie
   whom hee hath dearly bought,
The living and the dead also,
   whom hee hath made of nought:
And in the holy Sprite of God
   my faith to satisfie,
The third person in Trinitie
   believe I steadfastly.

The holy and Catholick Church
   that Gods word doth maintain,
And holy Scripture doth allow
   which Sathan doth disdain.
And also I do trust to have
   by Iesus Christ his death
Release and pardon of my sins,
   and that only by faith

What time all flesh shall rise again
   before the LORD of might,
And see him with their earthly eyes,
   which now do give them light.
And then shall Christ our Saviour
   the sheep and goats divide:
And give life everlastingly
   to those whom hee hath tride.

Which is the realme celestiall,
  in glory for to rest:
With all the holy company
  of Sainctes and Angels blest.

Who serve the LORD Omnipotent
  obediently each houre:
To whom bee all dominion
  and praise for evermore.

THE HUMBLE SUTE OF A SINNER

Sing this as the 22. Psalme

O Lord on whom I do depend,
  behold my carefull heart
And when thy will and pleasure is,
  relieve me of my smart.
Thou seest my sorrowes what they are
  my grief is known to thee:
And there is none that can remove,
  or take the same from mee.

But only thou whose aid I crave
  whose mercy still is prest
To ease all those that come to thee
  for succour and for rest.
And sith thou seest my restless eyes
  my teares and grievous groan:
Attend unto my sute, O Lord,
  mark well my plaint and moan.

For sin hath so inclosed mee,
  And compassed about,
That I am now remeedilesse,
  if mercy help not out.
For mortall man can not release,
  or mitigate this pain:
But even thy Christ, my LORD and GOD,
  who for my sins was slain.

Whose bloody wounds are yet to see,
  though not with mortall eye,
Yet do thy Sainctes behold them all,
  and so I trust shall I.

Though sin do hinder mee a while,
  when thou shalt see it good
I shall enjoy the sight of him,
  and see his wounds and blood.

And as thine Angels and thy Sainctes
  do now behold the same,
So trust I to possesse that place,
  with them to praise thy Name.
But whiles I live heere in this vale
  where sinners do frequent:
Assist mee ever with thy grace
  my sins still to lament.

Lest that I tread in sinners trace,
  and give them my consent,
To dwell with them in wickednesse,
  whereto nature is bent.
Only thy grace must be my stay
  lest that I fall down flat:
And being downe, then of myselfe
  can not recover that.

Wherefore this is yet once again
  my sute and my request,
To grant me pardon for my sin,
  that I in thee may rest.
Then shall mine heart my tongue and voice
  bee instruments of praise:
And in thy Church and house of Sainctes
  sing PSALMES to thee alwayes.

THE LAMENTATION OF A SINNER

Sing this as the 6. Psalme.

O LORD, turn not away thy face
  from him that lyes prostrate:
Lamenting sore his sinfull life
  before thy mercies gate:
Which gate thou openest wide to those
  that do lament their sin:
Shut not that gate against mee LORD,
  but let mee enter in.

And call me not to mine accompts
  how I have lived heere
For then I know right well, O LORD,
  how vile I shall appeare.
I neede not to confesse my life
  I am sure thou canst tell,
What I have done and what I am
  I know thou knowst it well.

O LORD thou knowes what things bee past,
  and eke the things that bee:
Thou knows also what is to come,
  nothing is hid from thee.

Before the Heavens and earth were made
  thou knewst what things were then:
And all things else that have been since
  amongst the sons of men.

And can the things that I have done
  bee hidden from thee then?
Nay, nay, thou knowes them, all O LORD
  where they were done, and when.
Wherefore with tears I come to thee,
  to beg and to entreat,
Even as the child that hath done evill,
  and feareth to bee beat.

So come I to thy mercies gate,
  where mercie doth abound:
Requyring mercie for my sin
  to heal my deadlie wound.
O Lord, I neede not to repeat
  what I do beg or crave:
Thou knowes O LORD before I ask
  the thing that I would have.

  Mercie, good LORD, mercie I ask,
    this is the totall summe:
  For mercie, Lord, is all my sute
    LORD, let thy mercie come.

THE COMPLAINT OF A SINNER

Sing this as the 143. Psalme.

Where righteousnesse doth say,
LORD, for my sinfull part,
In wrath thou souldest mee pay
Vengeance for my desert.

I can not it deny
But needes I must confesse:
How that continuallie
Thy Lawes I do transgresse.

But if it bee thy will
With sinners to contend,
Then all thy flock shall spill
And bee lost without end:
For who lives here so right,
That rightly hee can say,
Hee sins not in thy sight
Full oft, and everie day.

The Scripture plaine tels mee,
The righteous man offends
Seven times a day to thee,
Whereon thy wrath depends.
So that the righteous man
Doth walk in no such path,
But he falls now or than
In danger of thy wrath.

Then sith the case so stands,
That even the man right wise
Fals oft in sinfull bands,
Whereby thy wrath may rise.
Lord, I that am unjust,
And righteousnesse none have,
Whereto then shall I trust,
My sinfull Soule to save?

But truely to that Post
Whereto I cleave and shall,
Which is thy mercy most,
Lord, let thy mercy fall.

And mitigate thy mood,
Or else wee perish all,
The price of this thy blood:
Wherein mercy I call.

The scripture doth declare,
No drop of blood in thee:
But that thou didst not spare,
To shed each drop for mee.
Now let those drops most sweet,
So moist mine heart so dry:
That I with sin repleat
May live, and sin may die.

That being mortified,
This sin of mine in mee
I may bee sanctified
By grace of thine in thee.
So that I never fall
Into such mortall sin,
That my foes infernall
Rejoice my death therein.

But vouchsafe mee to keep,
From these infernall foes,
And from the lack so deep,
Whereas no mercy growes.
And I shall sing the songs,
Confirmed with the Iust:
That unto thee belongs,
Who art mine only trust.

The Song of the Blessed Virgine Mary.

Sing this as the 19. *Psalme.*

My Soul do magnifie the Lord,
 my Spirit eke evermore:
Rejoyceth in the Lord my God
 who is my Saviour.

And why? because hee did regard
 and gave respect unto
So base estate of his Handmaid,
 and let the mighty go.

For now behold all Nations,
  and Generations all,
From this time foorth for evermore
  shall mee right blessed call.
Because hee hath mee magnified,
  who is the Lord of might
Whose Name bee ever sanctified,
  and praised day and night.

For with his mercy and his grace
  all men hee doth inflame:
Throughout all generations,
  to such as fear his Name.
He sheweth strength with his right arm,
  and made the proud to start:
With all imaginations
  that they bare in their heart.

Hee hath put down the mighty ones,
  from their supernall seat:
And did exalt the meek in heart,
  as he hath thought it meet.
The hungry hee replenished,
  with all things that were good:
And through his power hee made the rich
  oft-tymes to want their food.

And calling to remembrance
  his mercies every deale,
Hath holpen us assistantly
  his servant Israel.
According to his promise made
  to Abraham before,
And to his seed successively
  to stand for evermore.

THE LAMENTATION.

*Through perfect repentance the sinner hath a sure trust in God, that his sins
shall be washed away in Christs blood.*

Sing this as the 59. Psalme.

O Lord in thee is all my trust,
Give eare unto my wofull cry:
Refuse mee not that am unjust,
But bowing down thine heavenly eye
Behold how I do still lament
My sins, wherein I do offend:
O Lord, for them shall I be shent,
Sith thee to please I do intend.

No, no, not so thy will is bent
To deal with sinners in thine ire:
But when in heart they shall repent,
Thou grantest with speed their just desire.

To thee therefore still shall I cry,
To wash away my sinfull crime:
Thy blood O Lord is not yet dry,
But that thou mayest help me in time.

For why? while I on earth remain
Opprest, alace, with woe and grief:
My feeble heart plunged in pain
Doth sigh, and sue for thy relief.
Sweet Christ, wilt thou not then appear?
To comfort them that comfort lack:
Wilt thou not bow thine ear to hear?
Lord Iesus come, and bee not slack.

For then shall thine receive their rest,
Their joy, their blesse, their perfect peace:
And see thy face of treasure best,
O LORD that doth our joyes encrease.
Then shall thou give those noble crownes,
Which thine own blood hath dearly bought:
Then shall those gifts and high renownes
Bee given in grace most richly wrought.

Then shall thy Saincts redeemed dear
From baile to blesse removed bee:
And blessed CHRIST thy sweet voice hear,
Come unto mee Babes, come to mee.

Come reigne in joyes eternally,
Come reigne in blesse that hath none end,
Come therefore LORD come CHRIST wee pray
Our pressed grief with speed amend.

Haste thee O LORD, haste thee, I say,
To powre on mee thy gifts of grace,
That when this life shall flite away,
In Heaven with thee I may have place:
Where thou dost reigne eternally
With GOD who once did thee down send,
Where Angels sing continually,
To thee bee praise world without end.

THE SONG OF MOSES. DEUTERON. XXXII.

Sing this as the 32. Psalme.

Take heed O Heaven and hearken Earth
    and hear my mouth rehearse,
In chosen tearmes and sentence great
    this high and heavenly verse.
2. As dew distils on tender hearbs
    so shall my doctrine flow:
I shall powre out my speach as showers
    makes corne and grasse to grow.

3. For I Iehovahs Name will preach,
    and set it foorth abrod:
Therefore see that yee give with mee
    all glory to our GOD.
4. Unto that Rock, who perfect is
    in all his works his wayes
In right and wise discretion
    are brought to pass alwayes.

Hee is a strong and trustie GOD
    without iniquitie:
Whole, upright, just in all respects,
    and righteous is hee.
5. A generation perverse,
    and wicked in their heart:
Corrupted hath their wayes and done
    was not his childrens part.

6. Yee foolish people and unwise,
    should yee have thus requite
Your Father I'OVAH, and your LORD
    freed you from bondage great?
Who made you grow in number huge,
    and honour high withall,
And stablisht you in such a state
    as none could make to fall.

THE SECOND PART.

7. Remember now the days of old,
    and yeers of ages past;

Ask at thy Fathers they will tell,
    and thy Fore-fathers ask.

They will thee shew, and orderly
    recount, how God on hie,
8. When hee divyded all the earth
    possessed for to bee.

Hee Nations great of Adams seed
    dispersed to and fro:
Hee set the bounds of people twelve
    in number and no mo.
According to the number just
    of Israels sons twelve:
9. For I'ovahs people in his part
    with Iaakob hee will dwell.

10. He found him in the Desert dry,
    and in the wildernesse
Of mone and lamentation
    with deep and great distresse.
Hee compast him about and did
    instruct and keepe him sure:
Even as the apple of his eye
    hee had of him such cure.

11. And as the eagle steireth up
    her nest, and sits upon
Her birds and stretcheth out her wings,
    to carrie them thereon
12. So only Iovah led them right
    without the companie
Or help of strange and unquoth god
    no help thereof had hee.

13. Hee set him up upon the hight
    of a most fertile land,
That hee might eat and use the fruits
    therof at his command.
And suck the honie of the mount
    and oyle of stonie rock:
And eat the butter of the heards,
    and milk out of the flock.

14. And fatnesse of the tender lambs,
    and of the sheep so great,
And Bucks of Bashan with the fat,
    and finest of the wheat.
Thou also drank the juice like blood
    of berries noble wine:
And that unmixed whole and douce,
    and pickand wonder fine.

THE THIRD PART.

15. But Iesurun when hee grew fat,
    then he began to fling:
Thou'rt foule, and fate, and finger-fed,
    thy paunches down do hing.
For why? he did forsake that God
    who life and honour send:
The rock of his Salvation
    he did him vilipend.

16. They mooved him to jealousie,
    with unquoth idols vain:
And with abominations
    they wrought him great disdain

17. They sacrificed unto devils,
    and not unto the Lord:
Of whom their fathers did not know
    nor from their fear abhord.

To new invented gods, of whom
    they did not understand;
Whereof the fashion and the guise
    came from their neighbour land.
18. Thou hast forgot that Rock, that did
    beget thee Fatherly
And cast into oblivion
    the God that formed thee.

The Fourth Part.

19. These things when I the LORD beheld
    into his children bad:
Through wrath and indignation
    he cast them off, and said,
20. Now I will hide my face from them,
    and yet will look, and see
What misery shall them betide,
    and what their end shall bee.

They are a generation
    given to perversednesse:
A sort of children into whom
    there is no faithfulnesse
21. By such as were not gods of might
    they have provoked mee:
And griev'd mee at the very heart,
    with foolish vanitie.

Therefore will I reject them now,
    and take into their place
A naughty people, whom they thought
    should ne'r have found my grace.
Whereby I sorely shall provoke,
    and move them to despight:
When they shall see a people naught
    embraced for my delight.

22. For there is kindled in my wrath
    a furious fire and fell,
Which shall burn up, and all consume
    even to the ground of hell.

Which shall eat up the earth and eke
    her great fertilitie;
And set on fire the fundaments
    of mountains hudge and hie.

23. I'l spend amongst them many ills
    and ware mine arrowes all,
To punish their enormities
    I'l shoot them great and small,
24. The hunger horrible I will
    send out, and eke the pest:
And bylefull botch shall them destroy
    with murther manifest.

The bloody teeth of cruel beasts
    I will among them send,
And venome of the serpents fair,
    of them to make an end.
25. Without the sword shall all consume,
    and in the minde within:
The terrour and the trembling fear
    without end shall begin.

The galland young man, nor the age
    of lofty virgine mild
Shall not escap this just revenge,
    old man, woman, or child.
26. Thus had I said, I will go to,
    and spoil them utterly:
And blot away from mortall men
    their rotten memory.

The Fift Part.

27. Were not I feard the enemies
    misknowing pridfull boasts:
Saying, Our hand hath done all this,
    and not the LORD of hoasts.

28. They are a clan of counsell void,
    and of intelligence:
29. Now would to God that they were wise
    and had some providence.

That they might know and understand,
   and rightly comprehend,
How that their matters do proceed
   and what shall bee their end.
30. Oh, how is't come to pass that one
   should thus a thousand chase?
And only two sum of your troups
   ten thousand to deface.

If that the LORD your Rock had not
   inclosd you in their hand:
And cast you under (as a prey)
   Your enemies command.
31. For why? their Rock is not like ours,
   to be a sure refuge:
Although the enemies themselves
   were set down to be judge.

32. The Vines of Sodom and Gomorah
   are not so ill as theirs:
Which grapes and berries venemous,
   and bitter clusters beares.

33. Their wine is venome dangerous
   which dreadfull Dragons cast,
And like the deadly poyson strong
   of the most cruell Asp.

34. And is not this laid up in store,
   and keeped mee beside:
And sealed in my treasure fast
   there ready to abide.

35. Vengeance is mine and recompence
   in their own proper time:
Their foot shall slip, and they shall fall,
   and turn to dust and slime.

For why? of their calamitie
   the day drawes very near:
And of the things will them befall
   the tyme shall soon appear.

36. When I'HOVAH shall begin, and judge
   his people whom hee bought:
Hee will repent him of that evill,
   against his servants thought.

THE SIXT PART.

Even when he shall perceive and see
   all power to bee gone:
And neither captive nor escapt
   able to fight again.
37. Then shall hee say, where are the gods
   which they took for to bee
Their strong and fenced rock, to whom
   in danger they might flee?

38. Who feed upon the fat of all
   their sacrifices slain,
And of their offrings drank the wine,
   now seek their help again.

Now let them rise, and succour you,
   and aid you in this need:
Now let them bee your lurking place,
   if they be gods indeed.

39. At last bee wise, see, and behold,
   that I, even I am hee,
And that there is none other God,
   to bear mee company.
Its only I that casteth down
   and strike unto the dead
And do restore to life again,
   when there is no remead.

I wound and I do heale again,
    all is at my command
And there is none that can escape
    the force of my right hand.
40. For I lift up mine hand unto
    the Heaven, and thus I say:
As I did live before all tyme
    and so shall live for ay.

41. When I shall sharp my glancing sword
    and draw it out to strike,
And put mine hand to execute
    my wrath amongst the thick.
Then shall I rightly recompense
    with vengeance, wrake, and shame
Mine enemies, and well repay
    all those that hate my Name.

42. I shall make drunken all my shafts
    into their bulyering blood.
My sword shall eat up and consume
    their filthy flesh and rude.
Even in the blood as well of them
    that shall be tane as slain:
Down from the first, on all their sins
    this vengeance shall remain.

43. Yee nations sing, and make a noise,
    praise Him his people all:
For he revengeth well the blood
    of such as on him call.
Hee vengeance for his servants sake
    upon his foes will cast,
And with his land and people bee
    well pleased at the last.

A THANKSGIVING after the receiving of THE LORDS SUPPER.

Sing this as the 137. *Psalme.*

The LORD bee thanked for his gifts,
    and mercies evermore,
That hee doth shew unto his Saincts
    to him bee laude therefore.
Our tongues cannot so praise the LORD
    as hee doth right deserve:
Our hearts can not of him so think
    as hee doth us preserve.

His benefits they bee so great
    to us, that bee but sin:
That at our hands for recompence
    there is none hop to win.
O sinful flesh? that thou shouldst have
    such mercies of the LORD:
Thou dost deserve more worthilie
    of him to bee abhord.

Nought else but sin and wretchednesse
    doth rest within our hearts:
And stubbornly against the LORD
    wee dayly play our parts.
The Sun above the Firmament,
    that is to us a light
Doth shew it self more clear and pure
    than wee bee in his sight.

The Heavens above, and all therein
    more holy are than wee:
They serve the Lord in their estate
    each one in his degree.
They do not strive for Mastership,
    nor slack their office set:
But serve the LORD, and do his will,
    hate is to them no let.

Appendix.

Also the Earth, and all therein
  of God it is in aw:
It doth observe the formers will,
  by skilfull natures law.
The Sea, and all that is therein
  doth bend when God doth beck:
The sprits beneath do tremble all,
  and feare his wrathfull check.

But wee alas for whom all these
  were made, them for to rule,
Doth not so know or love the Lord,
  as doth the Oxe or Mule.
A law hee gave for us to know
  what was his holy will:
Hee would us good, but wee would not
  avoid the thing is ill.

Not one of us that seeketh out
  the Lord of lyfe to please:
Nor do the thing that might us joine
  to Christ and quyet ease.
Thus are wee all his enemies
  we can it not denie:
And hee again of his good-will
  would not that wee should die.

Therefore when remedie was none
  to bring us unto life,
The Son of God our flesh hee tooke,
  to end our mortall strife.
And all the law of God the Lord
  hee did it full obey:
And for our sins upon the crosse
  his blood our debts did pay.

And that we should not yet forget
  what good hee to us wrought
A signe hee left our eyes to tell,
  that hee our bodies bought.

In bread and wine heere visible
  unto thine eyes and tast:
His mercies great thou maist record,
  if that his Sprit thou hast.

As once the corn did live and grow,
  and was cut down with sith:
And threshed out with many strips
  out from his husk to drive
And as the Mill with violence
  did tear it out so small:
And made it like to earthly dust,
  not sparing it at all.

And as the Oven with fire hot
  did close it up with heat:
And all this done as I have said,
  that it should be our meat.
So was the Lord in his ripe age
  cut down by cruell death:
His Soul hee gave in torments great,
  and yeelded up his breath.

Because that hee to us might bee
  an everlasting bread:
With much reproach and troubles great
  on earth his life hee led.
And as the grapes in pleasant time
  are pressed very sore:
And plucked down when they bee ripe
  and let to grow no more.

Because the juice that in them is
  as comfortable drink
Wee might receive, and joyfull bee,
  when sorrows make us shrink.
So Christ his blood out pressed was
  with nailes and eke with spear:
The juice whereof doth save all those
  that rightly do him fear.

And as the cornes by unitie
　　into one leafe are knit
So is the LORD and his whole Church
　　though hee in heaven sit.
As many grapes make but one wine,
　　so should wee be but one,
In faith and love in CHRIST above,
　　and unto CHRIST alone.

Leading a life without all strife,
　　in quyet rest and peace:
From envie and from malice both
　　our hearts and tongues to cease.
Which if wee do then shall wee shew
　　that wee his chosen bee,
By faith in him to lead a life,
　　as ever willed hee.

　　And that wee may so do indeed
　　　　GOD send us all his grace
　　Then after death wee shall bee sure
　　　　with him to have a place.

A SPIRITUALL SONG.

Sing this as the 110. *Psalme.*

What greater wealth than a contented minde?
What povertie so great as want of grace?
What greater joy than find IEHOVAH kind?
What greater grief than see his angrie face?
What greater wit than run CHRIST IESUS race?
What greater follie nor defections fell?
What greater gaine than godlinesse to embrace?
What greater loss nor change the Heaven for hell?
What greater freedome nor in CHRIST to dwell?
What greater bondage nor a Soule to sin?
What greater valiance nor subdue thy sell?
What greater shame than to the divell to run?
　　And leave the Lord who hath so dear us bought.
　　Judge yee his Saincts if this bee true or nought.

VIII.

Reasons against the reception of King James' Metaphrase of the Psalms.

MDCXXXI.

IN the first Vol. of the Bannatyne Miscellany, pp. 227, &c., Papers of Reasons against the reception of King James' Metaphrase are reproduced from a Vol. of MS. in the Advocates Library, collected by Mr. David Calderwood, by whom they are generally supposed to have been prepared immediately after the issue of King James' first edition—the Oxford—in 1631. They are elaborated with great care, and enter into very curious and interesting details, and are as follows:—

I. THE PSALMES OF DAUID IN MEETER ALLOWED BE THE GENERAL ASSEMBLIE, SHOULD BE SUNG IN THE KIRKS OF SCOTLAND, AS THEY HAVE BEEN SINCE 1564, FOR THE REASONS VNDER WRITTEN.

THE reformed kirke of Scotland, being subject to no other kirk in the world, bot independent and frie, hes power to interpret and apply the word, to her awin purgation, conservation, and edification.

BE vertue of this power, the pastors of this Kirk, at command of the great counsall of this kingdome, penned certane heads of reformation whilk wer allowed and subscryved in Januar 1560.

IN these articles it is expreslie provyded, that men women and childrene be exhorted to exercise themselvis in psalms, that whene the kirk conveenes and sings they may be the moir able together with commoun heartes and voyces to praise God.

IN the Generall Assemblie conveened at Edinburgh in December 1562, for printing of the psalmes, the kirk lent Robert Licprivick printer, tua hundreth punds to help to buy irons, ink, and paper, and to fie craftsmen for printing.

IN the Generall Assemblie holden at Edenburgh in December 1564 it was ordeaned that everie Minister, Exhorter, and Reader, shall have one of the psalme books printed in Edinburgh, and shall use the order therein conteaned in Marriage, Ministration of the Sacraments &c.

IN the Generall Assemblie holden at Stirline in Februar 1569 the kirk in testification of ther contentment with the works printed be Robert Licprivick did assign to him in pension fiftie punds.

IF anie person or persons had required reformation of the psalmes in whole or in pairt, that mater would have been done in right tyme and place *animo edificandi non tentandi*, conforme to the order agried vpon at Glasco, April 1581, and at Perth 1596.

IF the law of prescription, as it is respected be the civil law, the lawes of nations, and the lawes of this kingdome, be a just exception against pleyes moved efter the expyring of threttie or fourtie yeirs, and if it wer extended, as it should be, not onlie to privat mens rightes but to publict saiftie and tranquillitie, then all actions moved, or to be moved efter thriescoir and eight yeirs against the Scots Psalmes, receaved and retained vpon so good grounds, and so profitable and confortable to Christianes his Majesties good subjects, would be judged moir then void and vneffectuall.

IF *decennalis* and *triennalis possessio*, be law and custom have the nature of a perfite right, whereby things perteaning to the kirk, may be peaceablie possest, then this kirk sould reteane the possession of the Psalmes, ay and while ther possession be lawfullie declared to be groundles and vitious.

FOR forder confirmation of the kirks right and possession of the Psalmes, in the year 1579, it is statute and ordeaned, by our Soverane Lord and his three estates in Parliament, that all gentlemen householders and all others worth thrie hundreth merks of yeirlie rent or above, and all substantious yeamen, men, or burgesses, likewayes householders esteemed worth five hundred punds in lands or goodes, be holden to have ane bible and psalme booke, vnder the paines conteaned in the said act.

SUNDRIE Musitians of best skill and affection for furtherance of the act of Parliament anent the instructing of the youth in Musick, have set downe common and proper tunes to the whole psalmes according to the diverse formes of the meteer.

BOTH pastors and people be long custome, ar so acquanted with the psalmes and tunes thereof; that as the pastors ar able to direct a psalme to be sung agrieable to the doctrine to be delyvered, so he that taketh vp the psalme is able to sing anie tune, and the people for the most pairt to follow him.

BOTH people and pastors have some psalmes, or parts of psalmes, be heart, as may best serve for ther different disposition and case of concience, and for the chainges of ther externall condition.

BY the lose of that heavenly treasure in ther hart alreadie, they would be farder greived, and prejudged in ther spirituall estate than they could be hurt in bodie or goodes suffering for retention of ther owne psalmes.

IN other reformed kirks, as Ingland, France, Germanie, Netherlands, etc. ther psalmes in meeter ar not so absolutely perfite, and frie of blame that nothing can be censured in them, and yet nether have they, nor will they reject the comelie face of ther own psalter, for a small blott, one or mae, bot still reteane what they have had in long continued and comfortable practise.

IF it should happen (as God forbid) that our psalme bookes in meeter, with the commoun order prefixed unto them, and the catechise following them now printed *cum privilegio regiae majestatis* wer removed, it might be justlie feared as the kirk decays in moyane and means that the confession of faith, the order of the election of ministers, of the ecclesiasticall discipline, and of excommunication and publike repentance, the visitation of the sick, the buriall of the deade, the commoun prayers, the formes of the Lordes supper, of baptisme and mariage, the booke of fasting, and Calvines catechise, should be supprest to the great hinderance of publict and privat vses.

IT were a shameles ingratitude to extinguish the memorie of so many worthie men by whose caire and paines God had vouchsafed to bestow so manie benefites vpon his kirk, and a great testimonie against the pastors and professors of this aige, who having these psalmes and vther meanes, hes gained so litle by them for ther comfort and edification that they are readier to quyte them than to keip them.

IN the Generall Assemblie holden at Brunteland in Maij 1601, the occasion of a certane motion maid be some brether, concerning our vulgar translation of the Bible, the Common prayers, and the Psalmes in meeter. It wes ordeaned that Mr. Robert Pont sould revise the psalmes, and that his labours sould be revised at the nixt assemblie, bot as the motion above written proceeded from personall respects, so it is to be supposed, that if that faithfull man who was both holy and learned, had found anie just cause of alteration, nether he to whom the mater was recommended, nor the assemblie who should have taken compt of his diligence, would have suffered that mater to be buried in oblivion.

IF it had bene found expedient to alter these psalmes, Montgomerie and som others, principalls of English poesie in ther tymes, as they gave ther assayes of som psalmes yet extant, so they offered to translate the whole book frielie without anie pryce for their paines, ather frae the public state or privat mens purses.

As the kirk refused the offer of these poets as neidles for the privat and publict worship of God, so it is statute and ordained in the generall assemblie holden at St. Johnstoun in Junii 1563, and in sundrie other assemblies, that no work be sett forth in print, nor published in writ vnto such tyme as it sall be advysed and approven be the kirk, conforme to the order sett doun be the generall assemblie.

SINCE it hath pleased God to raise some hope of deliverance to the kirks of other countries so long troubled with bloodie persecution, and to stretch out the hand of his power against superstition and idolatrie, pietie and compassion, would that we sould hold fast what we have, and ferventlie pray to God to vindicat his truth fra the tyrannie of idolators, and to delyver his distressed people fra the craft and cruelty of men that praises may be given to his Majestie be all kirks and persons whom he hes blessed with anie measure of mercifull reformation.

IN respect of the premises and other reasons to be eiked as occassion shall requyre, the psalmes in meeter as they have bene, and ar vsed privatlie and publictlie in Scotland, ought to be reteaned and no wayes suppressed for anie thing sein or hard yet.

II. REASONS AGAINST THE PUBLICK VSE OF THIS NEW METAPHRASE OF THE PSALMES.

JOHN of Lincolne, in his sermone preached at the funerall of King James, reporteth that he was in hands, when God called him, with the translation of our Church Psalmes, which he entended to have finished, and to dedicat to the sainct of his devotion the Church of Great Britaine, and that of Ireland; and that this work wes stayed in the threttie one psalme. This controlleth the title. The people call them Menstries Psalmes. Bot we heir that another, if not others, also hath had ane hand in them, and that these have revised King James his part. Of these, then, we mene in speciall when I speik of the new metaphrase. I have not as zit compared ther translation with the originall, nor considdered what libertie they have takin in the metaphrasing, to add, insert, or degresse. But suppose ther war na faill in these, zit I vouch and many ane that they can not be soong in our kirk for these Resones following:—

1. First, this labour is vndertaken without direction of the kirk, or offer made to the kirk before. Alexander Montgomrie has a singular vaine of poesie, zit he

tuik a more modest courss, for he translated bot a few for a proofe, and offered his travells in that kynde to the kirk. Joseph Hall (Bishop of Exeter and Norwich) metaphrased also some few psalmes and offered his endevour to do the lyk in the whole, if he sould be employed be authoritie. Bot our new metaphrasts endeavour to have the whole metaphrase of there making emposed vpon the kirk without direction or employment of the kirk, or offer made efter proof before.

2. Nixt the people ar acquainted with the old metaphrase more than any book in scripture, zea, some can sing all, or the most pairt without buik, and some that can not read can sing some psalmes. Therfor our kirk wold not accept of anie other. Howbeit some pairts might be bettered, zit they would not admitt that the whole sould be chainged. Bot in the Assemblie holdin at Bruntiland, anno 1601, appointed Mr. Robert Pont, a man skillfull in the originall toungs, to revise the translation of the psalmes in meeter, and ordeaned that his travell sould be revised at the nixt Assemblie. And for the same cause, it appeareth, Joseph Hall's offer was not accepted. And this same new metaphrase is rejected, as we heir, be the cheef bischops in England. Neither can they accept it without consent of ther Convocation hous. These new metaphrasts have had such a spite at the old metaphrase that they have not left nothing of it for man's memories, even wher ther was no necessitie of a change, when they could not avoyd the words, as Psal. 1. v. 2, Bot of the Lord he on the law, for the old | Bot in the law of God the Lord.

3. Thirdlie, it is a discredite to the clergie and the kirk that the psalmes sould be soong in the kirk translated in meeter be a courteour or commone poet when ther is no such raritie among theme of learned men, skilfull both in poesie and the originall toung: yea gif such war not be found, the most famous amangst the saincts for holines, wisdome, gravitie, sould be appointed be the kirk to that effect. For courteours ar commonlie suspected be the people as prophane, becaus they imploy often there vane on bad purposes as often as on good, and both toung and pen against the best of God's servants: a courteour like Abadiah or Nehemiah is als rare as a wedg of gold. The papists casts in the teeth of the professors of France, that they sing the psalmes translated be Clement Marot, a courtlie gentleman, who translated onlie fiftie. Sall we suffer the lyk to be cast in our teeth, and suffer God's service to be loathed.

4. Fourthlie, this work of metaphrasing the psalmes is holie and strict, and abydes not anie youthfull or heathenish libertie, but requireth hands free frome prophannes, loosnes, affection, sayeth Joseph Hall. Scultingius, a professor in

Colene, in his Anacrisis, and the author of the book intituled Caluino Turcismus, jest at the commendation made be one of Clement Marot that he was so wele sene in Catulus, Tibullus, Propertius, and other poets as gif, say they, the elegancies and pleasant conceats of prophane poets might be broght in into so grave and austere a work. Have we not such heathenish libertie and poeticall conceats in this new metaphrase? Tak these for a taste: Psal. 69. 7. And with the hue that blushes die | shame covered hath my face. Psa. 72. 6. Or like soft pearles of quickening showers | on earth that num'rous fall. Psal. 78. 20. Loe wounded rockes gave cristall blood | which straight a torrent roar'd. Psa. 89. 1. The mercies of the Lord I still | will sing with sacred rage. Psa. 104. 26. There walke the ships amidst the floods | where captiu'd aire commands. Psa. 105. 32. And in their countrey ominous flames | like fatall fires did burne. Psa. 147. 16. He gives the snow like labour'd wooll | whose liquid threds oft turne. Psa. 148. 3. You flaming Lord of light | and with the starres in state | pale Lady of the night.

5. Fyftlie, the people must be first taught to vnderstand these and the lyk French, Latine, and hard English tearmes, and harsh phrases following, before they can sing with vnderstanding:—as regall | opposites | vastnes | various | vindicate | invoke | torrents | brandisht | vsher | guerdoned | obloquie | appall | gratefullie | sinistrous | verdure | billowes | site | cite | depraue | portend | portentuous | prodigies | divulge | tumide | exorbitant | vilified | dignified | rayes | impetuous | accumulat | emulate | exhilirat | reside | spheares | vases | shelfs | liquid | declind, for crooked | harmonious rounds | cristall rounds | &c. Our awin metaphrase hath non bot such as may be understood, except tuo or three that war wele knowin to that tyme when the psalmes war translated in meeter and may be easilie changed. Bot to bring in a number of words which have need of a dictionarie in the end of the metaphrase, is to mak worse and not better. As for harsh phrases, tak for example Psa. 9. 6. Destructions vastnesse now my foe | a period still doth bound.

6. Sextlie, our kirk sall be infected with the error of the locall descent of Christis saull to hell, be the metaphrasing of the 16 psalme, if this new translation shall be allowed, which is sufficient to reject the whole: for sall we be so stupid as to honnor the works of such as ar erroneous, or entertain error?

7. Seventlie, it sall mak vther kirkis call vs lightheaded Scotts, inconstant and vnsetled in our orders, changing without anie necessitie, if we will put quit doun the metaphrase which was recommendit to all the professors be the Generall Assemblie, and sett vp another.

Others have observed that there is a whole double verse wanting in the 43 psalme: and another psalme hath tuell lynes in the double verse.

III. Reasons against the private Vse.

The verie privat vse aucht to be suppressed, First becaus some perhaps will labour to have them by heart, who sould rather labour to have these in memorie which ar soong in the church; for who will studie to both? And therefor a metaphrase of the psalmes different from that which is vsuall in the church is the most unprofitabill work that may be; yea prejudiciall to that which is publictlie receaved, onless it be in Greek or Latine, which ar not, nor cannot be vsed in publict. Therefor, ye see the lyk doth not occur in any vther reformed church, French, Dutch, or Italian. A learned paraphrase vpon the psalmes is permitted to any that hath the gift, and is commendable. But another metaphrase is nevir convenient, bot prejudiciall to that which is vsed in the kirk, and serveth onlie to mak people glaik. Nixt, the printing of this book *cum privilegio* and the allowing of it to be red in privat, importeth allowance of the error above mentioned. Thirdlie, it may justlie be feared that in schort proces of tyme it may pass frome privat vse to publict. For have not some alreadie vsed this metaphrase when the congregation wer singing the old. A door sould not be opened to such light heads and prophane hearts.

A Caveat for the Burghs.

We can not deeme that the burrowis will commit such ane absurditie as, for the recommendation of vsurping bischops, medle with that which the Convention of the three Estates wold be loath to medle with, and which belongeth to a frie and right constitute Generall Assemblie. Can they appoynt some to try? or whome will they appoynt? or will they receave without triall? Then may they luik for the new service to be recommended to them, the nixt day the organes, &c. Bot we hope better things.

[Another paper is given in the *Miscellany*, entitled "Reasons against the receaving of this new Metaphrase of the psalmes," but they are chiefly condensed from the former. Only two of the reasons contain new matter—viz., the 6th and the 9th, and are as follows:—]

Sixtlie, the metaphrasts have taken great libertie to add matter of their awin to the text of scripture, which may be seen almost in everie psalme. Luther requesting Spalatinus to translate some of the psalmes in Dutch meeter, desyreth with all that he abstain from new coined and court tearms, and to content himself with such as were vulgar, and meetest for the capacitie of the people.

Ninthlie, the countrie shall be burdened with the loss of thrie hunder thousand buiks of the old, and with the cost of sex hunder thousand of this new meeter, during the privelige which we heir is to be granted to the cheef author.

As these Reasons serve for rejecting of it, so some of them also serve against the committing it to revising. For to commit it to some to revise tendeth to the approbation of it, if it be approved be the revisers, which may be easily obteaned. If any ought to be revised it is the old, and non hath power to commit it to be revised in prejudice of the old bot the Generall Assemblie; And speciallie seeing the General Assemblie hath ordeaned alreadie that the old be revised, which be reason of the troubles that followed efter wes not yit performed. The pretendit prelats therfor can not medle with this busines.

IX.

Letter to Sir William Mure.

THE following *Letter to Sir William Mure of Rowallan, from the Rev. Thomas Wyllie, Minister of Fenwick,* is deemed worthy of reproduction, as illustrating in some measure the spirit of the times in which he lived, as well as being in itself a curious document:—

27 May. 1676.

Right Worshipfull,

I am informed that upon invitation from John Paton in Middow-head & some in Loudounside, there is a young man expected to keep conventicle the morne with the people in the heads of the three parishes, either at the Croilburn or above Craiginduntan. I shall not be apt to think that any man of discretion will be so easily drawn to come within the bounds of planted congregations, yet because there be frolichness aneugh in some young men, I will wad upon none. Their preaching in vacant congregations and in places where curates are has some ground for it, & I should allow their preaching in *transitu* even in planted congregations on week days when there is no sermon in public, but to fall in upon planted congregations on the Lords day to make a diversion from the public, is not reasonable in them, nor ought it to be tolerat. I thought fit to shew your worship this that you may tak some course to crush such beginnings even in the outbreaking, *principiis obstare* is a good apothegm, for if such a wild course go on it will occassion much confusion in the three congregations, and occation much detriment among the people. I leave it to yourselve and the gentlemen to think upon the most effectual way to prevent this and the like in all times coming, in the meantime it will not be amiss to cause wairn all your people to come to the Kirks the morrow. I know not how long the Lord may continue his hand upon me, but if any I employ be once deserted upon such an occasion I need look for no more help. Whether the young man answer their desire or not the wairning of the people will do no skaith, but testify to them your worships dislike of such a way in such a case.

I am assuredly
Your worships most humble and real servant
THOMAS WYLIE.

X.

XTRACTS from the LAST WILL AND TESTAMENT OF FRANCIS ROUS, dated March 18th, 1657. These are curious and interesting, and leave do doubt as to his piety and conscientiousness.

"Forasmuch as to put houses in order, before our departure, is pleasing to the God of order, I do dispose of my affairs and estates in manner following. There is a youth in Scotland concerning whom, (because they call him my grandson) it is perchance expected that I should do some great matters for him; but his father marrying against my will and prohibition, and giving me an absolute discharge before the marriage under his hand, not to expect any thing from me if he did marry contrary to my prohibition, I hold myself discharged from the father, and consequently from the son of that father, the son having no interest in me but by the father.— And I hold it a good example for the benefit of the Commonwealth, that matters of discouragment should be put upon such marriages, being assured that their parents will not disinheritt or lessen them, especially if they have but one son; and though his mother is bound to maintain him, yet because I wish he might be a useful member of Christ and the Commonwealth, towards which I think she is not well able to give him an answerable education, I have in this my Will, taken course for a competent maintenance for him towards a profession, and it is utterly abhorring to give him an estate as the heir of idleness—Wherefore to the forementioned purpose, I desire my executor to give him £50 a year, so long as he shall be in preparation towards a profession, or shall really and seriously be in the practise of it, and as many of my books as may be fitt for him in the profession he shall undertake, and shall not be given to Pembroke college." "I desire my body may be interred and put to rest in the chapple of Eaton College, a place that hath my dear affections and prayers that it may be a flourishing nursery of piety and learning to the end of the world. And for a profession of my faith I refer myself to the works which I not long since published in one volume, wherein I have professed a right and saving faith and hope to continue therein until faith shall be swallowed up of sight, laying hold of the free grace of God in his beloved son as my only title to eternity, being confident that his free grace which took me up lying in the blood of irregeneration, will wash away the guilt of that estate, and all the cursed fruits of it, by the precious blood of his Son, and will wash away the filth of it by the Spirit of his Son, and so present me faultless before the presence of Gods glory with joy." Signed, "FRANCIS ROUS."

XI.

Boyd Caricatured.

WE cannot part from honest "Master Zacherie" without a word of protest against the execrable and unprincipled treatment to which portions of his poetry have been subjected at the hands of certain parties. He has been grossly burlesqued and caricatured, and made a laughing-stock of—whilst we believe that in spite of occasional quaintnesses and oddities of expression, he was heartily devout and in earnest. We append a few specimens of the liberty that has been taken with his productions. The true versions are quoted from his "Garden of Zion," and "Zion's Flowers," popularly known as "Boyd's Bible;" and the burlesques from "The Whiggs' Supplication, or the Scotch Hudibras, a Mock Poem, by Sam. Colvill," and other sources.

TRUE VERSIONS.

Rebekah fat and in body lusty,
A wife for Isaac, pleasant to the eye:
Bethuel's Laban's father's brother's love,
Her heart to stay from Isaac could not move;
Heare now said they, the Damsell's yea or no,
I will, she said, most gladly to him go:
She meeting *Isaac* in the evening tide,
Under a vaile her comely face did hide.

("GARDEN OF ZION," Vol. 1. p. 32.)

PARODIES.

Rebekkah was very blythe and bonnie
And pleased Isaac's wanton e'e
He took her to his mother's tent,
* * * * * *
* * * * * *
He begat Esau and Jacob.

In Uz a man cal'd Job there was
both perfect and upright;
Who feared God and did eschew,
evill even with all his might.

("GARDEN OF ZION," Vol. 2. p. 2.)

There was a man called Job
Dwelt in the land of Uz;
He had a good gift of the Gob
The same case happen us.

(COLVIL.)

Then said his (Job's) wife, Retain'st thou still
   thine old integritie
What meanest thou, O foolish man,
   now curse thou GOD and die;
But he again said unto her,
   his witlesse wife to schoole,
Thou speakest now thou knowes not what
   thou speakest like a foole.
        ("GARDEN OF ZION," Vol. 2. p. 8.)

Job's wife said to Job,
   Curse God and die;
Oh no, you wicked scold,
   No, not I.

Thus afterward these noble brethren two,
Went on and stood before the great Pharo;
Commanding him with great authoritie,
To free God's people from captivitie;
Because this King thus hardened his heart,
Of ten great plagues his Kingdom felt the smart.
        ("GARDEN OF ZION," Vol. 1. p. 53.)

And was not Pharaoh a wicked and har-
   den'd rascal,
Not to allow the men of Israel with their
   flocks and herds their wives and their
   little ones to go a forty days journey
   into the wilderness to eat the Pascal.

There Absolom a Rebell and a Foole,
Among the rest was riding on a mule;
By his long haire a branch caught him that day,
There he did hing when the mule went away:
Then Joab with his three darts came anone,
And thrust them through the heart of Absolom.
        ("GARDEN OF ZION," Vol. 2. p. 8.)

Absolom hang'd on a Tree,
   Crying God's mercy;
Then Joab came in, angry was he,
   And put a Spear * * *
        (COLVIL.)

But Jeshurun, who should have beene
   most righteous, did kick;
Thou art exceeding waxed fat,
   thou art also grown thick;
Thou covered art with fatnesse, then
   His Maker he forsook,
And of his sure salvation's rock,
   no care at all he took.
        ("GARDEN OF ZION," Vol. 1. p. 67.)

Jeshurun waxed fat,
   And down his paunches hang;
And up against the Lord his God,
   He kicked and he flang.

Jacob to Rachel.

Yea for your sake this little Joseph more,
I love than all that born were him before;
A lovely lade hee is, also his very birth
Unto us all presaged holy worth;
He surely is the darling of mine age,
He of our love is a most sacred pledge;
Him I doe count from Heav'n to be our lot,
Let us make him a particolour'd coat.

And Jacob made for his wee Josie,
A tartan coat to keep him cosie;
And what for no, there was nae harm,
To keep the lad baith saft and warm.

(ZION'S FLOWERS, MS., p. 403.)

The following is the true reading of the famous lines about Jonah in the whale's belly:—

> Here apprehended I in prison ly,
> What goods will ransom my captivity?
> What house is this, where's neither fire nor candle,
> Where I no thing but guts of fishes handle?
> I, and my table, are both here within,
> Where day ne'er dawn'd, where sun did never shine.
> The like of this on earth man never saw,
> A living man within a monster's mawe;
> Buried under mountains which are high and steep,
> Plunged under water hundrethe fathomes deep.
> Not so was Noah in his house of tree,
> For through a window hee the light did see:
> Hee sailed above the highest waves a wonder,
> I, and my boat are all the waters under.
> Hee in his ark might goe and also come,
> But I sit still in such a straiten'd roome
> As is most uncouth, head and feet together,
> Among such grease as would a thousand smother
> * * * * * *
> Where I entombed in melancholy sink
> Choak't, suffocat, with excremental sti..k.

(ZION'S FLOWERS, MS.)

Apropos of the story of Jonah, Boyd relates the following characteristic anecdote in one of his sermons:—" In the time of the French Persecution, I came by sea to

Flanders, and as I was sailing from Flanders to Scotland, a fearfull tempest arose which made our mariners reele to and fro, and stagger like drunken men. In the mean tyme there was a Scots Papist who lay near mee. While the ship gave a great shake I observed the man, and after the Lord had sent a calme, I said to him, 'Sir, now yee see the weaknesse of your religion; so long as yee are in prosperitie yee cry to this Sainct and that Sainct; in our great danger I heard you cry often, Lord, Lord, but not a word yee spake of our Lady.'"

This anecdote also is worth repeating. Finding on one occasion that several of his hearers went away after the forenoon sermon, he used this expression in his afternoon prayer,—"Now, Lord, thou sees that many people go away from hearing the word, but had we told them stories of *Robin Hood* or *Davie Lindsay*, they had stayed, and yet none of them are *near so good* as the word that I preach."

XII.

Logan and Bruce.

THE list of authors to whom the Paraphrases are ascribed is given as it was submitted to, and approved by the General Assembly of the Scottish Church, and the Assembly's Committee on Psalmody. Logan was a member of that Committee. We have no wish to take any part in the controversy that subsequently arose between the friends of Logan and those of Bruce regarding the authorship of the Paraphrases and other pieces around which the controversy turns. We would simply refer the reader who may be anxious to investigate the question, to two works in which it appears to be minutely discussed, and in which a strong case is apparently made out against Logan, and in favour of Bruce, viz.—"Lochleven and other Poems, by Michael Bruce, with a life of the Author from original sources, by the Rev. William Mackelvie, Balgedie, Kinross-shire. Edinburgh, 1837;" and "The Works of Michael Bruce, Edited, with memoir and notes, by the Rev. Alexander B. Grosart, Kinross. Edinburgh, 1865." Mr. Mackelvie conducts his investigation with great coolness, and sums up in the following temperate language:—"We have now done with this controversy, and after the proof we have led, cannot think it possible that any reflecting mind will regard Logan innocent of the dishonourable conduct which we have laid to his charge. We have no wish that the charge should continue to rest against him, and shall be pleased to find him successfully vindicated, and even to see the evidence which we ourselves have furnished made to tell in his favour." (p.p. 146. 147.) Mr. Grosart indicates his convictions in terms much more forcible and decisive. His "Introduction to the Poems" opens thus:—"I feel that it is a pity to perturb so meek and gentle a life as was that of Bruce, with controversy. But unfortunately the first editor of his Poems so dealt with the MSS. entrusted to him, and subsequently so asserted for himself the authorship of the 'Ode to the Cuckoo,' and the well-known 'Paraphrases' or 'Hymns,' that no choice is left. I have gone over the whole of the evidence *pro* and *con* after Dr. Mackelvie, with a single eye to ascertain the truth—nothing more, nothing less, nothing else; and the result has been a conviction of the utter untenableness of the claims of Logan. I use no stronger word at present. I would narrate the facts, adduce the evidence, and fortify our conclusions; and I am mistaken egregiously if any capable of weighing 'proof' will refuse acquiescence in the last." (p. 51.)

XIII.

Versions of Psalms by the Free Church.

THE "Versions of the Psalms," by a Committee of the General Assembly of the Free Church—alluded to in the text—consist of new renderings of forty of those which have so long been used in the service of the Church, given in a great variety of measures. As a specimen, we subjoin a portion of the 84th, setting over against it Dr. Watts' Version of the same verses. Both are in the same peculiar style of metre, and both have the same translation of the second verse, so significantly different from that which has been so long adopted.

Ps. LXXXIV. *Free Church Version.*

1. How lovely are thy tents,
O Lord of hosts to me!
My spirit longs, yea faints
The Lord's own courts to see.
    To his abode
    My heart aspires;
    My flesh desires
    The living God.

2. An house wherein to rest
The sparrow finds alway:
The swallow builds a nest
Where she her young may lay;
    Ev'n so would I,
    My King, my God,
    Make mine abode
    Thine altars nigh.

Ps. LXXXIV *Dr. Watts' Version.*

1. Lord of the worlds above,
How pleasant and how fair
The dwellings of thy love,
Thy earthly temples are!
    To thine abode
    My heart aspires,
    With warm desires,
    To see my God.

2. The sparrow, for her young,
With pleasure seeks a nest;
And wandering swallows long
To find their wonted rest:
    My spirit pants,
    With equal zeal,
    To rise and dwell
    Among thy saints.

Appendix.

3. O happy they that be
   Within thy house always;
   For there they wait on thee
   And ever give thee praise.
     Yea, happy they
     Whose strength thou art,
     And in whose heart
     Is found thy way:

4. Who passing Baca's vale,
   Therein do dig a well;
   The rain shall never fail
   The water-pools to fill.
     From strength to strength
     They go until
     To Zion hill
     They come at length.

3. O happy souls that pray
   Where God appoints to hear!
   O happy men that pay
   Their constant service there.
     They praise thee still;
     And happy they
     That love the way
     To Zion's hill.

4. They go from strength to strength,
   Thro' this dark vale of tears,
   Till each arrives at length,
   Till each in heaven appears:
     O glorious seat,
     When God our King
     Shall thither bring
     Our willing feet!

XIV.

Music Schools.

USIC Schools existed in this country during the time of the Reformation. The following items shew the support which they received compared with that accorded to Grammar-schools.

EXTRACTS FROM ACCOUNTS OF THE COMMON GOOD OF VARIOUS BURGHS IN SCOTLAND, PRESERVED IN THE GENERAL REGISTER HOUSE, RELATIVE TO MUSIC SCHOOLS, &c.

Aberdeen. 1594-5.

Item, to the maister of the grammer schoil for his fee of the twa termis	xxxiij.li. vj.s
Item to the maister of the sang schoill	xiiij.li.xiij.s. iiij.d.

Air. 1627-8.

Item to the Mr of the gramer scule, his stipend,	jc li.
Item to the Mr of musik scule, for teaching of the musik scule, and taking up the psalmes in the Kirk x. bolls victuall, and xlji.li.vj.s. viij.d. of silver	

Couper. 1581.

Item to the maister of the sing scole fe	vj.li. xiij.s.iiij.d.
Item to Mr Alexander Tyllideaphe, Mr of the Musick scol	jc li.

Dumbarton. 1621.

Item to Mr Alexander Home, scholemaster, for his feall and hous mail, 1621.	iiijc lxvj.li.xiij.s.iiij.d.
Item to the teicher of the Inglische schoole and musick	jc li.

Appendix. 193

Dundee. 1602.

Item, to the maister of the grammer scole,	ijc merkes.
Item, to the master of the sang scule,	lxxx.li.

1603.

Item, the masters of gramer and sang schol,	lxx.li.xiij.s.iiij.d.

1621-2.

Item, to Mr John Mow, Mr of the music schoole, for his fee and hous maill	ccl.li.

1628.

Item, to Mr John Mow, maister of the music scule	ijc lxvj.li.xiij.s.iiij.d.

Elgin. 1622.

First, to the master of the gramer scole	lxvj.li.xiij.s.viij.d.
To the master of the music scole	jc li.

Inverness. 1634.

Item, giffen to the Mr of the gramer scoil	iiijxx.li.
Item, giffen to Mr of the musick scoil	xxxvj.li.

Irving, 1633.

Our schoolmaister	lxxx. merkis.
Our doctour and musicianer	jc li.

Lanark, 1627-8.

Item, to the scholemaister of the said bruche, that teiches the gramer for the saidis tua termes, (Mertimes and Witsonday,)	jc li.
Item, to ane wther scholemaister, that teiches the musick	iijxxvj.li.xiij.s.iiij.d.

St. Andrews, 1626-27.

Item, to the publict reader	jc li.
Item, to the maister of the musik scholl, and for taking up of the psalme at preaching and prayeris of fie	ijc li.

2 c

Tayne. 1628.

Item, to Mr Thomas Ross, master of the gramour schooll. je li.
Item, to Mr John Tullidef, reider and master of the musick school je li.

Wigton, 1633.

Imprimis gevin to ane schoolmaister for teiching the grammer schole, reiding and raising the psalmes in the kirk yeirlie. iije merkis.

In a minute of the Town Council of Glasgow, dated 24th December, 1588, "the scuile, sumtyme callit the sang scuile," is mentioned as a part of the common good, which it was resolved to appropriate in order to liquidate the heavy charges which the town had incurred in consequence of the pest, &c. And in the Treasurer's accounts for the same burgh, in 1609, we find the following item—"Giffen upon the third of Marche 1608, to John Buchan, Mr of the sang scole, for Witsonday and Martymes termes, maill of his hous, L.xx.

These Music Schools existed in terms of *Royal enactment.* On the 11th November, 1579, the following STATUTE was passed:—

"For instruction of the youth in the art of musik and singing, quhilk is almost decayit, and sall schortly decay, without tymous remeid be providit, our Soverane Lord (James VI.), with avise of his thrie estatis of this present parliament, requeistis the provest, baillies, counsale, and communitie of the maist speciall burrowis of this realme, and of the patronis and provestis of the collegis, quhair sang scuilis are foundat, to erect and sett up ane sang scuill, with ane maister sufficient and able for instructioun of the yowth in the said science of musik, as they will answer to his hienes upon the perrel of their fundationis, and in performing of his hienes requeist do unto his Majestie acceptable and gude plesure."

These Schools were in existence previous to the Reformation, and would originate in the necessities of Popish worship. Boys required to be trained for chanting, and to be able to read Latin, so far at least as the church services were concerned. The "Sang Schule," therefore was the Elementary Seminary, as compared with the "Grammar Schule;" and the two in combination seem to have formed the preparatory course to attendance upon College. While primarily intended for church students, they were also open to others. They seem also to have included the departments of writing and arithmetic, and probably reading in the vernacular. After the Reformation, when it was no longer deemed essential to maintain a company of singing boys, besides an adult choir, in every considerable place of worship, and when the dissemination of knowledge in reading and writing had become a primary object to the church, it is natural to suppose that the musical element in these seminaries would descend, and the other elementary branches rise in public estimation. It may, however, be supposed that the edict of James would in some degree arrest the progress of decline in musical teaching, and would lead to an increase of the number of the "Sang Schules." There is no definite information respecting the musical materials used in these "Schules," during this period, but it cannot be doubted that the tunes of the Church Psalter would form a leading ingredient.

XV.

Rochester's estimate of the singing of Sternhold and Hopkins' Psalms.

JOHN WILMOT, Earl of Rochester, was a witty and profligate nobleman of the Court of Charles the Second, and a personal friend and favourite of his Sovereign. The levity and recklessness of his disposition frequently brought him into disgrace with his royal master, who, however, found his companionable qualities so necessary to his amusement, that the favourite's occasional exile was always of short duration. His constitution gave way under the violence of his excesses; and, exhibiting all the debility of an old man, he died in 1680, at the early age of 32. It is gratifying, however, to know that ere his death he exhibited symptoms of sincere repentance and reformation. His satirical powers were keen and clever, and deeply tinged with impiety. The following anecdote is characteristic of the man. Walking on one occasion in company with his Majesty, their way happened to lead them past a chapel at the time the precentor was singing a Psalm from Sternhold and Hopkins' version. The music, perhaps, did not come up to Rochester's ideal of what music should be—or at any rate he deemed the opportunity too rare to be lost of shewing his remarkable readiness of wit and powers of satire—and he at once saluted the ear of his royal companion with this impromptu,—

> "Sternhold and Hopkins had great qualms
> When they translated David's Psalms
>   To make the heart right glad.
> But had it been king David's fate
> To hear thee sing and them translate
>   By . . . 'twould set him mad."

XVI.

The decadence and revival of the Psalter Music.

HE music of the old Scotch Psalter, in common with that of kindred churches, formed part of a method of worship set up in opposition to that of the Church of Rome—a method differing not only in regard to the use of the vernacular language of the worshippers, and the adoption of metrical psalms, but also in regard to the principles of the musical department. Rome practises the chanting, or recitative singing of prayers. In her service books, or liturgies, everything is set to music. And moreover, before the Reformation, in those portions of her Ritual which admitted of it, she had set aside the more simple Gregorian song in favour of compositions in Canon, and other elaborate and shewy materials, which were necessarily monopolized by the professional performers; and in which, as asserted by Romish writers themselves, display was far more thought of than the spiritual good of the hearers. The Scottish Reformers discarded the whole system of chanting prayers as unnatural, and not adapted to edification in public worship—substituting the ordinary speaking voice. And they employed only such music as seemed capable of acquirement by an assembly of ordinary worshippers—music of a plain and simple nature, consisting of tunes popular in character, and fitted to move from stanza to stanza of metrical composition.

In regard to the origin of this particular style of church music, it is necessary to look backward considerably beyond the movement of Luther. Centuries before the Reformation, bodies of Christians, dissentients from the Church of Rome, existed under such names as Waldenses, Culdees, Lollards, Hussites, &c., with whom, or with parties similarly situated, such simple music would naturally originate, and form a vehicle for their praise, doubtless both from choice and from the necessities of their position. It could not be expected that worshippers in their condition—comparatively poor, widely dispersed, and exposed to much trouble and danger—could conduct their worship by companies of trained performers. Their service of song, if to be enjoyed at all, behoved to be by their common action; hence also with all simplicity, and with that nervous rythm and natural melody that easily affect the ear and engage the memory. And the social feelings aroused by their common circumstances, would find vent in the united burst of song. Portions of the Gregorian Tones, tunes attached to the old Latin hymns, and even secular airs of the graver sort, were probably impressed into this service—subjected perhaps more or less to a process of modification to adapt them to the measures with which they were associated; whilst it may be supposed original compositions were produced, expressive of the deep emotions awakened by the circumstances of the time. These views appear to be borne out by some of the oldest specimens of this style of music. It is stated by those who have examined it, that the Bohemian book of 1538 includes numerous Gregorian passages, but it only partially contributed to the full supply of Protestant Church Song. When Luther undertook to furnish appropriate tunes to metrical psalms and hymns, he found a considerable accumulation of such simple materials; but it is generally admitted that the best models in this style emanated from his own genius, or from that of his co-adjutors stimulated by his example.

The reign of this fine old music was, however, of but brief duration. It was soon allowed to fall into oblivion, and to vanish almost entirely from public view; a fact so discreditable as to have elicited from a foreigner, the late Dr. Mainzer, the following rebuke :—"While the protestants of Germany, Switzerland, Sweden, and Bohemia, cling with veneration and almost filial devotion to the psalm tunes of the Reformation, and consider them as a sacred trust, as a national legacy, to be transmitted from father to son, from generation to generation, the Presbyterians of Scotland have been taught melodies of other countries, of which many have not even borrowed their inspiration from the church—their own national psalmody, one of the most beautiful musical remnants of the Reformation, being allowed to perish unnoticed, and fall into oblivion."

Various reasons might be assigned for such a state of things. The new version of the psalms—1650—was printed without tunes, without compensation for the loss by having the tunes issued in a separate form, whilst very many of the old styles of metre were discarded. The Church ceased to protect her music, but turned it adrift to seek refuge wherever a private individual might be found willing to afford it. A depreciated estimate of the place and power of music in religion began to prevail—occasioned, amongst other causes—by the recoil from the pressure of the five Articles of Perth, the Service Book, and other features of the Episcopal movement which ended in 1637. A jealousy of, and aversion to, every indication of an interest in the external elements of worship, seem to have been thus engendered. The old psalm books, with the music, became increasingly scarce; " Sang Schules" became extinct, and the fallacy laid hold on

Appendix. 199

the Scottish mind that it matters not about the quality of the musical material or its execution if the heart be rightly exercised. Ultimately, Scotland seems to have become chiefly dependant on England for its supply of music; only some half dozen of its old Psalter tunes being retained, and nine-tenths of its precentors, it may be affirmed, being entirely ignorant that such a book ever existed.

Of recent years, however, there has been a partial return to the tunes of the Reformation, and in a variety of ways a revived interest has been indicated in the subject of Sacred Music. In England, Mr. W. Cross of Christ Church, Oxford, has issued a compilation consisting of old tunes to the extent of about a half, and accompanied with an able preface recommendatory of their style. Rev. W. H. Havergal's "Old Church Psalmody" has exerted a powerful influence in the same direction. Various more recent works include a large number of the ancient tunes, and others of similar structure. A kindred process has been going on in Scotland. Dr. Andrew Thomson's "Sacred Harmony" did good service. More recently, Mr. T. L. Hately and Dr. Mainzer have awakened an interest more especially in the Scottish Psalter tunes. And the publication of the "Scottish Psalmody," about 21 years ago, was quite an era in the modern history of music. The cause has been ably forwarded by public advocacy, and by the institution throughout the country of music classes and lectureships, which continue to be well patronised; and the ability to teach music in our ordinary schools is reckoned a special recommendation in a teacher. We would here simply refer to the EUING MUSIC LECTURESHIP, GLASGOW, as deserving of honourable mention. On the 31st of May, 1866, Wm. Euing, Esq., Insurance Broker, of that City, executed a "Deed of Trust," settling £3000 for the purpose of instituting and permanently establishing a Chair of Music in the Andersonian University. The first Course of Lectures in connection with this Institute was delivered in 1866-67, by Mr. John Curwen, of *Tonic Sol-Fa* notoriety; the second, in 1867-68, by Mr. H. Lambeth, City Organist; and the third, by Mr. Colin Brown of Glasgow, in 1868-69. In consequence of the successful attainments of his students, who have carried off the greater part of the honours and prizes bestowed by the Society of Arts of London, Mr. Brown still continues Lecturer to this Institution. Some of our "merchant princes" might do worse than imitate the example so worthily set by Mr. Euing in this respect.

The subject of the Old Psalter Music is ably and exhaustively treated by Rev. N. Livingstone, in his elaborate dissertations and notes annexed to his beautiful Reprint of the Psalter of 1635.

XVII.

The various Measures used in the Old Psalter. *(See Doxologies, App. V.)*

THE subjoined stanzas, selected from the Psalter of 1635, shew the style of poetical composition. They are given, however, chiefly as specimens of the various measures in which the Psalms are versified, shewing the number of lines required for each tune.

Psalm I.—C.M. 8.6. 8.6. 8.6 8.6.

1. The Man is blest that hath not bent,
   to wicked red his eare:
   Nor led his life as sinners doe,
   nor sate in scorners chaire.

2. But in the Law of God the Lord
   doth set his whole delight:
   And in that Law doth exercise
   himselfe both day and night.

Psalm XXV.—6.6. 8.6. 6.6. 8.6.

1. I Lift mine heart to thee,
   my God and guide most just:
   Now suffer mee to take no shame,
   for in thee do I trust.

2. Let not my foes rejoyce,
   nor make a scorn of mee:
   And let them not bee over-thrown,
   that put their trust in thee.

Psalm XXVII.—L.M. 8s. Eight lines.

1. The Lord my light and health will be,
   For what then should I be dismaide?
   My strength and life also is hee,
   Of whom then should I bee afraide?

2. When that my foes (men vile and vain)
   Approached neare my flesh to eat:
   They stumbled in the self-same train,
   Which they for me laid by deceit.

Psalm XXXVI.—8s. Five lines.

1. The wicked deedes of the ill man
   Unto mine heart do witnes plaine:
   That feare of God in him is none,
   Though hee himselfe would flatter faine:
   His wickednesse is judgde and known.

Appendix.

PSALM XLVII.—5s. Twelve lines.

1. Let all folk with joy
   Clap hands and rejoyce,
   And sing unto GOD
   With most chearfull voice.
2. For high is the LORD,
   And feared to bee,

   The Earth over all
   A great King is Hee.
3. In daunting the folk
   Hee hath so well wrought,
   That under our feete
   Whole Nations are brought.

The doxology to this Psalm contains only eight lines, but the twelve are made up by adding the four odd lines at the end of the Psalm.

PSALM L.—4.6. 4.6. 4.6. 4.6. 4.7. 4.7.

1. The mightie GOD
   th' Eternall hath thus spoke:
   And all the world
   hee will call and provoke,
   Even from the East,
   and so foorth to the West.

2. From toward Sion,
   which place him liketh best,
   GOD will appear
   in beautie most excellent:
   Our GOD will come
   before that long time be spent.

PSALM LXII.—4.7. 4.7. 4.6. 4.7. 4.7. 4.6.

1. Although my Soule
   hath sharplie been assaulted,
   Yet towards GOD
   in silence have I walked:
   In whom alone
   all health and hope I see.

2. He is mine health
   and my salvation sure,
   My strong defence,
   which shall for ever endure,
   Therefore afraid
   I neede not much to bee.

Four lines added to the doxology, as in Psalm XLVII.

PSALM LXVII.—5s. Eight lines.

1. Our GOD that is LORD
   and author of grace,
   Turn to us poor Souls
   his mercifull face.

2. His blessings encrease,
   defend us with might:
   And shew us his love,
   and countenance bright.

PSALM LXX. is in the same measure as Psalm XXVII.—8s. Eight lines. The four lines of its doxology are supplemented by the four at the end of the Psalm.

PSALM LXXVI.—8s. Seven lines.

1. In Jurie land GOD is well known,
   In Israel great is his Name.
2. Hee choose out Salem for his own,
   His Tabernacle of great fame,

Therein to raise, and Mount Syon
To make his habitation,
And residence within the same.

PSALM LXXX.—6.5. 6.5. 5.5. 5.5.

1. O Pastor of Israel!
   like sheep that dost lead
   The linage of Joseph,
   advert and take heed:

That sittest betweene
the Cherubims bright,
Appeare now and shew
to us thy great might.

PSALM LXXXI.—9.8. 9.8. 6.6. 5.6. 6.5.

1. To GOD our strength most comfortable
   With merrie hearts sing and rejoice:
   To Iaakobs GOD most amiable
   Make melodie with chearfull voice.
2. Go take up the Psalmes,

The timbrell with shalmes:
Bring foorth now let see
The harp full of pleasure,
With Viole in measure,
That well can agree.

PSALM LXXXIII.—4.6. 4.6. &c. Fourteen lines.

1. GOD for thy grace
   thou keep no more silence,
   Cease not O GOD,
   nor hold thy peace no more.
2. For lo, thy foes
   with cruel violence
   Confedered are:

and with an hideous roar,
In this their rage,
these rebels brag and shoar:
And they that hate
thee most maliciously.
Against thy might
their heads have rais'd on hie.

PSALM LXXXV.—8.8. 6.8. 8.6.

1. O LORD, thou loved hast thy land,
   And brought foorth Iaakob with thine hand,
   Who was in thraldome strait.
2. Thy peoples sins so great and hudge,
   Thou covered hast and didst not judge,
   Thy mercies were so great.

Appendix.

Psalm CIIII.—5.5. 5.5. 6.5. 6.5. 5.5. 5.5. 6.5. 6.5.

1. My soul praise the LORD,
speak good of his Name:
O LORD our great GOD,
how dost thou appear:
So passing in glory,
that great is thy fame;
Honour and Majestie
in thee shine most clear.

2. With light as a robe
thou hast thee beclad,
Whereby al the earth
thy greatness may see,
The heavens in such sort
thou also hast spred,
That it to a curtain
compared may be.

Psalm CX.—4.6. 4.6. 4.6. 4.6. Doxology in 10s.

1. THE LORD most high
unto my Lord thus spake,
Sit thou now downe
and rest at my right hand,

Untill that I
thine enemies doe make,
A stoole to bee
whereon thy feet may stand.

Psalm CXI.—6.6. 6.6. 6.6. 6.6. 7.6. 6.7. Doxology in six lines, adjoined to the last six lines of the Psalm.

1. With heart I do accord,
To praise and laud the Lord,
In presence of the just.
2. For great his works are found
To search them such are bound,
As do him love and trust.

3. His works are glorious,
Also his righteousnesse
It doth endure for ever.
4. His wondrous works hee would
We still remember should,
His mercy faileth never.

Psalm CXII.—8s. Six lines.

1. The man is blest that GOD doth fear,
And that his Lawes doth love indeed:
2. His seed on earth GOD will uprear,

And blesse such as from him proceed:
3. His house with good hee will fulfill,
His righteousnesse endure shall still.

Psalm CXIII.—8s. Twelve lines.

1. Yee children who do serve the LORD
Praise yee his Name with one accord.
2. Yea blessed bee alwayes his Name.

3. Who from the rising of the Sun,
Till it returne where it begun,
Is to bee praised with great fame.

4. The LORD all people doth surmount,
   As for his glorie wee may count
   Above the Heavens high to bee.

5. With God the Lord who may compare?
   Whose dwellings in the Heavens are,
   Of such great power and force is hee.

PSALM CXVIII.—9.8. 9.8. &c. Eight lines.

1. Give to the LORD all praise and honour,
   For hee is gratious and kind:
   Yea, more his mercie and great favour,
   Doth firme abide world without end.

2. Let Israel now say thus boldlie.
   That his mercies for ever dure:
3. And let Aarons whole progenie,
   Confesse the same stable and sure.

PSALM CXX.—6s. Six lines. Doxology as CXI.

1. In trouble and in thrall
   Unto the Lord I call,
   And hee doth mee comfort.

2. Delyver me, I say,
   From lyers lips alway,
   And tongues of false report.

PSALM CXXI.—8.6. 6.8. 7.7.

1. I lift mine eyes to Sion hill,
   From whence I do attend,
   That succour GOD mee send:

2. The mightie GOD me succour will,
   Who Heaven and Earth framed
   And all things therein named.

PSALM CXXII.—6.6. 8.6. 6.8. 6.6. 8.6. 6.8.

1. I did in heart rejoice,
   To heare the peoples voyce,
   In offering so willinglie
   For let us up, say they,
   And in the Lords house pray:
   Thus spake the folk full lovinglie.

2. Our feete that wandered wide,
   Shall in thy gates abide:
   O thou Ierusalem full fair:
3. Which art so seemly set,
   Much like a Citie neat,
   The like whereof is not els where.

PSALM CXXIII.—4.6. 4.6., &c. Ten lines.

1. Now Israel
     may say, and that truely,
2. If that the LORD
     had not our cause maintained,
   If that the LORD
           had not our right sustained,
     When all the world
           against us furiouslie
     Made their uproares,
     and said wee should all die

Psalm CXXV.—8.8. 8.8. 6.6.

1. Such as in GOD the LORD do trust,
   As Mount Syon shall firmly stand,
   And bee removed at none hand:
   The LORD will count them right & just
   So that they shall bee sure
   For ever to endure.

Psalm CXXVI.—4.8. 4.8. 4.8. 4.8. 4.6. 4.6.

1. When that the Lord
     again his Syon had foorth brought
   From bondage great,
     and also servitude extream
   His works was such,   [thought:
     and did surmount mans heart and

   So that we were
     much like to them that use to dreame
2. Our mouths were with
     laughter filled the-en
   And eke our tongues
     did shew us joyfull men.

DOXOLOGY TO PSALM CXXVII, same measure as Psalm CXII.—8s. Six lines.

Psalm CXXIX.—4.6. 4.7. 4.6. 4.7.

1. Of Israel
     this may now bee the song,
   Even from my youth
     my foes oft have me noyed.

2. A thousand ills
     since I was tender and young
   They have me wrought
     yet was not I destroyed.

Psalm CXXX.—7.6. 7.6. 7.6. 7.6.

1. Lord to thee I make my mone
   When dangers me oppresse:
   I call, I sigh, plaint and grone,
   Trusting to find release.

2. Heare now, O LORD, my reqyest,
   For it is full due time,
   And let thine eares ay be prest,
   Unto this prayer mine.

DOXOLOGY TO PSALM CXXXII, same measure as Psalm XXXVI.—8s. Five lines.

Psalm CXXXVI.—6.6. 6.6. 4.4. 4.4.

1. O laud the LORD benigne,
   Whose mercies last for ay:
2. Give thanks and praises sing
   To GOD of gods I say:

   For certainlie
   His mercies dure
   Both firme and sure
   Eternallie.

PSALM CXXXVIII.—4.6. 4.7. 4.6. 4.7. 4.7. 4.7. This Psalm is referred to Doxology of Psalm L, though the measure is not the same.

1. With my whole heart
   the Lord now praise will I:
   Before the Gods
   I will him praise for ever:
2. Towards thy Church
   and Temple will I cry,

   Because thy love
   and kindnes faileth never:
   Thy godly name
   thy word hath most advanced,
   Which doth excell,
   and ought to bee inhanced.

PSALM CXLII.—9.8. 9.9. 8.6.

1. Vnto the Lord I cry did and call:
   Yea, with my voice I him besought,
   And my requests before him let fall:

2. So that my griefes and troubles withall,
   Before his presence I foorth brought,
   To stay my troubled thought.

PSALM CXLIII.—6s. Eight lines.

1. Oh hear my prayer, LORD,
   And unto my request,
   To bow thine eare accord,
   And as thou thinkest best:
   According to thy truth,
   And for thy justice sake,
   O Lord on me have ruth
   And answer to me make

PSALM CXLIX.—5s. Six lines.

1. Sing unto the LORD,
   With heartie accord,
   A new joyfull song:
   His praises resound,
   In everie ground,
   His Saints all among

XVIII.

The Twenty-third Psalm in Forty-two different versions.

From "ANE COMPENDIOVS BOOKE OF GODLY AND SPIRITVALL SONGS." By the
WEDDERBURNS. *Circ.* 1542.
Dominus me regit. PSAL. XXIII.

The Lord God is my Pastour gude,
Aboundantly mee for to feid;
Then how can I bee destitute
Of any gude thing in my neid?
Hee feid mee in feildes faire,
To riuers sweit, pure and preclair,
He dryues me bot ony dreid.

My saull and lyfe hee dois refresh,
And mee conuoyes in the way
Of his justice and righteousnesse,
And mee defendes from decay.
Not for my warkes verteousnesse,
But for his name so glorious
Preserues mee baith night and day.

And though I wander, and goe will,
Or am in danger for to die,
No dreid of deid sall come mee till,
Nor feare of cruell tyrannie:
Because that thou art me beside,
To gouerne me and bee my gyde
From all mischiefe and miserie.

Thy staffe whereof I stand great aw,
And thy schiep huke me for tae fang;
They nurture mee my faults to knaw,
When fra the hie way I gae wrang:
Therefore my sperit is blyth and glad,
When on my flesh thy scourge is laid,
In the right way to gar me gang.

And thow ane tabill does prouyde
Before mee, full of all delyte,
Contrair to my perseuars pryde,
To their displeasure and dispyte.
Thou hes annoynted my head,
And full my cup thou hes made,
With many dishes of delyte.

Thy gudnesse and benignity,
Let euer bee with mee therefore;
And while I live, untill I die,
Thou lay them vp with mee in store;
That I may haue my dwelling place
Into thy house, before thy face,
To sing with thee for evermore.

PSALM XXIII—*as composed by* WHITTINGHAM *in* 1556, appearing in Version of
that date, and subsequent editions.

1. The Lord is only my support,
    and hee that doth mee feede;

How can I then lacke anie thing
whereof I stand in neede?

2. Hee doth mee fold in coates most safe
    the tender grasse fast by;
    And after driv'th mee to the streames
    which run most pleasently.

3. And when I feel myself neare lost
    then doth hee mee home take;
    Conducting mee in his right pathes
    even for his own Names sake.

4. And though I were even at deaths
    yet would I feare none ill: [doore,
    For by thy rod and sheepheards crooke
    I am comforted still.

5. Thou hast my table richly deckt
    in despite of my fo,
    Thou hast my head with balme refresht
    my cup doth overflow.

6. And finally, while breath doth last
    thy grace shall mee defend;
    And in the house of God will I
    my life for ever spend.

PSALM XXIII.—by STERNHOLD. 1562. Version adopted by English Chuch.

1. My Shepheard is the living Lord,
    nothing therefore I neede;
    In pastors fayre with waters calme
    he set me for to feede.
2. He did conuert and glad my soule,
    and brought my mynde in frame,
    To walke in pathes of righteousness
    for his most holy Name.

3. Yea though I walke in vale of death,
    yet will I feare none ill,

Thy rod, thy staffe doth comfort me,
    and thou art with me still.
4. And in the presence of my foes
    my table thou shalt spread,
    Thou shalt (O Lord) fill full my cup,
    and eke anoynt my head.

5. Through all my lyfe thy favor is
    so frankly shewed to me,
    That in thy house for euermore
    my dwellyng place shal be.

PSALM XXIII. *by* A. MONTGOMERY, 1606:—from "THE MIND'S MELODIE; containing certain Psalmes of the Kinglie Prophet David, applied to a new pleasant tune," &c.

I.

The LORD maist hie,
    I knaw will be,
    An hird to me,
I cannot lang haif Stress nor stand in Neid;

He makes my Lair,
    In Fields maist fair,
    Quhair I bot cair,
Reposing at my Pleasure safely feid.

He sweitly me convoyis
To pleesand Springs,
Quhair naething me anoyis,
But Pleasour brings;
He brings my Mynde, fit to sic Kynd,
That Forss or Feir of Fae cannot me grieve;
He dois me leid in perfyt Freid,
And for his Name he will me never leive.

II.

Thocht I wald stray,
Ilk Day by Day,
In deidly Way,
Zit will I not dispair, I feir none ill;

For quhy thy Grace,
In every Place,
Dois me imbrace,   [still.
Thy rod and Shiphirds Cruke comfort me
In dispyt of my Foes,
My Tabill grows,
Thou balmis my Heid with Joy,
My Cup owreflows.
Kindness and Grace, Mercy and Peice,
Sall follow me for all my wretched Days,
And me convoy to endless Joy
In Hevin quhair I sall be with thee always.

MONTGOMERY was one of the most popular of the old poets of Scotland. The author of "Reasons against the reception of King James' Metaphrase," says of him and his "Melodie"—"Alexander Montgomery has a singular vaine of poesie, zet he tuik a more modest courss (than King James) for he translated bot a few for a proofe, and offered his travell in that kynde to the kirk."

PSALM XXIII :—From "THE BOOK OF PSALMS: *By* H. A., *Amsterdam*, A° D! 1612."

1. Jehovah feideth me, I shall not lack,
2. In grassy folds, he dooth make me lye;
   he gently-leads me quiet waters by.
3. He dooth return my soul; for his name
   sake
   in paths of iustice leads-me-quietly.
4. Yea, though I walk, in dale of deadly
   shade,
   ile fear none yll: for with me thou wilt be:
   thy rod thy staff eke they shall comfort me.

5. Fore me, a table thou hast ready-made:
   in their presence that my distressers be;
   Thou makest fat mine head with
   oincting-oil.
6. My cup abounds. Doubtless good and
   mercie
   shall all the days of my life follow me;
   also within Jehovahs howse, I shal
   to length of days repose-me-quietlie.

210   *The Scottish Metrical Psalms.*

PSALM XXIII:—*from* "THE PSALMES OF KING DAVID, TRANSLATED BY KING JAMES.—Oxford, printed by William Turner, 1631."

1. The Lord of all my Shepheard is,
   I shall from want be free;
2. He makes mee in green pastures lie
   and neare calme streames to be.
3. He doth restore my weary soule,
   that it new strength may take:
   And in the pathes of righteousnesse
   mee leads for his names sake.
4. Yea though I through deaths shadow walk
   yet feare I in no sort

   Thou art with me, thy rod and staffe
   with comfort me support.
5. Thou for my food, before my foes
   a table dost bestow:
   And dost with oyl annoynt my head
   and makes my cup o're flow.
6. Thy goodness and thy mercy sure,
   shall whilst I live blesse mee:
   And of the Lord I in the house
   a dweller still will be.

The London Edition, 1636, has considerable variations.

PSALM XXIII:—From "DIVERS OF DAVID'S PSALMES; according to the French form and metre; by JOHN VICARS; London, by Thomas Purfoot, for Henry Sale, 1631." (These Psalms appear in Vicars' "England's Hallelujah.")

1.

Isr'ells great Shepheard is my Shepheard kind,
In him (therefore) all needfull things I finde;
Corporall comforts, aliment externall
Spirituall Dainties, Manna, food supernall
In fields he foulds mee, full of tender Grasse,
Where silver streames doe smoothlie, sweetly passe

2.

And when my soul with sorrow seems deprest,
The Lord re-cheers it, with sweet peace and Rest,
And me with rules of righteousness instructeth,
And me in Goodnesse graciously conducteth:
So that in Death's dire Dale I walk secure,
Thy rod, thy Staffe, supporting me most sure.

3.

And, maugre all the malice of my foes,
My cuppe with all choice Blessings overflows,
My Table is with Dainties well appointed:
My head with Oyle of Gladnesse is annointed;
And, all my daies, God's Grace shall me defend
And in his holy-house, my life I'le spend.

PSALM XXIII:—*From* "THE PSALMES OF DAVID TRANSLATED INTO LYRICK-VERSE, *by* GEORGE WITHER. Imprinted in the Neatherlands by *Cornelis Gerrits van Breughel*, 1632."

1. The Lord my Pastor daignes to be
   I nothing now shall need;
   To drink sweet springs he bringeth mee
   And on green meads to feed.
   For his Name-sake, my heart he glads,
   He makes my wayes vpright;
   And I the vale of deaths black shades,
   Cann pass, without affright.
2. Thy staffe, thy presence and thy rodd,
   My joyfull comforts are

And thou before my foes (oh God)
My table shalt prepare.
Oyle on my head pour'd out thou hast
My Cupp doth over-flowe;
And thou on me whilst life doth last
Thy favours wilt bestowe.
3. Yea, Lord, thy goodness and thy grace,
   Shall always follow me;
   And, in thy house, my dwelling place
   For evermore shall be.

PSALM XXIII:—*From* SIR WM. MURE'S VERSION (M.S.) 1639.

1. The Lord my sheepherd is, of want
   I never shal complaine.
2. for mee to rest on hee doth grant
   green pastures of the plaine.
3. Hee leads mee stillest streames beside,
   and doth my soul reclame,
   in righteous paths hee mee doth guide
   for glorie of his name.
4. The valey dark of deaths aboad
   to passe, I'le feare no ill;

for thou art with me Lord; thy rod
and staffe me comfort still.
5. For me a Table thou dost spread
   in presence of my foes,
   with oyle thou dost anoint my head,
   by thee my cup o'erflows.
6. Mercie and goodnes all my dayes
   with me sall surely stay
   and in thy house, thy name to praise
   Lord I will duell for ay.

PSALM XXIII:—*From* FRANCIS ROUS' VERSION—1643.

1. My shepheard is the living Lord,
 and he that doth me feed;
 How can I then lack any thing
 whereof I stand in need?
2. In pastures green and flourishing
 he makes me down to lye:
 And after drives me to the streames
 which run most pleasantly.

3. And when I feele myself neare lost
 then home he me doth take;
 Conducting me in his right paths,
 even for his owne Names sake.

4. And though I were even at deaths doore
 yet would I feare none ill
 Thy rod, thy staffe, do comfort me
 and thou art with me still.

5. Thou hast my table richly stor'd
 in presence of my foe;
 My head with oile thou dost anoint,
 my cup doth overflow

6. Thy grace and mercy all my daies
 shall surelie follow me;
 And ever in the house of God,
 my dwelling place shall be.

PSALM XXIII:—*From* ZACHARY BOYD'S *Version*, 3rd Edit.:—1646.

1. The Lord's my Shepheard, I'le not want
2. He makes me by good will
 Ly in green pastures, he me leads
 beside the waters still.
3. My soul likewise he doth restore
 and me to lead doth take,
 Into the paths of righteousnesse
 and that for his Name's sake.

4. Yea though through valley of death's
 I walk; I'le fear no ill, [shade

For thou art with me, thy rod and
 thy staffe me comfort still.
5. Thou set'st in presence of my foes
 a table me before
 Mine head with oyl thou dost anoint,
 my cup it runneth o're.

6. Goodnesse and mercy all the dayes
 of my life surely shall
 Me follow, and in the Lord's house
 for ever I will dwell.

PSALM XXIII:—*From* ZACHARY BOYD'S *Version*:—An Earlier Edition.

1. The mighty Lord my shepheard is,
 Who doth me dayly feede:
 Therefore I shall not want the thing,
 Whereof I stand in neede.

2. He makes me in the pastures green
 Ly down by his good will;
 He in his mercy doth me leade,
 Beside the waters still.

Appendix. 213

3. My wearied soul he doth restore,
   He also me doth lead
   Into the paths of righteousnesse
   For his Name's sake indeed.
4. Though through the valley of death's
   I walk I'l fear no ill;   [shade,
   Thou art with me, thy rod and staffe
   Me comfort ever still.

5. Thou sets in presence of my foes,
   A table me before;
   Mine head with oyl thou dost anoynt
   My cup it runneth o're.
6. Goodnesse and mercy all my life
   Shall heer me follow still;
   And in the house of GOD the Lord
   For ever dwell I will.

BOYD's Edition of 1648 varies considerably from both of these.

PSALM XXIII:—*From* FRANCIS ROUS' *Version*,—1646.

1. The Lord my Shephard is, I shall
   not want: he makes me ly
2. In pastures green, me leads by streams
   that do run quietly.
3. My soul he doth restore again
   and me to walk doth make
   On in the paths of righteousnesse
   ev'n for his own name's sake.

4. Yea though I walk in death's dark vale,
   I'le fear no evil thing;

Thou art with me, thy rod, thy staffe,
to me do comfort bring.
5. Before me thou a table fit'st
   in presence of my foes;
   My head thou dost with oile anoint
   my cup it overflowes.

6. Goodnesse and mercy all my life
   shall surely follow me;
   And in God's house for evermore
   my dwelling place shall be.

Psalm XXIII:—*From* VERSION *of* 1650, *authorised, and still used, by Church of Scotland.*

1. The Lord's my Shepherd, I'll not want.
2. He makes me down to lie
   In pastures green; he leadeth me
   the quiet waters by.
3. My soul he doth restore again;
   and me to walk doth make
   Within the paths of righteousness,
   even for his own name's sake.

4. Yea though I walk in death's dark vale,
   Yet will I fear none ill:

For thou art with me; and thy rod
and staff me comfort still.
5. My table thou hast furnished
   in presence of my foes;
   My head thou dost with oil anoint,
   and my cup overflows.

6. Goodness and mercy all my life
   shall surely follow me:
   And in God's house for evermore
   my dwelling-place shall be.

214   *The Scottish Metrical Psalms.*

PSALM XXIII:—From "SAMUELIS PRIMITIAE, or an ESSAY towards a METRICAL VERSION of the WHOLE BOOK OF PSALMES. By SAMUEL LEIGH;—London; —by Tho. Milbourn, 1661."

1. God is my Shepheard, I shall never need;
2. I drink sweet waters, in good ground I feed.
3. When I'm nigh lost, then home he doth me take
   And lead me in his paths for his own sake.
4. Though I were at deaths door, I'll feare none ill.
   For with thy staff thou comfortest me still.
5. Thou spread'st my table in presence of my foes,
   Thou nointst my head with oile, my cup ore'flows,
6. While breath doth last, thy grace shall me defend,
   And in thy house my life I'le ever spend.

PSALM XXIII:—(In two Versions)—*From* "THE PSALMS OF KING DAVID, Paraphrased and turned into English Verse, according to the Common Metre, as they are usually sung in Parish Churches:—By Myles Smith, London,— for T. Garthwaite, 1668."

1. God by whose Providence we live,
   Whose care secures our rest,
   My Shepherd is, no ill can touch,
   Nor want my soul infest.

2. He makes Luxuriant flowry Meads
   Serve me for food and Ease;
   And leads me where the cooling Streams
   My thirsty heat appease.

3. He, by his Sp'rit my Soul restores
   And doth my feet reclaim
   Unto the peaceful Paths of Grace
   That I may praise his Name.

4. Were I to pass that Vale where Death
   Dwells in a dismal Shade,
   Thou present with thy Rod and Staff
   No fear should me invade.

5. My full-ser'ved Table thou sett'st forth
   Before my envious Foes
   My head rich oyles perfume; my Cup
   With Gen'rous wine o'reflows.

6. Mercy and goodness all my Days
   Shall me pursue, and I
   Will in thy Temple dwell, till time
   Put off Mortality.

Or thus:—

1. The Lords My Shepherd, Therefore I
   Can nothing want; In flowery Meads
   And Pastures green He makes me lie,
   And to the quiet waters leads.

2. He by his Spirit's sweet access
   Restores my Soul, And doth reclaim
   My Feet to Paths of Righteousness,
   That I may Praise His Glourious
   Name.

3. Yea though I pass the gloomy Vale
   Where Death in Horror dwell: No ill
   Since Thou art with me, shall appall
   Thy Rod, thy Staff's my Comfort
   still.

4. My Table thou hast fairly spread
   In presence of my vexed foes;
   Rich Oyles perfume my envi'd head
   My Cup with Gen'rous wine o're-
   flows.

5. Mercy and Goodness all my days
   Shall surely follow me; And I
   Will in Thy Temple sing Thy Praise
   Till Life puts off Mortality.

PSALM XXIII:—(In two versions:)—*From* "THE PSALMS OF DAVID; *by* JOHN PATRICK, D.D. Preacher to the Charter House, London:—London 1679."

1. God is my Shepherd who will see
   That all my wants be still supply'd;
   I shall not be expos'd to wrong
   Nor left to stray without a guide.

2. The Pastures they are fresh and green
   Where I have ease and sweet Repast;
   The Streams are cool and quiet where
   I quench my thurst and please my tast.

3. His Comforts which revive my Soul
   Life's tedious Journey pleasant make;
   And in the peaceful ways of Grace
   He leads me for his Goodness sake.

4. Tho' I should walk where black despair
   And sorrow cast a dismal shade,
   Thy Power and thy tender Care
   Would chase my fears and make me
   glad.

5. Thou spread'st my Table where my foes
   Behold thy Bounty and repine
   To see rich Oyls anoint my Head
   To see my Cup o'erflow with wine.

6. Surely the goodness of the Lord
   Shall still surround me all my days
   I will frequent thy House, and there
   Display thy love and sing thy praise.

Another Metre.

1. The Lord my careful Shepherd is
   I to his flock belong;
   I shall not stray without a Guide
   Nor be expos'd to wrong.

2. The pastures they are fresh and green,
   Where I have food and ease;
   He leads me to the quiet stream,
   Where I my thirst appease.

3. His comforts which refresh my soul
    Life's Journey pleasant make;
   He guides me in his righteous paths
    For his own Goodness sake.
4. Tho' I should walk where black despair
    Reflects a dismal shade,
   Thy Rod and Staff would chase away
    my fears and make me glad.

5. In presence of my foes thou spread'st
    My Table, who repine
   To see rich Oyles anoint my Head,
    My Cup o'erflow with wine.
6. Surely the Goodness of the Lord
    Shall Crown my future days;
   I will frequent his House, to shew
    His Love, and sing his praise.

PSALM XXIII:—(In three versions.) *From* WM. BARTON'S *Edition of* 1682.
Metre 1.

   My Shepherd is the Lord most high,
    I shall be well supply'd;
2. In pastures green he makes me lie
    by silent waters side.
3. He doth restore my Soul that strayes,
    and then he leads me on
   To walk in his most righteous ways,
    for his Names sake alone.

4. Yea though through deaths dark Vale I go
    yet will I fear none ill;

   Thy rod and staff support me so
    and thou art with me still.
5. My Table thou hast furnished
    in presence of my foe,
   With Oyl thou dost anoint my head
    my cup doth overflow.

6. Surely thy goodness and thy grace
    shall always follow me,
   And my perpetual dwelling place
    thy holy house shall be.

Metre 2.   *Imitatio Herberti.*   *Have mercy &c.*

1. The Lord my shepherd is,
   and he that doth me feed:
   Since he is mine and I am his
   what comfort can I need.

2. He makes me to lie down
   upon the flowery grass;
   Then to the streams he leads me on
   where waters gently pass.

3. And when I go astray
   he doth my soul reclaim:
   Conducting me in his right way
   for his most holy Name.

4. Yea though the paths I trod,
   through Deaths dark Vale should be,
   I would not fear, for there's my God,
   a staff of Strength to me.

5. And in mine enemies sight
   thou mak'st me sit and dine:
   Anoint'st my head, in foes despite
   and fillst my cup with Wine.

6. Surely thy grace and love
   shall measure out my days:
   And from thy house I'le not remove,
   nor there from thee my praise.

Appendix.

Metre 3.

1. The Lord's my shepherd to provide,
   I shall be sure to be supply'd:
   And by this means,
   In pastures green, I couch between,
   the silent streams.

2. He doth restore my Soul that strayes,
   He leads me in those righteous ways,
   Which I should take;
   And therein he, still guideth me,
   for his Names sake.

3. Yea though I walk through deaths dark Vale
   No evil will I fear at all:
   For there thow art
   With me, O God, thy staff, thy rod
   uphold my heart.

4. Thou spread'st my Table in despite
   Of envious foes, and in their sight
   Anoint'st my head
   And fillest up, my bounteous cup
   until it shed.

5. Thy goodness and thy mercy sure
   Shall follow me whilst I endure:
   And I therefore
   Will have abode i' th' house of God
   for evermore.

Considerable variations occur throughout the different editions of Barton's version of the Psalms.

PSALM XXIII:—(In two versions.)—*From* "A NEW VERSION OF THE PSALMS OF DAVID. By SIMON FORD D.D., and Rector of Old Swinford in Worcestershire. London: by J. H. for Brabazon Aylmer, 1688."

To the Tune of Psalm 113. Ye children, &c.

1. The Lord my faithful Shepherd is,
   Of nothing therefore can I miss
   Which to promote my good I need:

2. In pastures fair he doth me place
   All over spred with tender grass
   Where to the full he doth me feed.

   He leads me by the waters' side [glide;
   Whose streams with pleasant smoothness

3. He comforts me when faint I am:
   And lest at any time I stray,
   In every good and righteous way
   Guides me for th' honour of his name.

4. Yea in the vale where death doth throw
   Its dismal shade, I fearless go;
   For thou art with me even there:
   Thy rod and staff do comfort me

5. Thou, (which my foes repining, see,)
   A table for me dost prepare.

   Thy oyl anoints my head, and thou
   Makest my cup to overflow:

6. Mercy and goodness shall attend
   Me surely, while I here ab de;
   And in thy house I will reside,
   Till parting breath my life shall end.

218 *The Scottish Metrical Psalms.*

The same in other Metre.

1. The Lord my faithful shepherd is,
    A sheep of his am I:
    With all that may promote my bliss
    He will my needs supply.
2. In pastures cloath'd with tender grass
    He makes me rest and feed:
    Pastures, through which smooth streams do pass
    By which he doth me lead.

3. To strengthen me when faint I am,
    Sound med'cines he provides;
    And for the honour of his name
    In righteous paths me guides.

4. Yea though in death's black shade I live
    No evil will I fear:
    Thy Rod and Staff me comfort give
    For thou art with me there.

5. In presence of my mortal foes
    My Table thou hast spread:
    Filled by thee my cup o'er flows,
    Thy oyl anoints my head.
6. Mercy and goodness all my days,
    Shall surely me attend:
    And in God's house, to sing his praise,
    My life I'll wholely spend.

PSALM XXIII:—From "A NEW VERSION OF THE PSALMS OF DAVID; Fitted to the Tunes used in CHURCHES. By N. TATE, and N. BRADY. London: Printed by M. Clark; for the Company of Stationers, 1696." (The version adopted by the English Church. The second and subsequent editions differ from this.)

1. Since God does me, his worthless charge
    Protect with tender Care
    As watchful Shepherds guard their Flocks,
    What can I want or fear?
2. In shady Pastures fresh and green
    He makes me feed and lie;
    Then leads me to the silver streams
    That gently murmur by.

3. My wandering Soul by him restor'd
    To his immortal Praise
    He taught with humble Zeal to walk
    In his most righteous ways.

4. Though through Death's gloomy Vale I march
    Yet safe and undismaid;
    His Presence cheers, his Rod and Staff
    Afford me constant Aid.

5. By him in sight of all my Foes
    My Table's richly spread
    My Cup o'erflows with genrous Wine
    With pretious Oyls my Head.
6. Since God thus shews his wondrous Love
    Through all my Life's extent
    My time to come shall in his House
    In Pray'r and Praise be spent.

PSALM XXIII:—From "THE PSALMS OF DAVID. Paraphrased and interpreted according to the New Testament. By HENRY MUGGLETON, Carolina, 1696."

1. My God's my Shepherd! I'll not care
   For any breath of moved air;
   The winds may blow, the storm may roar;
   Jehovah will preserve his store;
   He'll hide me from the stormy wind,
   And calm the tumults of my mind;
   He'll shade me from the scorching heat,
   And lull my soul in soft retreat.

2. He'll lead me to the pastures green,
   And from the wolves my life will screen;
   He'll feed me by the gentle streams
   Where I shall bask in sunny beams.

3. Although amazed for a while,
   Unconscious of his wonted smile,
   O'erwhelmed with grief, o'erwhelmed with pain,
   My soul the Lord restores again.

4. Yea though I walk in death's dark vale
   No terror shall my heart assail;
   I'm with my God, I fear no ill
   Thy rod and staff me comfort still.

5. My table thou hast furnished
   Thy holy oil anoints my head,
   Thou fill'st my cup with heavenly wine
   Thou mak'st my face with joy to shine:

   And to confound my foes the more,
   These triumphs of thy love, before
   Their very presence thou hast shewn
   And glorified thy HOLY ONE.

6. Thy love and mercy, all my days,
   Shall fill my life with joy and praise;
   And when the blessed hour is come
   Thou'lt take me to thy glory home.

   My Father, Shepherd, Lord, and God,
   For ever bless'd in thine abode,
   I'll shout and sing to thee, along
   With all my circling elect throng:
   What thou, my Father, art to me,
   Thy Son to all thy flock shall be,
   Till I thy kingdom perfect bring,
   Their Father, Shepherd, Lord and King.

PSALM XXIII:—From "PSALMS HYMNS AND SPIRITUAL SONGS. By REV. DANIEL BURGESS. London, 1714."

1. The Father, Son, and Holy Ghost
   My gracious Shepherd is
   My Wants will always be supplied
   By tender Care of his.

2. As Shepherds find their helpless Flocks
   Places for food and Rest;
   My ever-blessed Shepherd finds
   And leads me to the best.

3. He doth my straying soul restore,
   He my sick soul doth raise:
   Of Grace, and no Desert of mine
   He leads me in his ways.

4. I walk in a most gloomy Vale
   A Vale of Snares and Tears;
   But never am I over-whelmed,
   His Grace my Heart so cheers.

5. The Bread, the Wine, the Oil he gives,
   Makes spightful Enemies pine;
   So doth thy Bounty over-flow,
   Bounty entirely thine.

6. Sure then thy wondrous rich free grace
   Will reach through my few Days,
   And let my Life be long or short
   It shall be spent in Praise.

PSALM XXIII:—(In three versions), From "THE PSALMS OF DAVID, imitated in the language of the New Testament, and applied to the Christian State and Worship. By ISAAC WATTS, D.D., London 1719."

God our Shepperd. (L.M.)

I.
My Shepherd is the living Lord;
Now shall my wants be well supply'd;
His providence and holy word
Become my safety and my guide.

II.
In pastures where salvation grows
He makes me feed, he makes me rest;
There living water gently flows,
And all the food divinely blest.

III.
My wandering feet his ways mistake,
But he restores my soul to peace
And leads me, for his mercy's sake
In the fair paths of righteousness.

IV.
Tho' I walk thro' the gloomy vale
Where death and all its terrors are
My heart and hope shall never fail
For God my Shepherd's with me there.

V.
Amidst the darkness and the deeps
Thou art my comfort, thou my stay;
Thy staff supports my feeble steps,
Thy rod directs my doubtful way.

VI.
The sons of earth and sons of hell
Gaze at thy goodness, and repine
To see my table spread so well
With living bread and cheerful wine.

VII.
How I rejoice when on my head
Thy Spirit condescends to rest!
'Tis a divine anointing shed
Like oil of gladness at a feast.

VIII.
Surely the mercies of the Lord
Attend his household all their days;
There will I dwell to hear his word,
To seek his face, and sing his praise.

The Same. (C.M.)

I.
My shepherd will supply my need,
  Jehovah is his name;
In pastures fresh he makes me feed
  Beside the living stream.

II.
He brings my wandering spirit back,
  When I forsake his ways;
And leads me for his mercy's sake,
  In paths of truth and grace.

III.
When I walk through the shades of death,
    Thy presence is my stay;
A word of thy supporting breath
    Drives all my fears away.

IV.
Thy hand in spite of all my foes,
    Doth still my table spread;
My cup with blessings overflows,
    Thine oil anoints my head.

V.
The sure provisions of my God
    Attend me all my days;
O may thy house be mine abode,
    And all my works be praise!

VI.
There would I find a settled rest,
    (While others go and come)
No more a stranger or a guest,
    But like a child at home.

The Same. (S.M.)

I.
The Lord my shepherd is
    I shall be well supplied
Since he is mine and I am his
    What can I want beside?

II.
He leads me to the place
    Where heavenly pasture grows,
Where living waters gently pass,
    And full salvation flows.

III.
If e'er I go astray,
    He doth my soul reclaim,
And guides me in his own right way,
    For his most holy name.

IV.
While he affords his aid,
    I cannot yield to fear;
Tho' I should walk thro' death's dark shade
    My shepherd's with me there.

V.
In spite of all my foes,
    Thou dost my table spread,
My cup with blessings overflows,
    And joy exalts my head.

VI.
The bounties of thy love
    Shall crown my following days;
Nor from thy house will I remove,
    Nor cease to speak thy praise.

PSALM XXIII:—(In two Versions)—From "NEW VERSION OF THE PSALMS: by SIR RICHARD BLACKMORE, KT., M.D., London, 1721."

1. God is my Shepherd, can I Want?
2. He feeds me in delightful meads;
    Do's for my Rest green Pastures grant
    And me to gentle Waters leads.

3. 'Tis he restores my sinking soul
    And for the Glory of his Name,
    His Counsels so my Feet Controul
    That righteous Paths I make my Aim.

4. When I approach Death's silent Court
   To give me Aid He still is near
   Thy Rod and Staff are my Support
   They Comfort me and ease my Fear.

5. A plenteous Table thou hast spread
   For me before my envious Foe,
   And pour'd rich Oyntments on my Head,
   And made my Cup to overflow.

6. Surely thy mercy, often try'd
   Shall all my future life attend;
   I'll in thy sacred House abide
   Till my appointed Days shall end.

Another Metre.

1. God is my Shepherd, can I want?
2. He feeds me in the Meads:
   Do's for my Rest green Pastures grant
   And to still waters leads.
3. 'Tis He restores my sinking Soul
   And for his Glory's sake,
   His Counsels so my Feet controul
   That righteous Ways they take.
4. Tho' I approach Death's silent Court
   To help me He is near;

   Thy Rod and Staff are my Support
   And ease me of my Fear.
5. A plenteous Table Thou has spread
   For me before the Foe,
   And pour'd rich Oyntments on my Head
   And made my Cup o'erflow.

6. Surely thy Mercy, often try'd
   Shall all my Life attend
   And in thy House will I abide
   Till my set Days shall end.

PSALM XXIII:—*From* "THE PSALMS, HYMNS, AND SPIRITUAL SONGS of the Old and New Testament. Boston, N.E., 1737."

1. The Lord to me a shepherd is
   want therefore shall not I:
2. He in the folds of tender grass
   doth make me down to lie:
   He leads me to the waters still.
3. Restore my soul doth he;
   In paths of righteousness he will
   for his name sake lead me.
4. In valley of death's shade although
   I walk, I'll fear none ill:

   For thou with me, thy rod also
   thy staff, me comfort will.
5. Thou hast fore me a table spread
   in presence of my foes;
   Thou dost anoint with oyl mine head,
   my cup it overflows.
6. Goodness and mercy my days all
   shall surely follow me;
   And in the Lord's house dwell I shall
   so long as days shall be.

Appendix. 223

PSALM XXIII:—(In two versions)—*From* "A NEW VERSION OF THE PSALMS. BY JOHN BARNARD, Pastor of a Church in Marblehead. Boston, N.E., 1752."

1. Jehovah my kind shepherd is
   He doth my Wants supply
2. In pastures green by Waters still
   He makes me down to ly.
3. My soul so prone to go astray
   He mildly doth reclaim;
   And leads me on in righteous Paths
   For th' Honour of his name.

4. Tho' thro' Death's shady Vale I walk
   No evil will I fear:
   Thy Rod directs and Staff defends,
   For thou art with me there.
5. My Table thou hast richly spread
   In presence of my Foes
   Thou dost my Head with oyl anoint
   My Cup it overflows.

6. Goodness and Mercy surely shall
   Attend me all my Days;
   My fix'd Abode forever, Lord,
   Shall be thy House of Praise.

2nd Metre.

1. The gracious Lord is still to me
   A Shepherd kind and faithful Guide,
   Whate'er my wants demand, shall be
   By his indulgent care supply'd.
2. In pastures ever fresh and green
   He feeds, and makes me take my rest;
   He leads me to the silent stream,
   Or Pool which living Springs have blest.
3. My Soul, which his assistance needs,
   He doth restore, by sov'rain Grace:
   For his Name's Sake, he gently leads
   Me in the Paths of Righteousness.

4. Tho' thro' Death's gloomy Vale I glide
   No threat'ning Dangers will I fear;
   For thou art with me, Lord, to guide
   Thy Rod and Staff to Comfort there.
5. My Table's with thy Bounties spread
   In sight of all my spiteful Foes,
   Thou dost anoint with Oyl my Head,
   My cup with blessings overflows.
6. Goodness and Mercy from my God
   Shall surely crown my future Days,
   Therefore I'll make my fixt Abode
   Lord in thy House of Prayer and Praise.

PSALM XXIII:—*From* "THE PSALMS OF DAVID, translated into HEROIC VERSE. London; Printed for S. Birt, in Ave-Mary-Lane, and J. Buckland, in PaterNoster Row, 1754."

Jehovah tends me with a Shepherds care,
What pressing wants, what evil can I fear?

At rest he in the verdand pasture lays,
Or guides me, where the quiet current strays;
Whene'er I'm lost, his watchful eyes behold
My wand'rings, he restores me to the fold:
For his name's sake (lest I should tread amiss)
He points the path, which leads to virtuous bliss.
If bound to traverse o'er death's dreary vale,
Thine aid forbids my dreadless heart to fail;
Thy rod and staff supporting comfort yield,
And help me onward thro' the dismal field.
My foes observe me, and repining stand,
Feast on the choicest bounties of thine hand:
Thy sacred oyl makes glad my chearful face,
My cup is crown'd with thine o'erflowing grace.
Thus whilst thy love shall bless my latest days,
In Sion's courts I'll sing JEHOVAH's praise.

PSALM XXIII:—*From* "THE PSALMS, *translated* or *Paraphrased* in ENGLISH VERSE, by JAMES MERRICK, M.A.; *Reading*, by J. Carnan & Co., 1765."

Lo, my Shepherd's hand divine!
Want shall never more be mine,
In a pasture fair and large
He shall feed his happy charge,
And my couch with tend'rest care
Midst the springing grass prepare.
When I faint with summer's heat
He shall lead my weary feet
To the streams that still and slow
Through the verdant meadow flow.
He my soul anew shall frame,
And, his mercy to proclaim,
When through devious paths I stray
Teach my steps the better way.
Though the dreary vale I tread

By the shades of death o'erspread,
There I walk, from terror free,
While my ev'ry wish I see,
By thy rod and staff supplied,
This my guard and that my guide.
While my foes are gazing on,
Thou thy fav'ring care hast shewn;
Thou my plenteous board hast spread,
Thou with oil refreshed my head;
Fill'd by Thee my cup o'erflows;
For thy Love no limit knows:
Constant, to my latest end
This my footsteps shall attend,
And shall bid thy hallow'd Dome
Yield me an eternal home.

Appendix.

PSALM XXIII:—(In two versions.) *From* "A TRANSLATION OE THE PSALMS OF DAVID attempted in the Spirit of Christianity, and adapted to the Divine Service. By CHRISTOPHER SMART, A.M. London, by Dryden Leach, 1765."

The Shepherd Christ from heaven arriv'd,
My flesh and spirit feeds;
I shall not therefore be depriv'd
Of all my nature needs.

As slop'd against the glist'ning beam
The velvet verdure swells,
He keeps and leads me by the stream
Where consolation dwells.

My soul he shall from sin restore,
And her free powers awake,
In paths of heav'nly truth to soar
For love and mercy's sake.

Yea tho' I walk death's gloomy vale,
The dread I shall disdain;
For thou art with me, lest I fail,
To check me and sustain.

Thou shalt my plenteous board appoint
Before the braving foe;
Thine oil and wine my head anoint
And make my goblet flow.

But greater still thy love and grace
Shall all my life attend;
And in thine hallow'd dwelling place
My knees shall ever bend.

Or this.

Christ Jesus has my name enroll'd
And to his own peculiar fold
  Above all want consign'd;
Thou hast to ghostly welfare brought
The sheep, thy precious blood has bought
  O shepherd of Mankind.

Me placed beneath the blue serene
In pastures ever fresh and green,
  Where all is peace and still,
He feeds—and sets me on the brink
Of living waters, there to drink
  Of comfort and my fill.

He shall convert my carnal heart,
And every Christian grace impart,
  To fix me in his way;
For by his hallow'd name he swore,
And for the sake of that, no more
  Shall David ever stray.

Yea tho' from hence my journey lies
Down thro' the vale of tears and sighs,
  And up the steep of pain,
No terror shall my course withstand;
Thy rod and staff are still at hand
  To check me and sustain.

Thou shalt add plenty to thy grace,
And heap my board before their face,
  My troublers to confound;
The head that thou hast lifted up,
Thou hast anointed, and the cup
  Of my Salvation crown'd.

The goodness and the grace divine,
Shall constant all along the line
  Of utmost life extend;
And I shall in thy temple dwell,
In thankful psalmody to tell
  Of transport without end.

The Scottish Metrical Psalms.

PSALM XXIII:—*From* "THE PSALMS OF DAVID IN METRE, By Mr. GEORGE SCOTT, Gentleman. Edinburgh. 1768."

1. My Shepherd is the Lord most High
   who doth me guide and lead;
   Therefore no good thing want shall I
   which he doth see I need.

2. It's he who makes me down to lie
   in the green pastures fair,
   And he alone doth lead me by
   the still waters with care.

3. The Lord my soul doth from distress
   restore and me doth make,
   To walk in paths of righteousness
   even for his own name's sake.

4. Yea altho' I melancholly
   walk thro' the dismal val
   Of deaths dark shade, yet fear will I
   no ill, can me assail.

   Because that thou O Lord my God
   for ever art with me:
   Yea thy staff and likewise thy rod
   still my comforters be.

5. For me a table thou appoints
   in presence of my foes;
   Thou with thy oil, my head anoints
   and my cup overflows.

6. Surely shall mercy and goodness
   me follow all my days:
   And in God's house nevertheless
   there will I dwell always.

Psalm XXIII:—*From* "A NEW VERSION OF THE WHOLE BOOK OF PSALMS, by JAMES MAXWELL, S.D.P. Glasgow. 1773."

1. The Lord's my shepherd, by whose aid
   My wants are all supply'd;
   Of what should I be then afraid
   Since he's my constant guide?

2. He leads me forth to pastures fair
   Where sweetly I repose;
   And living streams pass gently there
   Wherein salvation flows.

3. My soul he doth restore again
   When from his folds I stray;
   And in his paths, by grace made plain
   He gently leads my way.

4. Yea tho' I walk through death's dark
   No danger will I fear;   [vale
   Thy presence, rod, and staff ne'er fail
   My drooping heart to cheer.

5. My table thou dost also spread
   In presence of my foes:
   Thine oil of joy anoints my head
   My gen'rous cup o'erflows.

6. Goodness and mercy sure shall still
   My future days attend;
   And I within thy house shall dwell
   Where pleasures never end.

Appendix.

A remarkable version of the Psalms has lately appeared—viz., "The Psalms: frae Hebrew intil Scottis. By P. Hately Waddell, LL.D., Minister. Edinburgh, 1871." It is a very curious production. Some of the renderings are strikingly emphatic. Though perhaps not in entire accordance with the plan of this work, we venture to give the translation of the XXIII Psalm.

The sheep-keepin o' the Lord's kind an' canny, wi' a braw howff at lang last: David keeps his sheep; the Lord keeps David.
Ane heigh-lilt o' David's.
THE LORD is my herd, nae want sal fa' me:

2. He louts me lie amang green howes; he airts me atowre by the lown watirs:

3. He waukens my wa'-gaen saul; he weises me roun, for his ain name's sake, intil right roddins.

4. Na! tho' I gang thro' the dead-mirk-dail; *een thar*, sal I dread nae skaithin: for yersel *are* nar-by me; yer stok an' yer stay haud me baith fu' cheerie.

5. My buird ye hae hansell'd in face o' my faes; ye hae drookit my head wi' oyle; my bicker is *fu'* an' skailin.

6. E'en sae, sal gude-guidin an gude-gree gang wi' me, ilk day o' my livin; an' evir mair syne, i' the LORD's ain howff *at lang last*, sal I mak bydan.

THE PLATES.

Mr. Gibb—of Messrs. Keith and Gibb, Lithographers, Aberdeen—who made the fac-similies from Wode's Manuscript Volumes for the Society of Antiquaries of Scotland, has subjected them to a careful revisal, to render them as near the original as possible, with the amount of colouring adapted to such a work as this. He says:—"The figure in Plate I., in the original, is dressed in a black gown and cap, his under dress—the sleeves of which only are seen—being yellow; while the border and the flowers are illuminated with bright blue, green, and yellow. The figure in Plate III. has a dress of brilliant green, slashed with yellow, and green stockings; the border being in the same style of illumination as Plate I., as also are all the others in the Volumes. The decorations are outlined in a dull, deep, pinky brown, and coloured over with bright tints of green, yellow, and red—blue being only used in the flowers ornamenting the figure pages. The workmanship of the original is evidently that of a clever and practised penman, but one whose eye has been dimmed and his hand shaken by age. This remark, however, does not apply to the initial capitals in Plates III., IV., and V., which are executed with a degree of sharpness and precision very remarkable, as if they were the work of a different scribe from that of the rest of the Volumes."

TENNOWR.

He mā is blest ẏ heth nō bēt, to wicked red his eare: Noꝛ led his lyfe as sinners do, noꝛ sat ī scoꝛners chaire. But ī ẏ lau of god ẏ loꝛd, doth set his whole delẏ. And ī ẏ lau doth exerrise, him selfe both day and nicht.

He man is blest that heth

not bẽt. to wicked rede his

eare: Nor led his lyfe as sinners do. nor sate

in scorners chaire. But in ye lawe of god the

lord. doth set his whole delȳ. And i ye lau doth

exercise. him selfe both day and nicht.

The first psalme. pag 1

♪ ♪ ♪

He mā is blest ẏ heth

♪ ♪ ♪ ♪

not bēt, to wicked rede

♪ ♪ ♪ ♪ ♪ ♪

his eare: Nor led his lyf as siners do, nor sate

♪ ♪ ♪ ♪ ♪ ♪

in scorners chaire. But in ẏ law of god ẏ

♪ ♪ ♪ ♪ ♪

lord, doth set his whole deliẏ: And ī ẏ law

♪ ♪ ♪ ♪ ♪

doth exercise; him selfe both day & nẏ

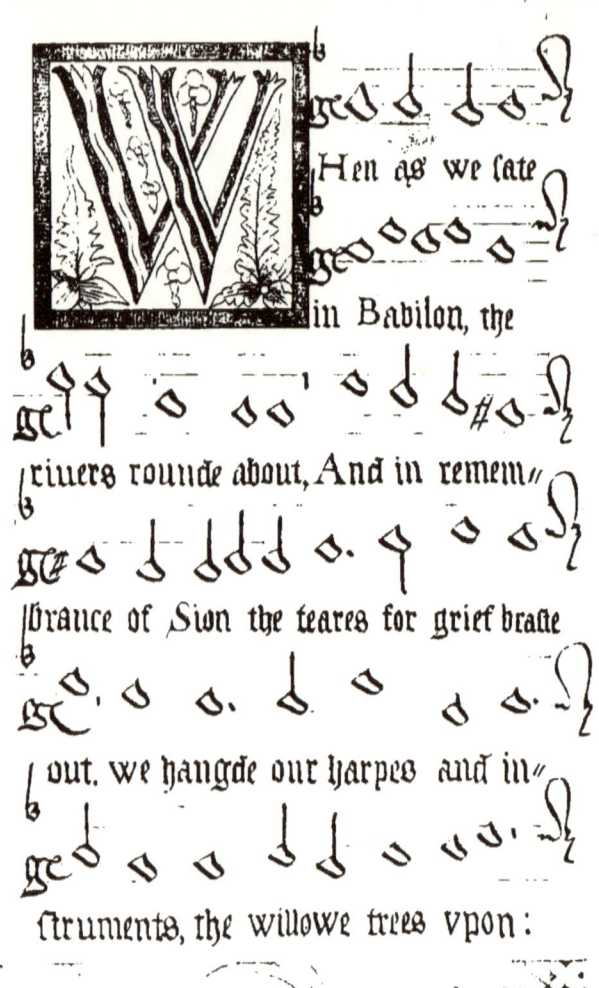

PSAL. CXXXVII.

For in that place men for their vſe

had planted mony one

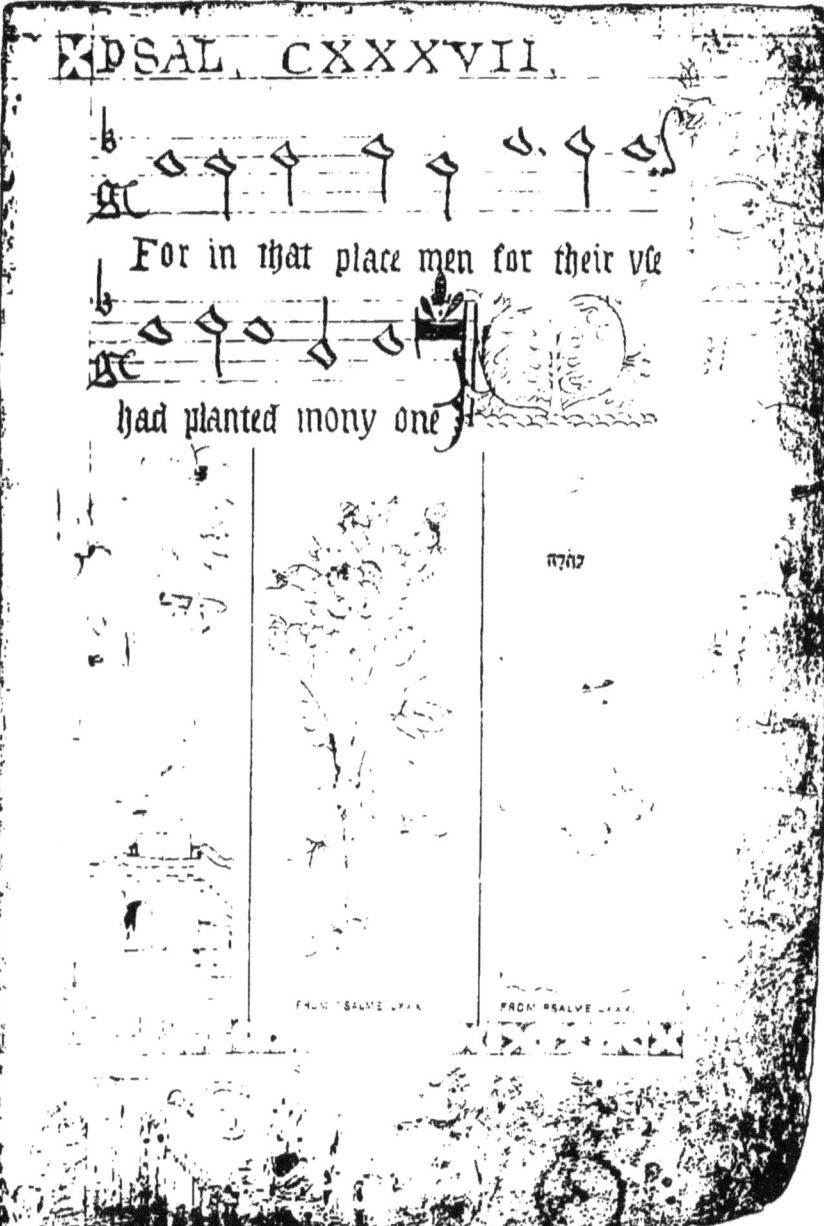

(TENOR)

Endis ye psalmes set furth i.iiii.partes
Conforme to the tenour of ye Buke.
1566

Be ane honorable and singulare cunnig
man Dauid Peables i Sanctandrous
And Noted or wreaten be me
Thomas Wode.

(TREBLE)

Set i iiii partes be ane honorable mā
Dauid Peables In Sanctandrous.

And Noted and wretin by me
Thomas Wode, in decēbar. 1566.

(BASSUS)

Set i iiii partes be ane honorable
mā Dauid Peables i.S. Noted or writtin
by me Thomas Wode of Sanctandrois.
1566

SUBSCRIBERS' NAMES.

Adair, John, Airdrie.
Addie, John, 144 St. Vincent-street, Glasgow.
Alexander, Edward, jun., 13 Claremont-gardens, Glasgow.
Alexander, George, Dowanhill-gardens, Glasgow.
Alexander, John, Menstrie Bank, Dowanhill, Glasgow.
Alexander, Rev. Dr. Lindsay, Pinkie Burn, Musselburgh.
Allan, Peter, Merchant, Lesmahagow.
Allan, William, Portland-street (S.), Glasgow.   2 copies.
Alston, William, of Stockbriggs, Lesmahagow.   10 copies.

Baillie, James W., of Culter Allers, Biggar.
Baird, James, Kirkmuirhill Tile Works, Lesmahagow.   2 copies.
Ballantine, Alexander, Artist in Stained Glass, Edinburgh.
Bartholomew, Hugh, of Glenorchard.
Baxter, Edmund, W.S., Edinburgh.
Baxter, John, Blackwood Saw Mills, Lesmahagow.   2 copies.
Begg, Rev. Dr., 50 George Square, Edinburgh.
Binnie, David, 29 Taylor-street, Glasgow.
Braidwood, James, Bookseller, Edinburgh.
Brown, Major, of Auchlochan, Lesmahagow.   15 copies.
Brown, James, Auchrobert, Lesmahagow.
Burness, Rev. James, Kirkfieldbank, Lesmahagow.

Campbell, Duncan, Parish Schoolhouse, Lesmahagow.   3 copies.
Campbell, James, Coalmaster, Netherhouse, Lesmahagow.   3 copies.

Church, William, 13 Queen's-terrace, Glasgow.
Cosh, Rev. Nathan, Douglas Water.
Cubbon, William, Broomhill, Dunipace, Denny.
Cunningham, William, Bunker, Manchester. 6 copies.

Daly, James, 150 Trongate, Glasgow. 2 copies.
Dalzell, John B., Merchant, Lesmahagow. 4 copies.
Davidson, Rev. Alexander, Kilbirnie.
Davidson, Hugh, P.-F., Lanark.
Davidson, John, Surgeon, Newmilns.
Dick, Rev. James, M.A., Wishaw.
Dodds, William, Lesmahagow.
Drew, William, 22 Renfield-street, Glasgow.
Duff, James, Factor, Blackwood, Lesmahagow. 3 copies.
Duncan, Mrs. W., 26 Percy-street, Liverpool. 2 copies.
Duncan, William, 65 Hamilton-drive, Glasgow.
Dunlop, Matthew, Bristol.
Dykes, James, Bent, Lesmahagow.

Easton, Rev. Thos., Stranraer. 3 copies.
Edmonstone & Douglas, Booksellers, Edinburgh.
Euing, William, Insurance Broker, Glasgow. 6 copies.

Fairbairn, Rev. James, Newhaven.
Fairley, Matthew, 105 Hill-street, Glasgow.
Fallow, James, Brackenridge, Lesmahagow.
Ferguson, James, of Wiston. 10 copies.
Ferguson, Peter, 15 Wilson-street, Hillhead, Glasgow.
Ferguson, William, F. C. Schoolhouse, Lesmahagow.
Frazer, James, 2 North Albion-court, Glasgow.

Gibb, Mr., of Keith & Gibb, Lithographers, Aberdeen.

Gibb, George, of Calver Lodge, Barlow.
Gibb, John, Banker, Lesmahagow. 3 copies.
Gilroy, Captain, Lanark.
Glasgow, Earl of, The Garrison, Millport. 2 copies.
Gow, Leonard, of Hayston.
Greenshields, James, West-town, Lesmahagow.
Greenshields, J. B., of Kerse, Lesmahagow. 30 copies.
Grossart, William, Surgeon, Salsbury, Holytown.

Hamilton, Andrew, of Garngour, Lesmahagow.
Hamilton, Gavin, of Auldtoun, Lesmahagow. 4 copies.
Hamilton, James, Millbank, Douglas. 3 copies.
Hamilton, James, Lesmahagow.
Hamilton, Major J. G., of Dalziel, M.P. 2 copies.
Hayes, Edwin F., 98 Argyle-street, Glasgow.
Henderson, William, Merchant, Lesmahagow.
Home, Earl of, Douglas Castle. 10 copies.
Hope Vere, W. E., of Blackwood and Craigie Hall. 2 copies.
Hope Vere, Miss. 2 copies.
Hunter, J. K. S., LL.D., of Daleville, Carluke.
Hunter, William, Nether Birkwood, Lesmahagow.

Jones, William, Bridge-street, Bristol.

Kay, Rev. John, Coatbridge.
Kerr, Rev. James, Greenock.
Kerr, Mrs., Whitehill, Dalserf.
Kirsop, John, 98 Argyle-street, Glasgow.

Laing, Rev. James, M.A., Free West Church, Glasgow.
Lang, Archibald, 144 St. Vincent-street, Glasgow.
Lang, John, Motherwell.

, Leadbetter, J. G., Gordon-street, Glasgow. 6 copies.
, Lindsay, Alexander H., Surgeon, Lesmahagow.
Lindsay, John, M.D., Lesmahagow. 2 copies.
, Lockhart, Andrew, Old Hall-street, Liverpool. 2 copies.
, Lockhart, Robert, Rumford-street, Liverpool. 6 copies.
, Lockhart, William, Old Hall-street, Liverpool. 2 copies.

Main, Rev. Thomas, 7 Bellevue-crescent, Edinburgh.
, Malcolm, Robert, Sheriff-Clerk, Nairn.
, Marshall, Rev. William, London. 3 copies.
, Maxwell, Andrew, St. James'-terrace, Glasgow.
, Middleton, David, LL.D., H.M. Inspector of Schools, Bothwell.
, Mosman, Hugh, of Auchtyfardle, Lesmahagow. 3 copies.
, Murdoch, William, 12 West Garden-street, Glasgow.

, McAlister, Robert, St. Flanan's, Kirkintilloch.
, McCaig, Rev. Charles N., Lochgilphead. 6 copies.
McCall, Mrs., Lanark.
, McGhie, David, of Auchren, Lesmahagow. 2 copies.
McGhie, James, Lochanbank Cottage, Lesmahagow.
, McKenna, James, Writer, Girvan.
McKenna, John, Bookseller, Girvan.
MacKinnon, Peter, 4 Pennyman-street, North Ormesby.
, McKirdy, J. Gregory, of Birkwood, Lesmahagow. 10 copies.
Macnaughton, Rev. Allan, D.D., Lesmahagow. 2 copies.
Macnaughton, Rev. N. M., Kinclaven. 6 copies.
, McNaughtan, Peter, Temple Back, Bristol.

Naismith, William, Printer, Hamilton.
, Neilson, M. G., 9 West Regent-street, Glasgow.
, Newton, James, 2 West Grove, Cotham, Bristol. 8 copies.

Paterson, Rev. John, Torryburn.
Paterson, Matthew, Elmbank-crescent, Glasgow.
Paton, Rev. James, Airdrie.
Pirie, A. G., Auchtyfardle, Lesmahagow. 5 copies.
Proudfoot, Rev. George, Glasgow. 6 copies.

Reid, Rev. William, Airdrie.
Robertson, J. M., 57 St. George's-place, Glasgow.
Rowatt, Thomas, 7 Palmerston-road, Edinburgh.
Rowatt, William, Paisley.

Sandilands, Gavin, of Longridge, Lesmahagow. 2 copies.
Sandilands, William, Cumberhead, Lesmahagow. 2 copies.
Scott, Gavin, Manufacturer, Lesmahagow.
Scott, George, Inspector of Poor, Lesmahagow.
Scott, James, Parish Schoolhouse, Douglas.
Scott, William, Princes-terrace, Dowanhill, Glasgow.
Semple, Andrew, Woodhead, Lesmahagow.
Shanks, Thomas, Drumshangie, Airdrie.
Simpson, John, 25 Centre Redcliffe-crescent, Bristol.
Slimon, Robert, Surgeon, Lesmahagow.
Smith, Miss, 4 Bellevue-crescent, Edinburgh. 2 copies.
Smith, Andrew, Writer, Lanark.
Smith, James, of Swanston Hill, Port-Bannatyne.
Smith, John, of Birkhill, Lesmahagow. 3 copies.
Smith & Son, Booksellers, Glasgow. 2 copies.
Sommerville, William, J.P., Bitton Hill, Bristol.
Sommerville, William, 9 South Apsley-place, Glasgow.
Steele, Gavin, of Holmhead, Lanark. 5 copies.
Stark, J. M., 25 Buckingham-terrace, Glasgow.
Stevenson, Robert, Engineer, Airdrie.
Stewart, Mr., of Symington & Stewart, 119 St. Vincent-street, Glasgow.
Stewart, R. B., 224 St. Vincent-street, Glasgow.
Stein, John, of Kirkfield, Lesmahagow.

Swan, Professor, University, St. Andrews.
Swan, James, of Collier-Hall, Douglas. 3 copies.
Symington, Andrew, 119 St. Vincent-street, Glasgow.
Symington, Rev. William, Glasgow. 6 copies.

Tait, M. S., George-square, Glasgow.
Taylor, James, Stockbriggs, Lesmahagow.
Taylor, J., Hamilton-square, Glasgow. 2 copies.
Thomson, Rev. J. H., Eaglesham.
Tudhope, Miss, Abbeygreen, Lesmahagow.
Tudhope, John Hamilton, Lesmahagow. 2 copies.
Turnbull, Rev. Thomas H., Lesmahagow.

Waddell, Rev. P. Hately, LL.D., Elmgrove-place, Glasgow.
Wallace, Rev. Robert H., Hill-street, Glasgow.
Watt, Mrs., Shotts Manse, Holytown.
Waugh, J. H. W., M.D., &c., &c., of Orchardville, Lesmahagow.
White, James, Optician, Union-street, Glasgow.
White, John, of Netherurd, Dolphinton.
White, Rev. John, Carluke.
Wilson, John, of Aucheneck. 6 copies.
Wilson, Rev. Thomas, A.M., Lesmahagow. 3 copies.
Wilson, William, 10 Abbotsford-crescent, Edinburgh.
Wyllie, D. & Son, Aberdeen.

M'CULLOCH AND CO., PRINTERS, 7 ALSTON STREET, GLASGOW.

www.ingramcontent.com/pod-product-compliance
Lightning Source LLC
Chambersburg PA
CBHW032122230426
43672CB00009B/1829